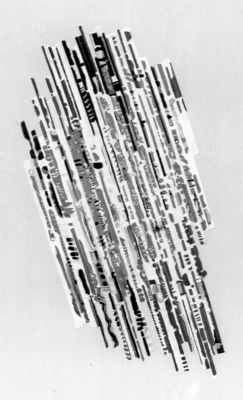

￥300

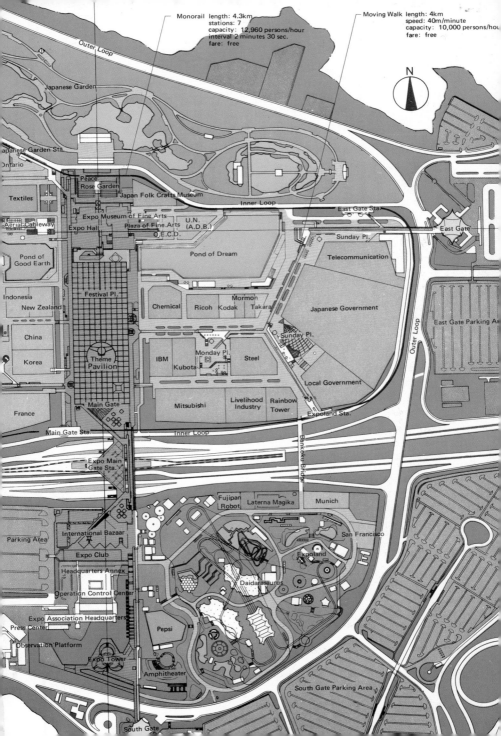

Monorail length: 4.3km
stations: 7
capacity: 12,960 persons/hour
interval 2 minutes 30 sec.
fare: free

Moving Walk length: 4km
speed: 40m/minute
capacity: 10,000 persons/hour
fare: free

N

Outer Loop

Japanese Garden

Japanese Garden Sta.

Ontario

Peace
Rose Garden

Japan Folk Crafts Museum

Inner Loop

East Gate Sta.

Textiles

Expo Museum of Fine Arts

Aerial Cableway

Expo Hall

Plaza of Fine Arts

U.N.
(A.D.B.)

O.E.C.D.

Sunday Pl.

East Gate

Pond of
Good Earth

Pond of Dream

Telecommunication

Outer Loop

East Gate Parking Area

Indonesia

New Zealand

Festival Pl.

Chemical

Ricoh

Kodak

Mormon

Takara

Japanese Government

China

Korea

Theme
Pavilion

IBM

Kubota

Monday Pl.

Steel

Sunday Pl.

Local Government

France

Main Gate

Mitsubishi

Livelihood
Industry

Rainbow
Tower

Expoland Sta.

Main Gate Sta.

Inner Loop

Bankoku Bridge

Expo Main
Gate Sta.

Parking Area

International Bazaar

Fujipan
Robot

Laterna Magika

Munich

Expo Club

San Francisco

Headquarters Annex

Operation Control Center

Expoland

Expo Association Headquarters

Daidarasaurus

Press Center

Observation Platform

Pepsi

Expo Tower

Amphitheater

South Gate Parking Area

South Gate

EXPO'70
OFFICIAL
GUIDE

Japan World Exposition

Type of exhibition:
A General Exhibition of the First Category in accordance with the "Convention regarding International Exhibitions"

Year: 1970

Duration: March 15 (Sunday) till September 13 (Sunday) (183 days)

Location: The Senri Hills in Osaka, Japan

Area: About 3,300,000 square meters

Exposition schedule

March 15 — April 28

Open	Open
Gates—9.30a.m.	Pavilions—10.00a.m.
Close	Close
Gates—10.00p.m.	Pavilions—9.00p.m.

April 29 — September 13

Open	Open
Gates—9.00a.m.	Pavilions—9.30a.m.
Close	Close
Gates—10.30p.m.	Pavilions—9.30p.m.

Organizer

The Japan Association for the 1970 World Exposition

Admission fees

	Adults	Youths*	Children
Ordinary tickets	¥800	¥600	¥400
Group discount	¥700	¥500	¥300
(groups of over 25)			
Coupons	¥3,800	¥2,850	¥1,900
(good for 5 visits)			
Night discount**	¥400	¥300	¥200
Special discount	¥300	¥200	¥100
(for physically			
handicapped, etc.)			

School Group discount   ¥200 (highschool student)

¥100 (primary or secondary school pupil)

Parking

March 15 — April 28
    Open: 8.30a.m.
    Close: 11.00p.m.
April 29 — September 13
    Open: 8.00a.m.
    Close: 11.30p.m.
Fees: Passenger car ¥500
    Buses with over 11 seats ¥1,000

EXPO'70 Inauguration Ceremony

Time   11:00 a.m.

Date   March 14, 1970

Place   Festival Plaza

1) "Ettenraku" — a composition of Imperial Court Music.

2) Entrance of Their Majesties, the Emperor and Empress, Their Imperial Highnesses, the Crown Prince and Princess, and other members of the Imperial Family.

3) Singing of "Kimigayo," the Japanese national anthem
Raising of the Flag of Japan

4) Raising of the flags of the participating countries

5) Raising of the International Exposition Symbol Flag and the EXPO'70 Flag.

6) Address by the Prime Minister of Japan
Address by the President of EXPO'70 Association
Message from the President of the Bureau of International Expositions

7) Declaration of the Opening of EXPO'70.

8) Fanfare, cannonade, fireworks, confetti, balloons
Start of the EXPO fountain
Lighting of the Electric Signboard — "Progress and Harmony for Mankind"

9) "Prelude to the Festival" — Musical program

10) World '70 Parade

11) Departure of Their Majesties, the Emperor and Empress, Their Highnesses, the Crown Prince and Princess, and other members of the Imperial Family.

12) Music and Fireworks.

The closing ceremony is scheduled for September 13, 1970

* Age: 15 to 22
** After 5:00 p.m.

Official Emblem of Universal and International Exhibitions

This is the official emblem of universal and international exhibitions as selected by the Bureau of International Exhibitions (BIE) at its executive committee meeting in November 1969. EXPO'70 is the first world exposition to use the mark. Within a circle symbolizing friendship, the emblem shows a series of surging, blue-purple waves denoting the progress of mankind. It was designed by Masanori Matsushita, at the time of the selection a 22-year-old art student.

EXPO'70 Emblem

The EXPO'70 Emblem was chosen after a competition of 15 designers and members of two groups of artists. Created by Takeshi Ohtaka, the winning design is patterned on the cherry blossom, perhaps the most typically Japanese of flowers. Five petals represent the five great continents and symbolize the coming of people from all over the globe to the Japan World Exposition. The central circle: Japan. But the overall impression of the Expo Emblem is one of deep harmony.

Message of His Highness the Crown Prince

It is a great pleasure for me to welcome visitors from all over the world to EXPO'70, a monument to culture, made possible by the enthusiastic cooperation of many countries.

The 20th Century has been an era of great achievements. These remarkable accomplishments, colourfully displayed here under the theme "Progress and Harmony for Mankind," have impressed me with the unlimited possibilities of human wisdom.

I believe that true progress of human society can only be achieved where harmony exists and harmony can so easily be lost in this age of rapid progress. I sincerely hope that with EXPO'70 as an incentive, the peoples of the world will deepen their mutual understanding and bring about true peace and progress for all.

Akihito 明仁

Beginning with the first world exposition held in London in 1851, a series of world expositions subsequently held in several countries, has conscientiously recorded the progress of mankind, especially man's scientific achievements. We may well say therefore, that a world exposition is a high watermark denoting the successive waves of human advancement.

I personally believe that progress can never be achieved without harmony. Mankind is assured of unending progress only through the achievement of harmony; harmony between mankind and nature, between mankind and his community, and above all among mankind.

Technology has created what may be called a "second spring" for society. The integration into our daily lives of improvements brought about by technical innovations lead to a more affluent life. I feel it is very significant that Japan is hosting EXPO'70 at this time in history.

I sincerely hope that with EXPO'70 as a springboard, technology will better serve men and men will deepen their mutual understanding.

Eisaku Sato
Prime Minister of Japan
President
Japan World Exposition

It was just before the collapse of the feudal regime that Japan participated for the first time in an international exposition, that of Paris in 1867. It has since then participated in nearly all the international expositions held in Europe and in America, and the Japanese people have always wished to organize one in Japan. It had indeed been scheduled in Tokyo for 1940 and the tickets were put on sale, but it had to be given up because of the War.

Now, at long last an international exposition, the first of its kind in Asia, is being held in Osaka. People from all parts of the world, unlike in 1940, can easily come to Japan by air, and foreign visitors to the exposition will far exceed a million. The Japanese people, who will flock to Osaka in tens of millions, will be virtually making a trip around the world in the exposition ground, where they can make a tour of 85 pavilions, with displays so painstakingly mounted by various countries, international organizations, provinces and municipalities. This, in itself, will signify a step toward "Harmony for Mankind."

The spectacular progress of science and technology may sometimes seem to bring about discord and danger to humanity. But the displays in the pavilions of this exposition will certainly make us think about "Harmony" sought after by Oriental philosophy. At the same time, this exposition will be a gay and enjoyable occasion, with something of traditional Japanese festivities. I hope it will be a brilliant success and you will find it enjoyable and fruitful.

萩原　徹

Toru Haguiwara
Commissioner General
of the Japanese Government

Welcome to EXPO'70.

I would like to express my heartfelt gratitude to all those participating countries, international organizations, territories, states, provinces, cities, organizations and enterprises whose splendid contributions have been instrumental in making EXPO'70 such a magnificent spectacle.

A world exposition is a wonderful opportunity for man to display his progress. It is also a place where the people of the world can meet and exchange ideas. It is my firm belief that EXPO'70 will greatly contribute to world peace, by offering an international forum where citizens of all countries, overcoming differences in language, race and religion, can promote mutual understanding and friendship.

I hope that all visitors to EXPO'70 will immensely enjoy the great variety of exhibits. I trust that all will find in them the key to the twenty-first century.

Taizo Ishizaka
President
Japan Association
for the 1970 World Exposition

EXPO'70 OFFICIAL GUIDE
Table of Contents

Cover "Shasen Toshi" by
Guen Inokuma

Published by
The Japan Association for
the 1970 World Exposition
Publisher:
    Shunichi Suzuki
Editor in chief:
    Shozo Ogiya
Consulting Editors:
    (in alphabetical order)
    Jun Eto
    Masaru Ibuka
    Hidetoshi Kato
    Seiji Kaya
    Yoshizo Kawamori
    Sakyo Komatsu
    Shigeharu Matsumoto
    Michio Nagai
    Taro Okamoto
    Saburo Okita
    Kenzo Tange
    Ayako Totsuka
    Samitaro Uramatsu

Paintings:
    Kaii Higashiyama
    Ikuo Hirayama
    Kenkichi Sugimoto
Contributions:
    Yukio Haruyama
    Ayako Totsuka
    Alice Shabecoff

Photography:
    Tadahiko Hayashi
    Jun Miki
    Tsutomu Ogura
    Kazuyuki Shinohara
    Masafumi Umeda
    Toshio Yoshida

Illustrators:
    Munetake Chuma
    Yoichi Kogire
    Hiroshi Ooba
    Susumu Takasuga
    Yasuo Terakado

Compiled with the cooperation
of Dentsu Advertising Ltd.
(Editorial Staff of EXPO'70
Official Guide headed by
Haruo Chijiiwa)
©Copyright, 1970, Japan
Association for the 1970
World Exposition

How to Use the EXPO'70 Official Guide

The "Official Guide" is designed as your best directory to the wonders and delights of EXPO'70. In addition, it is a souvenir of your visit to Japan's world exposition, a souvenir to recall pleasant memories of what you see, hear, feel and think at Expo.

Particular care has gone into the compiling of your "Official Guide." Whenever you want to locate a point of interest on the site and find out how to get there, refer to the map of Expo on the inside front cover. The inside back cover provides a map of the area around the Expo site.

Blue Pages Separate Each Chapter

The "Official Guide" is divided into eight chapters. These deal with the Expo Theme; Japanese Government Pavilion and Foreign Pavilions: Japanese Private Pavilions; Special Events and Entertainments; Services, Meals and Shopping; Expoland; and Japan and the World Exposition and a Compendium of Data. Each chapter begins with a blue page, enabling you to quickly find any information of interest.

Theme Chapter

This chapter explains the concept of the central EXPO'70 theme, "Progress and Harmony for Mankind," and the four sub-themes, as well as the philosophy behind the Symbol Area. For the first time in the construction of a world exposition, the theme was central to the development of the EXPO'70 site layout and theme architecture.

Japanese Pavilion and Foreign Pavilions

National pavilions and the pavilions of international organizations, territory, provinces and states, and cities, as well as non-Japanese private pavilions, are all introduced in this chapter.

(1) Pavilions are listed in order of nations, international organizations, territory, provinces and states, cities, and enterprises.

(2) In each of these categories, the pavilions are listed in order of dates contracts were signed.

(3) A layout map and alphabetical index are included at the beginning of this chapter for convenience in finding the descriptions of the respective pavilions.

(4) National names used in this guide are based principally on those used by the Japanese Foreign Ministry.

(5) The introductory descriptions place emphasis on the structure of the pavilions and their exhibits.

Domestic Pavilions

The chapter on Japanese Private Pavilions introduces them in order of local governments, public corporations, and enterprises. The enterprises are listed in order of dates contracts were signed.

A layout map and alphabetical index of these pavilions are to be found at the beginning of the chapter.

Entertainments

The chapter on Special Events and Entertainments lists the events and performances in chronological order. It gives time, place and detail of any entertainment you may find of interest.

For a Pleasant Visit to Expo

Before touring the Expo site, be sure to refer to the chapter on Services, Restaurants and Shopping. Expo's many varied services are projected from a large-scale, computerized information and telecommunication system.

NOTE:
All facts and figures in this book are based on the data and information confirmed as of February 1, 1970.

THEME
AND
ITS DEVELOPMENT

The Basic Concept

The grandeur of civilization built up by man through thousands of years of his history inspires us with awe when we turn our minds forward to imagine what might be in store for us in the infinite future unfolding before us. In particular, the progress made in recent years by science and technology has subjected every aspect of human life to changes such as could never have been dreamt of the day before. And the advance of civilization is still quickening its pace, promising for future mankind a mode of living far surpassing all present imagination.

Since the first universal and international exhibition was held in London in 1851, many such exhibitions have been organized in various cities of Europe and America. The events have played an important role in advancing the civilization of man, by collectively exhibiting the products of creative activity undertaken at the time by the peoples of the world, for all to see and ascertain the progress made to date, and inciting all to further efforts toward new developments. Japan has now the honor and privilege to organize, in Osaka in 1970, a universal and international exhibition in conformity with the Convention relating to International Exhibitions of 1928.

In planning this first universal and international exhibition ever to be held in Asia, it is our intent to realize an event that should leave its mark in the history of human civilization, and to this end, while duly respecting the customs and achievements of past universal and international exhibitions, we will base our plans on a new theme linking East with West. Our 1970 Exposition should indicate the progress made by modern civilization, and at the same time mark a turning point toward the development of a still better mode of living for future mankind.

Turning our eyes to the present world, however, we cannot but acknowledge that mankind with its glorious history behind it is still afflicted with many discords. The far-reaching developments of our technological civilization have brought about

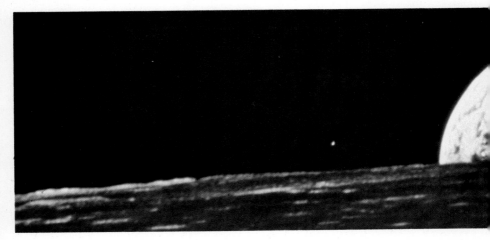

Theme & Its Development

PROGRESS AND HARMONY FOR MANKIND

radical changes to every aspect of our life today, and numerous problems arising therefrom are yet to be solved. Also there exist gross disparities in many parts of the world, while exchanges, both material and spiritual, between different regions are seriously deficient, often serving only to incite friction and tension through lack of understanding and forbearance. Even science and technology themselves are now adding a threat to mankind with the possibility of total destruction if once misapplied by those who have created them.

In full awareness of this actual state of our world, we still believe in the existence of human wisdom to open the door to the future prosperity of mankind. And this light of wisdom, we further believe, is not limited to certain parts of this earth but shines wherever there is man. With effective mutual communication and stimulation, the multifarious wisdom of the human races should gain higher levels, and serve mankind in harmoniously developing a better mode of life for all, through understanding and tolerance between the peoples of different traditions.

Such are the convictions and aspirations on which we will base our plans for the Japan World Exposition, Osaka, 1970. We look to all the peoples of the world to bring forth with pride the wisdom they have respectively developed and the fruits they have reaped therefrom. Here we shall see a happy forum of concord among men. It is the honor and pleasure of Japan to be able to organize this Exposition a century after her emergence from her isolation policy, which for nearly three hundred years had secluded her from the rest of the world.

And today, a new era must dawn on the world. The twentieth century is a period of great progress, but at the same time it has been far from free of suffering and disorder.

We desire to leave this world to the next generation as an abode ruled by peace and as a temple fit for praising the dignity and well-being of mankind. No honor could be greater for us than to see the place and opportunity we have provided for the World Exposition prove to be the turning point toward such a Golden Age.

This is the key Subject Theme in developing the Central Theme.

Progress and Harmony may seem to present an incompatible contradiction, but our expectation of a bright future for human civilization would depend on whether a way is found to reconcile the two propositions.

And the key to this problem must lie in respect for life itself: Every human individual must be accorded consideration for his worth as a being possessed of life, and this is the basic ground for equality of man regardless of race, nationality, sex, language, creed and social standing.

This Subject Theme 1 endeavors to throw light on the inherent nature of life, and also takes up the question of man's effort to fight diseases of mind and body that threaten life. But we are not to satisfy ourselves with the present state of human ife as we observe it objectively. We must keep in view a fuller life as our ultimate aim.

We must emphasize that to fully enjoy life is much more than merely to keep the body alive, but to strive for and to realize the true joy of living, a joy that every individual should have the right to feel as a human being.

14

The three Subject Themes 2 to 4 divide among them all subjects of possible relevance to living man in his environment.

The Subject Theme 2 deals with the relation between man and nature. Man has built up his present civilization by aggressively confronting and utilizing nature.

While on one hand man's concept of nature has come to cover the ocean depths, the polar regions and even interplanetary space, he has yet to fully and effectively utilize the soil of his own land where he has dwelt all these thousands of years. Thus we must let the results of science help us make better use of our earth, and yet at the same time we must not forget that man will, if he continues thoughtlessly to despoil and ravage nature, end by inviting disaster upon himself.

Nature poses upon us a question of *Harmony in Progress.*

Subject Theme 3 — Toward fuller engineering of our living environment

This Subject Theme deals with the products of man's work on material substances, in their relation to man in his life activities. We deal here mainly with the domain of technology. But we will look at technology, not only from the side of the manufacturer, but also through the eyes of man the user, to call for efforts to design better living with the use of the products of technology.

We aim at proving the ascendancy of man's freedom over machine, to defy the fallacy that the industrialized society is enslaving man to machine, while admittedly advancing human civilization. We see here again the problem of *Harmony in Progress,* as it presents itself to us in the domain of technology.

Tools and machines should naturally occupy an important position under all four Subject Themes, and in this particular instance, such Suggested Topics as clothing, food, housing, transportation and city development treat mainly of the impact of technology on mankind. The independent topic heading "Tools and Machines" is included for the purpose of covering cases where these implements make their appearance and contribution only in the intermediate stages of production processes.

The last topic "Time" is obviously a factor having increasingly important implications upon man's life, and we hope to see this actual yet ancient problem confronting man made an apposite subject for free play of imagination in planning fascinating displays for intellectual exercise.

Subject Theme 4 —— Toward better understanding of each other

In this last Subject Theme, we return to man himself, and take up the relation between man and his fellow men: To live is to live in a society.

Ever since antiquity, the supreme means of communication between men has been language. Language has not only provided man with the tool for verbally handing down the traditions of local society, but has lent itself to registration in writing, and now to transmission by radio wave, and we should like to see the technological problems involved given their due share of attention.

The Subject Theme should further transcend the category of spoken and written languages to consider the impact of communication on human society. Edu-cation should also be covered, for its function of imparting wisdom and experi-ence from man to man.

The human society has developed from isolated tribes into nations and is now advancing to constitute an international society in many domains. Social systems and customs are indispensable in the organi-zation of human society, but in striving to realise *Harmony in Progress* in this realm, we should not forget that, apart from the contribution to be expected from social systems contrived by human intellect, there is an important role to be played by the arts which appeal to the human emotion.

The urgent necessity of a better under-standing between nations and races cannot today be overemphasized.

Expo Site Master Plan

On September 14, 1965, the Bureau of International Exhibitions in Paris gave official approval to hold a universal and international exhibition in Japan. In the months that followed, the Theme Committee chaired by Seiji Kaya decided on "Progress and Harmony for Mankind" as the central theme for the exposition named EXPO'70. Then a study committee led by Kazumi Iinuma, Kenzo Tange and Uzo Nishiyama considered the best way to utilize the previously chosen site, the Senri Hills in Osaka.

The master plan was finalized by October 1966. Shigeru Ito became head of the five man Construction Advisory Committee and Kenzo Tage took charge of the basic site facilities. A group of 13 architects evolved the final construction blueprints in January 1968.

The unifying force in the evolution of the plan was the determination to give life to the theme "Progress and Harmony for Mankind". The result is that while EXPO'70 celebrates the history, culture and achievements of the past, it attempts to achieve a new milieu. A milieu in which people from all over the world can meet face to face, talk heart to heart and share the joy of peace and harmony. This milieu has been achieved, especially in Festival Plaza, the heart of EXPO'70.

The Theme Exhibits adjacent to the Festival Plaza form a display related to the main theme. Both the Exhibits and the Plaza are covered by the Grand Roof to emphasize their unity.

Dividing the site into Northern and Southern zones is the Osaka Central Loopway. In the northern zone are the Japanese Garden and Pavilions. Expoland and Administration facilities are contained in the southern zone. The 1,000 meter long and 150 meter wide Symbol Area, which includes the Main Gate, connects the two zones. Within the Symbol Area are the facilities devoted to the main theme.

Each national pavilion reflects the culture of that country. The diversity is great. Yet the master plan brings these differences together to produce a unique sense of harmony.

Picture the site as a tree with the Symbol Area as the trunk. The moving walks, the monorail and the seven sub-plazas serve as the boughs. All are painted a uniform white. Since they

are surrounded by the colorful "blossoms" of the pavilions, Expo presents a tree in full boom.

Yet the "tree" is in reality a city, a bustling center of activity. On weekends, with almost 600,000 visitors wending their way among the attractions, it will be a crowded city. However, Expo is a city of the future. The master plan incorporates forward-looking ideas, and the site is planned to serve man. Traffic will flow smoothly, people will easily find their way about, and areas of rest and relaxation are plentiful.

The planners gave close attention to the "Relations between Man and Nature". In doing so they made full use of the rolling hills of Senri. EXPO'70 may come to be termed the "exposition of the hills" because of

this. Canada's "Expo67" which was held in Montreal won the title "exposition of water" because it so utilized the grandeur of the St. Lawrence River.

In taking advantage of the topography, the planning committee situated the artificial Pond at the lowest point between the hills. Nearby are located the general exhibition area. Smaller pavilions are close to the Pond and larger pavilions are on higher ground. These follow the contour of the land and encircle the smaller pavilions. Another advantage of this arrangement is that it prevents a concentration of visitors in the central part of the site.

"Relations between Man and Technology" also received close scrutiny. Technology will enable visitors to achieve closer harmony with nature, especially during the hot, humid summertime in Japan. The Grand Roof will shade thousands from the sun. Covered, air conditioned moving walks, and regional air conditioning systems will make everyone's visit a comfortable one. The total capacity of Expo's regional air-conditioning equipment is the largest in the world.

Technology offers a wonderful future to man. The benefits of technology are incorporated into Expo. An efficient computer control system, will not only add to the ease of seeing Expo through traffic control and planning, it will also add to the spectacle of Expo by creating unique panoramas of light, color, sound and water. Everything possible has been done to make EXPO'70 a place for people.

Theme & Its Development

Symbol Area

The Symbol Area, the heart of Expo, is devoted to the central theme, "Progress and Harmony for Mankind." Gracious buildings and wide plazas present the historical experience of mankind while providing a forum for thousands of visitors of all nations, races and cultures.

Extending north and south from the Main Gate, the Symbol Area is 1,000 meters long, 150 meters wide and covers a total area of 118,000 square meters.

The Festival Plaza will be one of the liveliest parts of the Symbol Area. Here, many of the pageants of Expo will be held.

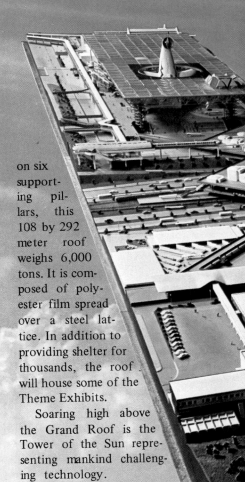

The Plaza itself and the Theme Exhibits are covered by the world's largest translucent roof. Rising 30 meters on six supporting pillars, this 108 by 292 meter roof weighs 6,000 tons. It is composed of polyester film spread over a steel lattice. In addition to providing shelter for thousands, the roof will house some of the Theme Exhibits.

Soaring high above the Grand Roof is the Tower of the Sun representing mankind challenging technology.

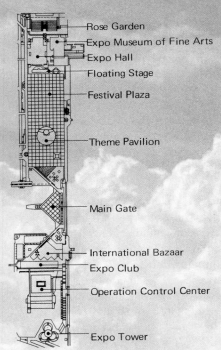

Rose Garden
Expo Museum of Fine Arts
Expo Hall
Floating Stage
Festival Plaza

Theme Pavilion

Main Gate

International Bazaar
Expo Club
Operation Control Center

Expo Tower

Theme & Its Development

Inside the Tower is an exhibition depicting the evolution of man. On either side stand two smaller towers, one representing Youth, the other Motherhood.

At the northern end of the Symbol Area is the artificial pond with its Fountains and Floating Stage. In front of the Pond is the ultra modern Expo Hall. An entire section behind the stage is glass, allowing spectators to enjoy the activities in Festival Plaza and on the Floating Stage. Performances will be staged at all three of these places.

A priceless collection of the world's masterpieces is displayed in the Expo Museum of Fine Arts, across from the Expo Hall. Varieties of roses create a galaxy of color in the Rose Garden located in front of the Museum.

To the south of the Main Gate is the International Bazaar. One splendid setting provides the opportunity to enjoy worldwide dining and shopping.

The Expo Association Headquarters and the Operation Control Center are behind the Bazaar.

At the southern tip of the Symbol Area, the Expo Tower extends a slender silhouette into the sky. The landmark of Expo, its many observation platforms provide people with varied views of the site and Osaka plain.

Theme Exhibition

A world exposition should be a festival in which the participants share in and increase each others' joy. This ideal guided Mr. Taro Okamoto, one of Japan's leading artists, in producing the Theme Exhibition.

In the space between the Main Gate and Festival Plaza he has given symbolic and concrete expression to the central theme, "Progress and Harmony for Mankind." Viewing these exhibits should involve all visitors in a shared experience that leads to mutual joy.

The exhibits, dominated by the Tower of the Sun, are located on three levels. In the subterranean hall visitors will be taken back to view the origins of life. At ground level they will be surrounded by impressions of today's world, and on the mid-air level their eyes will be focused on man's future.

Mid-Air Level (Future)
World of Progress

SYSTEM & INFOR-MATION
- Universe: Man & Nature
- Man: Man Himself
- World: Man vs. Man
- Life: Man & Technology

Ground Level (Present)

World of Harmony

ENERGY OF MODERN MAN
- Tower of the Sun
- Tower of Motherhood
- Tower of Youth
- All Expo Site and Pavilions
- Photo Exhibits

Subterranean Level (Past)

World of Mystery

MYSTERY OF LIFE
- Life: Man Himself
- Man: Man & Nature
- Mind: Man & Technology
  Man vs. Man

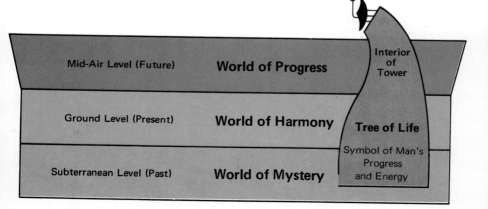

The World of Mystery

Subterranean Level

A moving walk takes visitors into complete darkness. Nebulous swirls of light appear, then glittering balls float around the people as they plunge into the origin of the universe. In the exhibition called "Life" visitors witness the first stirrings of life. Beginning with a model of the DNA molecule, they are present at the birth of various forms of life.

The next step is "Man." Within the

huge cave leading into this section are the wall paintings and drawings of primitive man. Further on, his struggle against nature and animals is depicted. Through a special screening system visitors are subjected to attacks by pre-historic animals, thus sharing their forbears' experiences.

In the final underground display entitled "Mind," the wisdom of early men is shown in their tools, weapons and utensils, while their religious experiences are reflected in their symbols for God, their idols, statues and masks.

The Energy of Life

Exhibition inside the Tower

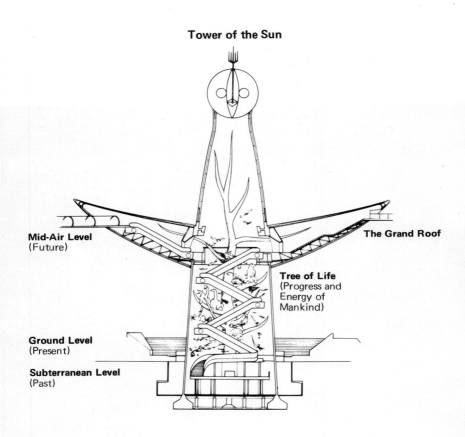

Tower of the Sun

Mid-Air Level
(Future)

The Grand Roof

Tree of Life
(Progress and
Energy of
Mankind)

Ground Level
(Present)

Subterranean Level
(Past)

Inside the Tower of the Sun rises the "Tree of Life" which dramatizes the story of evolution. Four escalators carry spectators up 45 meters past 300 models of simple cells, reptiles, birds, apes and homo sapiens. Lighting, sound effects and action displays intensify this trip through time. At the conclusion of their trip visitors step into the "Space of the Sun".

Theme & Its Development

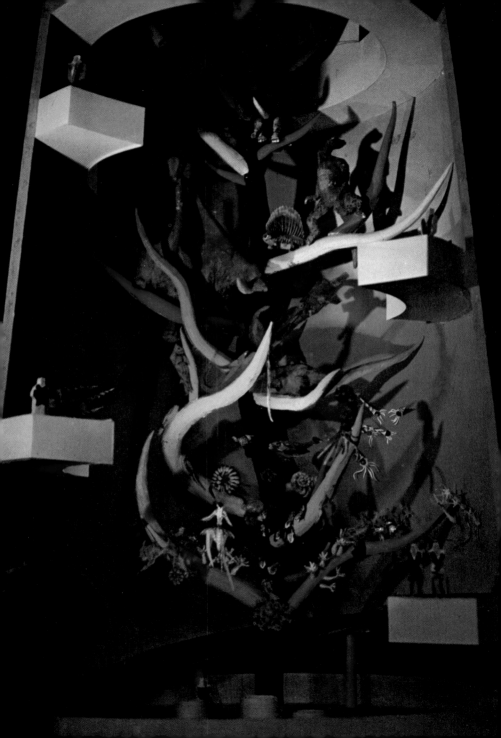

The World of Progress
Mid-Air Level

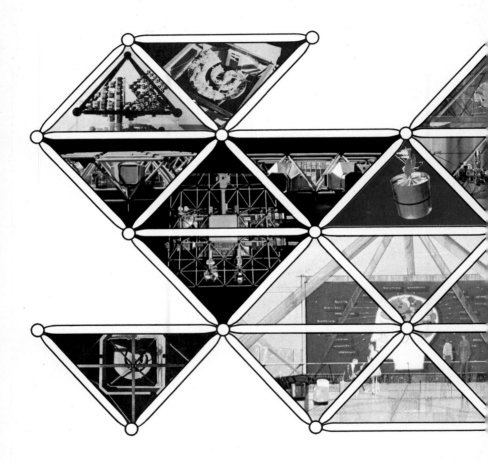

Now the visitor leaps through time and is transported into the "Universe." The exhibits in the Grand Roof propel the fairgoer through the solar system, along the Milky Way and out into the further reaches of space.

For the study of "Man" a huge profile of a man has been constructed.

Human emotions play across the face and a colored lighting system reveals the operations of the human brain. Here is the biggest picture book in the world. It measures 3.3 by 5 meters and uses 3D writing.

One hundred and ninety-two screens in the Mandarama depict fami-

lies living in different parts of the world. The physical vastness of the planet, the varieties of races who dwell on it are impressive. One world embraces a great deal of diversity.

A degree of unity has been achieved. Yet problems remain. These problems are recalled in vivid photo-graphs lining the walls of the entrance-way to the "World." Here the empha-sis is on human dignity and the im-portance of human life.

"Life" presents a picture of tomor-row. Futuristic homes, cities, tools and machines give everyone a preview of life in the not too distant future.

The World of Harmony
Ground Level

The 16,000 sq. meters surrounding the Tower of the Sun and the companion Towers of Motherhood and Youth, form the Plaza of Harmony. An eyecatching display of 500 photos depicts the joys and sorrows of ordinary people all over the world; a tribute to the "Anonymous People Who Support the World."

Piercing through the Grand Roof, the Tower of the Sun soars 70 meters into the sky. The magnificent Tower, symbolizing the dignity and unending progress of mankind, has three faces. The one facing the Main Gate is 12 meters in diameter. Overlooking Festival Plaza is the 8 meter "Black Sun" called the guardian deity of the Plaza. On the pinnacle of the Tower is the glorious "Golden Sun" which is 11 meters in diameter. Two arms, 25 meters long, are stretched in welcome.

The Tower of Motherhood express-es the bounty of maternal love. The graceful Tower links the World of Progress with the Plaza of Harmony. From its terrace, 5 meters above the Plaza, vistors can enjoy watching the crowds below.

Depicting the youthful energy of mankind, the needle sharp Tower of Youth stands 23 meters in height. Six ·modern sculptures cling to the steel pipe Tower, portraying different aspects of youth.

Around these three Towers visitors from every corner of the globe can share their excitement and joy.

Created by Taro Okamoto

Festival Plaza

This is the focal point of EXPO'70. A plaza that is constantly a festival — full of sound, color, light and movement that is a reflection of the world. A unique meeting place. A place for exciting and varied performance and presentations.

A grand roof covers the plaza, stretching north to south over an area equal to an entire baseball stadium.

On the southern end there are special seats for distinguished visitors. Along the western side is a long Terrace Cafeteria. The cafeteria can accommodate 400 — and it's possible to eat while watching performances.

Stacked up above the cafeteria are six unique grandstand units that are somewhat like petals of a flower.

Another six units — each capable of holding 200 — move about the area of the plaza to meet the needs of the various performances.

The grandstands, plus standing room, allows a total of 27,000 people to see Festival Plaza performances.

A giant "robot" is the technical director of the plaza — controlling electronically the lights, sound system and other equipment.

Celebrations of National Days of Expo participants will be held in Festival Plaza. A great variey of spectacular special shows are scheduled for the plaza — with something happening there almost every day. But even if a performance isn't going on in Festival Plaza, the plaza itself is a performance — an experience that shouldn't be missed. (Complete program: P.224—229.)

Theme & Its Development

Expo Hall
Floating Stage
Fountains

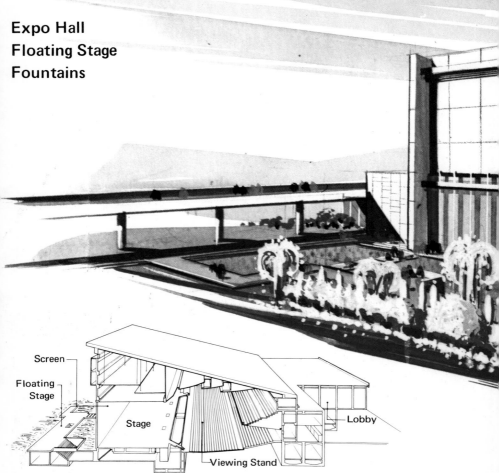

Screen —
Floating Stage —
Stage
Lobby
Viewing Stand

● Located at the north end of the Symbol Area, Expo Hall is a unique theater that denies distinction between indoors and out; its stage opens to reveal Expo's Floating Stage, the Pond and its fantastic fountains and, indeed, the entire Festival Plaza.

For Expo Hall, a total of 20 programs — including popular musicals and light music from around the globe — have been planned. One star attraction is America's Sammy Davis

Jr., called the most versatile entertainer of the century. But other shows include a chanson festival featuring France's Dalida; a Canadian musical comedy, "Anne of Green Gables;" the National Northern Russian Choir; a Cuban carnival, and many others.

● The Floating Stage, on the Pond between Expo Hall and Festival Plaza, features a variety of relaxing entertainment — a Hawaiian band, a water show, a festival of Italian songs and dances, a Caribbean steel band. Mostly

Theme & Its Development

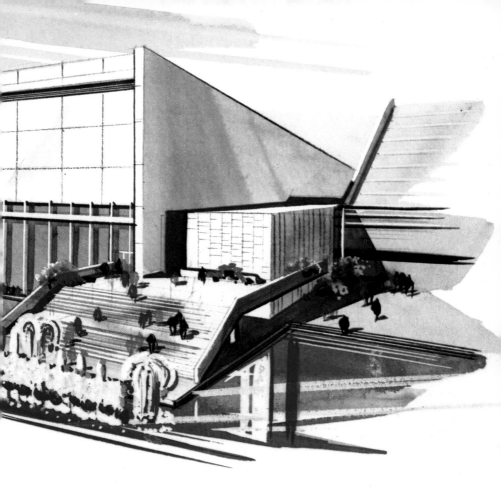

amateurs, the performers are all dynamic and enthusiastic.

The various shows make full use of unconventional techniques and ideas. One example: three shows under a common theme simultaneously in Festival Plaza and Expo Hall and on the Floating Stage. And rear-wall glass may be opened to let the Expo Hall stage 'borrow' a backdrop of the fountains, the Floating Stage and the Plaza.

● But there are other performers at EXPO'70: those fountains. Musical ones in the Pond jet water high or low, spheric or fan-shaped in form, and to colorful lighting variations. Nine fountains of the falling, rotary, up-and-down type play in front of the Japanese Pavilion. Also designed by Isamu Noguchi and also in the Pond, on the pavilion's west side, five funnel-shaped fountains artistically shoot great quantities of water downward and outward.

For details of performances in Expo Hall and on the Floating Stage, see Pages 232 to 237.

Expo Museum of Fine Arts

Art is a world language, the one that transcends the barriers of present-day tongues and communicates through the ages as well. From the birth of mankind, art has been with us. The arts have developed independently in various parts of the world and yet have also influenced one another. Art evolves parallel to human spirit and culture, providing a big clue to answering: "How have human beings been coming along?"

Displayed in the Expo Museum of Fine Arts are about 300 works from more than 40 countries, plus about 400 from Japan itself.

Under the following five themes, the exhibits are displayed in such a manner as to follow the historical streams of Western and Eastern arts, showing the harmony, contrast and integration of arts by times and regions.

Saria casket made about 700 B.C.
Tokyo National Museum

1. Soul of Primitive Ages: Dawn of Creation

The origin of the fine arts differs from place to place and from people to people. But joy in the beauties of nature is common to all ancient works.

These exhibits are roughly divided into two categories with examples from ancient Egypt, Greece and Mesopotamia, birthplaces of civilization. Included are the "Sumerian Statue" of Iraq, the "Standing Statue of Tutan-khammon" from Egypt and remnants of the Mayan and Incan civilizations, as well as works by natives of Africa and Australia.

2. East-West Exchange: Silk Road and European Culture

This theme studies how East and West began to exchange cultures and ideas as, in ancient times, the Silk Road of traders served as a bridge between the two.

Conveying the great influences of Europe and the Middle East are crystalware unearthed in the tomb of the Emperor Ankan and loaned by the Tokyo National Museum, the "Leather with Dyed Pattern" from the Todaiji Temple, and the "Camel, Three-Color Glaze" of the T-Ang Dynasty (Tokyo Museum).

3. Sacred Arts: Path of Faith

Religious faith was indispensable to mankind and a rich variety of art works developed from that fact. All Western works were once related to Christianity. Displayed here are "Pieta" by Van Dyck, "St. Peter the Martyr" by Fra Angelico, a life of Christ on nine tapestries for which Raphael made designs, and "Apocalypse", 16 woodcut prints by A. Durer.

Buddha images and Buddhist pictures on display include national treasures and important cultural assets such as the statue of "Miroku Bosatsu" from Koryuji Temple and "Kongokai Mandara-Zu" from Kyoogoku-ji Temple. There are also stone images of Buddha from Asian countries.

4. Progress Toward Freedom: Man, Nature and the World

This is a collection of works postdating the Renaissance, all depicting people yearning for freedom. From France are works of master artists of all schools from classicism to impres-

5. Dynamics of the Present

Introduced here are contemporary works expressing the dynamic spirit of today's world. With more examples of the abstract school than that of traditional realism, some of the masterpieces here are the works of Kandinsky, Klee and Mondrian. The "Three Musicians", one of Picasso's representative works, is hung along with "Premonition of Civil War" by Salvador Dali, "The Portrait of an Admiral" by Siqueiros and, as well, "Family Group" by Henry Moore.

sionism to realism, including Cezanne, Renoir and Gauguin. And there are works of Rubens, Van Gogh, and Delacroix.

The Japanese works in this section include such national treasures as "Portrait of Takami Senseki" by Watanabe Kazan (Tokyo Museum), the "Portrait of Minamoto-no-Yoritomo" (Jingoji Temple, Kyoto) and the "Scrolls of Frolicking Animals and People" (Kozanji Temple, Kyoto).

Also on display is pop art from the United States.

The Expo Museum of Fine Arts is run by a 25-member staff, headed by Director Soichi Tominaga, in cooperation with the 15 members of the EXPO'70 fine arts exhibition committee, the Cultural Agency, the National Museum of Fine Arts and many others. The splendid exhibits are housed in the latest of facilities.

"Pieta" (1636) by Antoine van Dyck (1599 — 1641)
Musées Royaux des Beaux-Arts, Antwerp

Above:
"Portrait
of Joahim
Gasquet" (1900)
by Paul Cézanne
National Museum
of Prague

"Tête d'Athlète"
sculptured
about 500 B.C.
The Louvre,
Paris

Expo Tower

A major landmark at the Exposition, the Expo Tower soars 120 meters (394 ft.) into the sky. It's on a 70-meter hill in the southern part of the Symbol Area.

New super strong steel and new design and construction techniques have eliminated the supports which would normally be required so the tower stands gracefully on three vertical pillars. Observation platforms, open to the public, are located up to the 75-meter level. The tower does more than offer a view: it's also a wireless relay station for the press and security officers.

Rose Gardens

The Expo Rose Gardens were born from an idea of the host city of Expo67. The Montreal Rotary Club suggested the gardens. 50 varieties of roses from throughout the world have been gathered as a Rotary project. 10,000 plants, carefully tended by the Osaka Rotary Club, have gone into the gardens. One is on the north side of the Symbol Area; the other on the east side of the Textile Pavilion.

Expo Club

Created by and for participants in the Exposition, the Expo Club has an auditorium, conference rooms, reception rooms and restaurants. It is a center for cultural and business ex-

changes for visiting officials and those who staff the big fair.

International Bazaar

Here is the world in a nutshell. Products, crafts, souvenirs and food from all over the globe in one compact, colorful area. Ten countries operate restaurants here, with staff members dressed in native costumes.

Thirty countries offer their products for sale. About a third of the goods for sale are special Japanese products. Special arrangements have been made so prices are quite reasonable.

The Main Gate

Over 150,000 people a day will go through the Main Gate.

Underneath the gate are the Osaka Central Loop Highway, the Chugoku Expressway, a station of the Kita Osaka Electric Railways plus bus and taxi stops. From there, visitors move to the gate's triangular deck by escalators.

Operation Control Center

Housed in an annex of the Association Headquarters, this is the "heart" of EXPO'70. Experts, aided by the latest computerized equipment, collect, process and distribute the great mass of information required to keep Expo going.

The center is linked electronically to points throughout the site. Information concerning the number of visitors and vehicles in parking areas, congestion in any area of Expo, daily events, detailed programs, property lost and found, etc. flow through the center to all pavilions and facilities.

The center is a good example of what the "information community" of the future may be like.

We're all you expect Japan to be.

Your Japan Air Lines hostess is much more
than an airline stewardess. She's an artful conjurer.
She brings to life the atmosphere of serenity and peace,
of welcome and personal attention, that is Japan
at its most charming. It's something you can expect
from us, wherever in the world you're heading. For we take
the legendary hospitality of Japan...everywhere.

JAPAN AIR LINES

Japan Air Lines—official airline for EXPO'70

FOREIGN PAVILIONS
AND
JAPANESE PAVILION

Index of Pavilions (1) — West of Senri Bridge Avenue —

Pavilions on this page are listed in alphabetical order.

Descriptions of pavilions are arranged in order of dates contracts were signed.

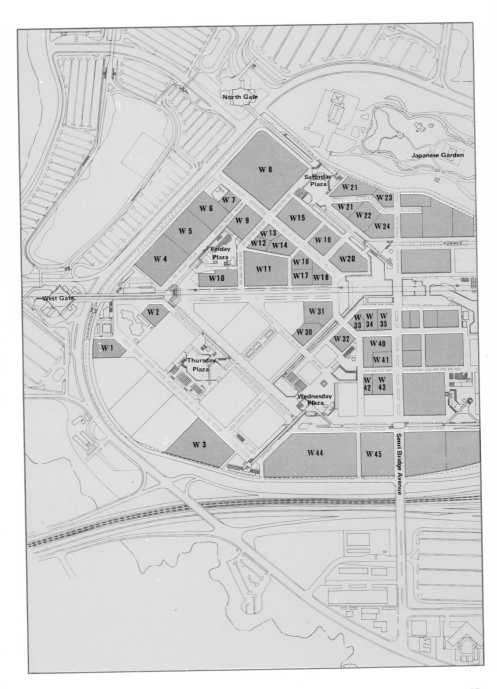

Index of Pavilions (2) — East of Senri Bridge Avenue —

Abbreviations:

I.P. = International Place

RCD = Regional Cooperation for Development, here used to indicate the joint pavilion of the RCD member countries.

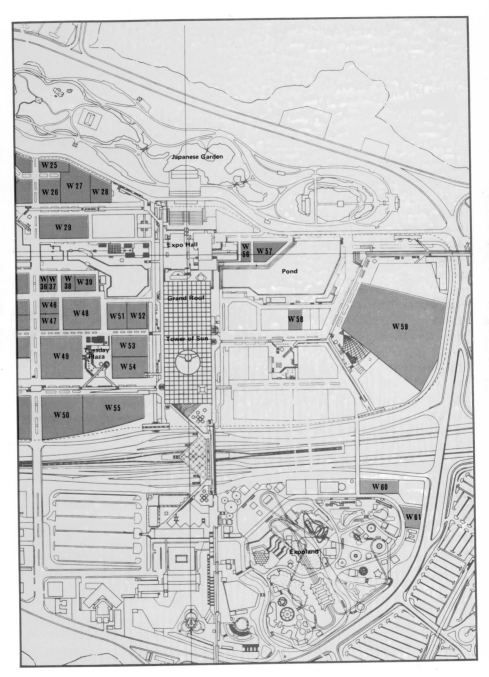

JAPAN

—Japanese Government Pavilion—

Producer: Takeji Tsukamoto
Architects: Nikken Sekkei
Exhibit Designer: Takashi Kono

As befits the host nation, Japan has built by far the largest pavilion at EXPO'70. It's as interesting as it is big.

Five drum-like elevated structures surround an 80-meter (260-foot) tower. From above, the grouping looks like a cherry blossom, which is both the Expo emblem and the national flower. Each of the five halls is 58 meters (190 feet) in diameter and 27 meters, nearly 90 feet, tall.

Under the theme "Japan and the Japanese," the pavilion presents the past and present of the land and its people in all their varying aspects. Then it delves into the future, when the world will have come to know Japan better and when the Japanese will have developed their dreams.

The Japanese Pavilion tells how the EXPO'70 theme, "Progress and Harmony for Mankind," has sprouted and will bloom, like a cherry blossom. Exhibits, therefore, stress the "progress" that has made the historical development of Japan more than a mere "lapse of time." You see contemporary industry and culture and hopes for the 21st Century. Exhibits also stress the "harmony" of a Japan that has drawn on both Eastern and Western cultures and has built upon this double foundation the structure of a vigorous and unique culture of its own.

Consequently, exhibits are arranged in the three sections of yesterday, today and tomorrow — Mukashi, Ima and Asu. All is understandable wherever you begin; but you may follow the flow of history by entering Hall 1 and proceeding clockwise through the others.

After being carried up by escalator 42 meters, nearly 140 feet, from below the tower, you are in Hall 1 and the Mukashi section — the past. Photos, replicas and other media show Japan's history. Immemorial times, as represented by "Haniwa" clay dolls. Olden times, when an aristocratic culture followed the introduction of Buddhism. Kamakura and Muromachi

eras: the absorption of China's Sung and Ming cultures as well as the creation of Japan's own Zen culture. Azuchi-Momoyama era, the "golden culture." Edo period, with its merchant culture. And the Meiji era, which ushered in Western culture and contemporary times.

Hall 2, under the theme Ima, or Today, demonstrates the huge scale and dynamic growth of Japanese industry and the great energy of the Japanese people. A giant steel wall, in the shape of a 300,000-ton-tanker's stern section, symbolizes this fast-growing industry. Its inside surface houses a mass of screens and models. This hall also shows the enriched daily life of the Japanese and their steady advance.

Also under the theme of Ima, Hall 3 puts an emphasis on sun and water. There's "Japanese Nature and Its Utilization" and an exploration of the relations between nature and man. There's a "Forest of Statistics" showing, by slides, the population, industry and life of Japan. There's the "Sea of Japan" where you'll enjoy a simulated underwater trip and learn about the fishing industry and power generation by waves.

Hall 4 is a sort of plaza where Japan's latest technology is demonstrated: a linear-motor car, items for exploring the Antarctic, an earthquake-proof structure. In addition, the "Little World Hall" shows you what's going on in 17 places in the world simultaneously and "Illusions" tests your sense of equilibrium.

Then you come to Hall 5. Asu, Tomorrow, is the theme and film called "Japan and the Japanese" is the main attraction. It is shown on a huge screen, 48 meters wide (157 feet); production became possible only with the development of an eight-lens camera of a quite special type. Among other features in Tomorrow is "Japan in the 21st Century;" four research organizations use animations and models to envisage an ideal of Japan in the future.

Japanese Pavilion

JAPANESE GARDEN

Japan is famed for its gardens. As famed as for its classic architecture.

EXPO'70' Japanese Garden — in the northern quarter of the site — is an area of calm, simple, natural beauty pleasingly in contrast with the technological glitter of the pavilion sections. But this area is also a visual demonstration of Japan's superb gardening techniques.

The Japanese Garden is designed to create a world of "Harmony between Nature and Man." A stream meanders through it, from west to east, tracing the course of Japanese gardening techniques from ancient to medieval to recent times — Jodai to Chusei to Kinsei Periods. The waters end with a demonstration of modern gardening techniques, fitting to the Expo theme of "Progress and Harmony for Mankind," where new ideas are combined with centuries-old traditions.

Some 1.3 kilometers (0.8 miles) long and 200 meters (about 650 feet) wide, the Japanese Garden area gently

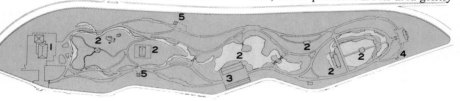

1 Guest House   2 Rest House   3 Main Entrance Administration Bldg.   4 East Entrance   5 Washroom

slopes to carry its waters eastward. The basic idea is "flow" — the natural flow of water through valleys and plains, at once symbolizing the flow of time and the progress of man through the eras.

A Guest House for visiting Heads of State and other prominent guests, in the west end, the Jodai section, is classic in style to harmonize with the garden. Firs, black pines and other conifers around it create the atmosphere of a remote mountainside in ancient Japan.

Nearby, from a fountain on a bluff, gushes the stream, soon to be divided by a hill planted with Japanese black pines and various species of azalea, typical of the Kansai area. On this hill is an observation tower as well as a rest house and ceremonial tea room — features of medieval-era gardens.

The streams rejoin by an extensive sandy beach suggestive of the origins of the "stone gardens" unique to Japan. Then the waters pour into a large pond of 11,000 square meters or about 13,000 square yards in size, north of the Symbol Area. A combination of hill and pond represents the style and technique prevalent in the early Edo Period.

At the eastern end of the garden is the modern area with its series of ponds — including a carp pond, a lotus pond and an iris pond — and a terraced flower bed. Here, as throughout the Japanese Garden, rest places and wide promenades abound for the convenience of strollers.

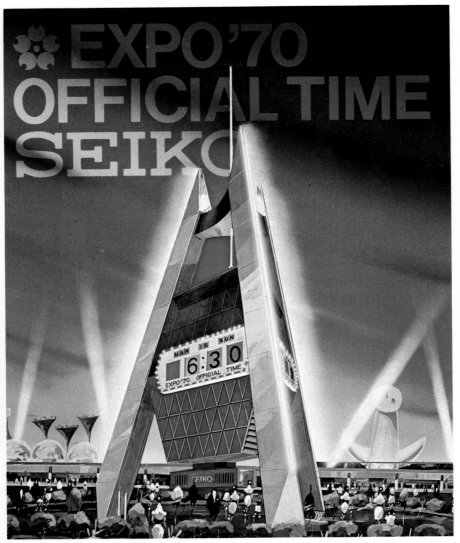

EXPO '70 TIME IS SEIKO TIME

From the time EXPO'70 opens until it closes, Seiko will be keeping time. Conveniently located at 50 sites throughout the fair, 110 Seiko clocks will be synchronized by UHF with a central atomic master clock. Seiko will be counting every second of time with an accuracy of ± one second for more than 1,000 years.

Head Office: Seiko Watches— K. Hattori & Co., Ltd., Ginza, Tokyo, Japan.

54

CANADA

Discovery. That's the theme of the Canadian Pavilion — an invitation to discover Canada but also an essential fact, that ever since its discovery Canadians have explored the vast reaches of their land and today bring this quality of adventure to industry, science and art.

Sheathed in mirrored slopes, the pavilion exterior reflects the sky. But illusion suggests arctic ice, the mass of mountains, vast prairie sky or the glitter of water, all aspects of the Canadian landscape.

In the courtyard the mood changes. A young country. "The Young Pavilion." Huge rainbow parasols revolve colorfully above young Canadian singers, dancers and musicians, performing every day.

The exhibits, underground, commence with a series of theaters. Computerized audio-visual displays and an avant-garde musical score introduce you to the expanse, grandeur and po-

tential of the Canadian land, to Canada as a Pacific-rim nation, to the accomplishments in urbanizing the country. On one wall, thousands of tiny electro-luminescent cells form a cartoon of people adapting their environment to themselves.

Concluding exhibits trace, by artifact and product, the origins and development of the Canadian people — from the original migrants from Asia, to the French and English, to recent arrivals from every part of the world. Amid evidence of a sophisticated economy, the presentation is climaxed by the largest mural ever carved by Eskimos.

As befits the holder of Expo 67, Canada was the first country to agree to participate at Osaka and the first to complete every phase of planning. Canada is also represented by the Provinces of Quebec, British Columbia and Ontario with their own distinctive pavilions.

KOREA
Republic of Korea

The Republic of Korea Pavilion, using as its theme "Better Understanding and Friendship" is a blending of the old and the new. It is surrounded by 15 huge steel columns, each 30 meters high and 4 meters in diameter, symbolizing the Korean people's accomplishments in industrialization.

At the entrance to the pavilion is a replica of the giant bell, "Shin Jong" (God's Bell), which was cast by a master craftsman in the 8th Century.

The exhibits reveal Korea's history and progress towards becoming a self-sufficient nation and its hopes for the future.

On the upper floor are examples of celadon and other ceramics, metal and art work, and traditional musical instruments. Also shown is Korea's greatest contribution to world progress — metal, movable, printing type. Such type was in use in Korea more than 200 years before Gutenberg

introduced similar methods in Europe.

The floor below reflects the remarkable progress of modern Korea. The exhibits consist mainly of photographs and mosaics illustrating the country's natural beauty, resources and its industrious people.

A special room on the same floor, staffed by capable personnel, provides foreign businessmen with detailed information about Korean products.

Future development plans are shown in the Annex, designed to resemble an ancient Korean ship. Each side has 13 oars in motion, symbolizing Korea's continuing advancement.

Visitors may purchase colorful souvenirs at a well-stocked concession shop in the lounge on the first floor.

The Korean Pavilion, on the west side of the Symbol Area, directly between the Tower of the Sun and Tuesday Plaza, is one of the closest to Expo's Main Gate.

UNITED STATES OF AMERICA

The United States Pavilion measures 83 by 140 meters and covers an area of 9,290 square meters. The elliptical translucent domed roof is the largest and lightest clear span, air-supported roof ever built.

The theme of the United States exhibit is "The Images of America" and through these images an attempt is being made to familiarize visitors with what Americans are like; where and how they live, and what they have created in the way of culture, science and technology.

"Ten Photographers" Exhibit — contains a contemporary photo documentary of the United States by 10 outstanding American photographers.

American Painting Exhibit — features select American paintings from the eighteenth century to the present, loaned exclusively for EXPO'70 display by the Metropolitan Museum of Art in New York.

Sports Exhibit — provides viewers with a panoramic view of U.S. sports including a collection of baseball memorabilia of such greats as Babe Ruth, Walter Johnson and Joe DiMaggio.

Space Exploration Exhibit — displays virtually all the space components which have either been retrieved from outer space or engineering test models capable of being flown. A key exhibit is an actual sample of moon rock retrieved by American astronauts during the Apollo 11 lunar mission.

Architectural Exhibit — the dynamics of American architecture is treated photographically to show a wide range of indigenous architecture.

Folk Art Exhibit — presents the most diversified single collection of American folk art objects ever shown in Asia.

New Arts Exhibits — selections from the results of an "Art and Technology" collaborative project now in progress under the auspices of the Los Angeles County Museum of Art.

CHINA

Republic of China

The Chinese Pavilion is based upon the theme "China — Heritage and Progress." Architecturally, it expresses the traditional philosophy of intricacy within simplicity. Two equal and opposite triangular towers are unified by a massive canopy of lights, echoing the majesty of a palace gate in the Han Dynasty. This gateway symbolizes cultural exchanges between China and other nations throughout her long history. Exhibit rooms are created by cantilevers thrusting into space between the two towers and linked by glass bridges that afford the visitors alternative experiences of openness and enclosure. At the back of the gateway are a cafeteria, a gourmet restaurant, and a plaza with a pool surrounding an ancient pine.

Of the ten distinct exhibit areas, the first four feature some of China's unique gifts to mankind, ranging from science and technology such as paper, printing, porcelain, and silk, to language and art, such as calligraphy and painting; the fifth area presents the story of transition from the dynastic past to the modern republic; the next four areas depict progress in education, transportation, communication, industry, commerce, science and agriculture, in Taiwan today; and the last area projects an enchanting panorama of the Island Beautiful. Throughout, modern techniques of audio-visual communications, such as films, slides, graphics, and photo-murals are used.

The pavilion, in depicting China's heritage and progress, aims to express the Confucian ideal of "tien-hsia wei-kung" or "One World for All Mankind."

The Pavilion of the Republic of China, which conveniently overlooks Expo's Festival Plaza and the Tower of the Sun, is just to the northeast of Tuesday Plaza.

Architectural design: Y.H. Peng and C.Y. Lee. Exhibits and graphic design: Wang R.C. Weng, Peter Yung, and Robert Yung. Coordinator: I.M. Pei.

Today is Suntory Day

Savor the quiet, good, taste of Old Suntory. Today. Anyday. Discover its classic flavor born in Japan ages ago . . . a fine blend of golden barley, pure spring water and time (lots of it). Shouldn't today be your Suntory Day?

See the "Water of Life" Suntory Pavilion (Wednesday Plaza). And, dine and drink heartily at the many Suntory EXPO '70 restaurants. Also, be sure to stop by the airport duty-free liquor shop and take home the good taste of Japan . . . Suntory.

Find a new world
in the old world of fairy tales...

Folk stories from around the world. Old, familiar tales — but shown
in a remarkable new way. It's at the Sumitomo Pavilion.
An insight into many cultures . . . interpreted by ultra-modern
techniques and age-old puppetry. A memorable, happy experience
brought to you by 46 leaders in Japan's world of business,
industry and finance.

 The Sumitomo Pavilion

NETHERLANDS
Kingdom of the Netherlands

The Netherlands Pavilion represents the three countries — the Netherlands, Surinam and the Netherlands Antilles — which together form a commonwealth: the Kingdom of the Netherlands.

In the pavilion's central hall, two large walls are devoted to Surinam and the Netherlands Antilles. Slide projections depict the openness of these two Caribbean countries to contacts with the world.

Progress through Openness, in fact, is the theme of the entire pavilion, in which the Netherlands is seen as an open country, both literally and spiritually. The Dutch people, at a junction of world traffic routes, regard contact with others as vital.

The Dutch Pavilion, in striking blue, silver and orange colors, is a series of cube-like tiered sections spiraling to a height of 30 meters (98 feet) and supported by four towers. Two access streets sloping under the building lead to an escalator which takes you into the central hall; three wings here contain a restaurant, a theater and a reception area.

The second floor is a service area. In the main structure, gained by escalator, there are three "cabins," the uppermost giving a panoramic view of Expo.

Throughout the pavilion, extensive use of a new "multiple screening" technique showing several films simultaneously, gives a many-sided and vivid impression of life in the Netherlands.

In the theater, documentary films are regularly screened and Dutch music is played daily. "Information units" at the rear of the building are another important source of specific information; you can operate them yourself. There is also a bookshop, a tourist information center and a stand where more detailed documentation can be obtained.

ZAMBIA
Republic of Zambia

Zambia was the first of the African nations to announce its intention to participate in EXPO'70.

The Zambian Pavilion is centrally located ·at International Place 1-A together with other members of the African group.

The Zambians staged a strong

nationalist movement after World War II to free themselves from British rule, realizing that there is nothing quite like freedom and independence. It was a long, hard fight but they finally won, gaining their independence at the time of the Tokyo Olympic Games in 1964.

The country has rich deposits of cobalt, manganese, zinc and lead which they exploit aggressively. Copper is especially important to Zambia and in its production, Zambia is important enough to rank fourth in the world.

However, Zambia is striving to reduce her reliance on copper as the main revenue earner by boosting agriculture. The people of Zambia strongly believe that it is of vital importance for them to establish a diversified economy.

Zambians feel that, at all costs, they must plan to be more than self-sufficient in foodstuffs; they must develop commercial farming of those products that can earn them foreign exchange. In the first category of products, experiments are being carried out in wheat and sugar production and fruit and vegetable canning.

Zambia is also finding new sources of revenue from the tourist industry, which they hope to develop and enlarge. More travelers all the time are becoming aware of the unspoiled scenic beauty of Zambia. They are discovering for themselves such places as the famed Victoria Falls; the Kariba Dam, which has formed the largest man-made lake in the world, and the large number of natural parks both large and small.

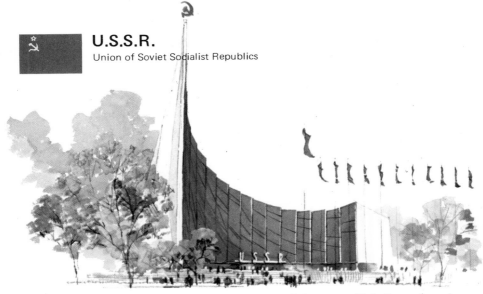

U.S.S.R.
Union of Soviet Socialist Republics

Capped by the hammer and sickle, a tower to socialist achievement, the Soviet Pavilion soars to the skies above. It's Expo's loftiest building at nearly 110 meters.

The pavilion, northwest in Expo, honors the centenary of the April 22, 1870, birth of V.I. Lenin, the Soviet Union's founding father and greatest thinker. Its first section introduces his life and activities. Films taken while he yet lived are seen on a large screen, and personal articles are displayed. Also, this section shows the origins and development of Soviet-Japanese relations.

"Harmonious Development of the Individual under Socialism" is the theme of the second section and you may witness the life of Soviet men, women, and young people. Exhibits include cultural and artistic articles, such as gold ornaments used by Scythians; pictures of ancient Russian

sacred images; old bells, and a piano once belonging to Tschaikovski.

The third area introduces you to the vastness of eastern and northern Siberia. Displayed are fine examples of Siberian natural resources.

Then you come to a hall all of 100 meters high. You find a space ship, a laser system, high-precision machinery to explore the depths of the earth and oceans — all demonstrating the high scientific achievement of the Soviet Union. A huge screen shows 10 films at the same time as if they were one.

The Soviet Pavilion also has a Concert Hall, where a variety of folk songs, music and dances is presented. And Russian, Gruziyan, Ukrainian and other local dishes equally tempting are served in the pavilion's restaurant.

The Soviet Pavilion, created under chief architect M. Posokhin and chief artist K. Rozdestvensky, is adjacent to Saturday Plaza, though it is easily spotted from most anywhere in Expo.

BELGIUM
Kingdom of Belgium

The Belgian Pavilion, under the theme "You and Us," gives to the millions of visitors the image of a true, simple and human Belgium; the image of a people striving for the betterment of the human condition in fraternity and peace.

A harmonious blend of certain traditional features of Belgian and Japanese architecture, the Belgian Pavilion with its severe white curved walls and its baked red tiles is located in a garden designed to represent the exiguity and total utilization of the national territory.

From this figuration of an intensive and diversified agriculture, the visitor enters the section of the "Present." Here is illustrated the Belgian people at work, around its institutions, through audio-visual means enhanced by large plastic studies and a harmony of lights and sounds representing the main national industries.

In the section of the "Past" a succession of paintings, tapestries, pieces of jewelry and other works of ancient art, depict the power and the dynamism with which the Belgians have fought through the ages for the progress of mankind.

The third section, that of the "Future," shows the complexity and the rapidity of today's technological evolution but emphasizes the Belgian vision that humanism will keep controlling the effects of mechanization.

From the main Exhibits Building, the visitor may proceed to the Entertainment Hall where he will find a small deluxe restaurant and a large, moderately-priced cafeteria where he will be able to partake of typical Belgian dishes.

Belgium was the host of the first universal and international exhibition following World War II — the Brussels Universal and International Exhibition of 1958. At EXPO'70, Belgium's pavilion is directly south of Saturday Plaza.

GERMANY
Federal Republic of Germany

The experience in store for the visitor to the "Gardens of Music," the Federal Republic's contribution to EXPO'70, is of a Germany cooperating in a worldwide partnership to build a peaceful future. It is a country which is fresh and cheerful, it is a wave of youth on an old, old sea. You meet both the vitality of Germany's present and the rich traditions of its past.

The fluorescent dome of the Music Auditorium rises amidst a charming garden landscape of German flowers of all seasons. This panorama of growing things includes a species of man-made life: dynamic creations by contemporary German sculptors in a variety of materials. You can stand on the roof of the pavilion and survey, through a periscope working in reverse, the exhibition's subterranean realms.

Appropriate to its name, the German pavilion provides a musical escort. Unobtrusively, loudspeakers are placed strategically in the auditorium's dome, in the subterranean theater, wherever the visitor may wander. The result is that the visual kaleidoscope is married to music — the music of contemporary German composers: Blancher, Eimert, Stockhausen, Zimmermann, Zacher. Much of their work has been newly created for this new kind of pavilion. Music will accompany the visitor through all parts of the pavilion, because it is the element which links the whole exhibit.

Mobility is the motif of the underground exhibition area, thanks to an interplay of movement and light, to devices like mirrors and projected films that defy dimension and seem to obliterate partitioning walls. Here you can explore the German scene from the North Sea to the Alps, encounter the old and new in architecture, share the achievements of research and technology, venture into the world of music and literature, witness the inspiring effort towards tomorrow and, above all, meet the people and their land.

SWITZERLAND
Swiss Confederation

Switzerland takes part in EXPO'70 under the motto of "Diversity in Harmony." Its participation consists of the Radiant Structure, a pavilion for a thematic show, and a restaurant.

The Radiant Structure symbolizes harmony and diversity, as well as "Swiss inventiveness, precision and appreciation of beauty." A steel construction 21 meters (69 ft.) tall and 55 meters (180 ft.) in diameter, it may be compared with a highly stylized tree; a sturdy trunk splits and vanishes gradually into ramifications, and the entire surface is decked with aluminum plates.

With 32,000 glass spheres flashing in the sunlight, and shining as electric lights in the evening, the tree transmits by day and by night something of the aura of a festive experience.

Under the structure, there is an air-conditioned area where electronic music creates an atmosphere of joy and relaxation.

An adjacent pavilion houses a thematic show, and a restaurant with a kiosk for the sale of Swiss souvenirs. In the exhibition hall, accessible from three sides, the image of modern Switzerland is displayed in 12 columnar supports which extend from the floor to the ceiling. The blue columns express pictorial sidelights on the diversity of the people and their culture, while the yellow columns show the manifoldness of the countryside, and the red and green columns the wide range of the country's economic production.

The restaurant seats 180 guests, and the bar and cocktail lounge offer visitors the opportunity of getting acquainted with luxurious Swiss gastronomy.

The information department will inform you about Switzerland, her geography, languages and culture, her science and economy. A richly illustrated 24-page prospectus with a record and 5 volumes on Switzerland in Japanese will complete the information.

Start your trip through EXPO '70 at the Pepsi Pavilion

Come see man's sixth sense, the wonders of the future, the new and the strange—all at the Pepsi-Cola Pavilion. Look for the intriguing Pepsi dome, wherever you are at EXPO '70. You can't miss it.

The Pepsi Pavilion is located at the foot of the EXPO Tower within EXPO Land.

Shaping
the total environment

World development is a monumental task. Some countries face the daily
problem of supplying the most basic necessities of life—water, food and shelter.
Other countries face far more sophisticated problems created by
industrialized living . . . cleaner air, better transportation and faster construction.
To meet those problems, Kubota supplies agricultural machinery,
irrigation systems to aid those struggling for basic necessities—new construction
materials and machinery to enhance efforts to make cities more livable.
Kubota invests its efforts in shaping the total environment.

The Basic Necessities Giant

Kubota, Ltd.
22, Funade-cho 2-chome,
Naniwa-ku, Osaka, Japan

Agricultural machinery/waterworks and
irrigation systems/housings/construction
materials/construction and other heavy
machinery/marine diesels/
materials handling equipment.

Visit the Kubota Pavilion. It's next to the Monday Plaza.

THAILAND

Kingdom of Thailand

The bright golden towers of the Thai Pavilion mirror across Expo's artificial pond, reflecting hope for worldwide peace and expressing Thailand's friendship to the peoples of the world regardless of nationalities or religious beliefs.

A group of three buildings, the Thai Pavilion is a fine reproduction of the many beautiful temples in which Thailand, and especially Bangkok, abounds and which are the highest expression of Thai architecture.

The pavilion consists of a rectangular exhibition hall flanked by imposing towers. Identical in design, the towers are blunt crosses in plan, with four frontals and covered with triple-tiered roofs, the eaves of which are supported by colonade. Richly ornate gables are of carved teakwood. From where the ridges meet rise tall towers, "prangs," of elaborately carved teak and encrusted with gilded glass mosaic; the entire work was done in

Bangkok and the finished prangs shipped piece by piece to Osaka for re-erection.

Pavilion displays emphasize Thailand's rich cultural heritage and the progress which it has made through peaceful cooperation. They cover a wide range of subjects, from aspects of Thai culture and history to economic and social development. A collection of priceless art objects has been brought from the National Museum in Bangkok and modern Thailand is represented by exhibits showing the progress of Thai industries.

On display also are famous Thai silk, beautiful Thai jewelry, Thai bronze and silverware, and samples of such export commodities as rice, rubber, maize, tapioca, minerals and forest products.

As noted, the Thailand Pavilion borders the Pond — south and west from the Expo Hall and near Senri Bridge Avenue.

PHILIPPINES
Republic of the Philippines

The exhibit at the Philippine Pavilion presents the modern Filipino and his institutions. Under the theme of "Progress through the Harmony of Diverse Cultures," the exhibits show the Philippines in terms of its people and their aspirations, activities and accomplishments.

The pavilion transmits its message through the use of idea centers, clusters of photographs, articles and artifacts in artistic arrangements designed to create an atmosphere rather than to express facts and figures.

It weaves an environment from one idea cluster to another so that an attentive visitor may run through an emotional experience, hopefully leaving the pavilion with the feeling that he has met the Filipinos at their best.

You enter the exhibit area through an escalator and at the first level where you are oriented to the location and position of the country. Walking down to the main level, you meet the Filipino at work in his political system, social milieu and economic enterprises. The basement level is phased into the infrastructures of the economy through architecture and then introduces you to Filipino arts, letters and music.

On an outdoor stage, a performing troupe demonstrates the evolution of customs, dance and song from aboriginal gongs and mountain wear, through Moslem institutions and the Spanish heritage, to the modern dancers and musical virtuosity.

But the main features of the pavilion are the Filipino hostesses, conversant in English and Japanese, and radiating the friendliness, hospitality and warmth of the Philippines.

Added to the main pavilion, which is on Senri Bridge Avenue, the Agricultural Industrial Commercial (AIC) Center is organized like a modern Filipino business office to give out data on investment opportunities in the Philippines.

ALGERIA
Democratic and Popular Republic of Algeria

Facing the mild Mediterranean Sea, the capital of Algeria is popularly known as "Alger la blanche" — Algiers the white — because of the beautiful white houses that line its eight kilometers of coastline.

The Algerian Pavilion, on a 2,000-square-meter lot facing the Japanese Garden, is a three-story structure — painted white as an expression of "Alger la blanche."

This pavilion has as many as 13 themes, including "International Cooperation Based on Freedom and Justice" and "Contributions to World Progress." Algeria hopes, through these themes, to contribute to human progress and harmony.

An escalator takes you to the top floor of the exhibition. Exhibits here are divided into four sections. In the first exhibition hall, you are given a sightseeing tour through the scenery of this lovely land. Many historical art works are featured in the second hall.

From Algerian museums, these pieces are but a small sampling of the great contributions to modern Algerian culture.

Then you pass on to the third hall to witness the economic and industrial growth of fast-developing Algeria. Your brief Algerian visit ends with a theater; here you feel as if you are yourself touring North Africa, these movies of Algerian history, art, culture, education and economy and other subjects are so engrossing.

On the ground floor of the pavilion, a 150-seat restaurant in Algerian motif serves foods typical of Algeria, including "couscous," made of wheat, and famous wines such as Mascara, Medea and Harrach.

Also, there is an Algerian shop in the International Bazaar for the exhibition and sale of popular Algerian handicrafts and art works such as jewelry, baskets, ceramics and leather goods.

MEXICO
United Mexican States

The Mexican Pavilion is a modern transposal of the spacious citadels of the Ceremonial Centers of Teotihuacan (City of Gods). The overall architectural effect symbolizes, with symmetrical dynamism, the pre-Colombian concept of Dualism and the Dynamic Union of Opposing Elements.

The theme is based on art-language which has no frontiers and which best expresses the creative genius and spirit of the Mexican people. The motto "Mexico, People of the Sun, at the encounter of Japan, country of the Rising Sun, and of all other nations of the World" is inspired on the profound desire rooted in the hearts of all Mexicans that there be prosperity and social justice for all the people on earth, showing forth the humanistic supremacy over the machine, technology and science, so that these may be used to bring about an era of peace and progress for humanity.

To illustrate these concepts, Mexico has used in her pavilion sculptural pictorial symbols, films, masterpieces in art from all epochs, crafts, music, dances and section of plastic arts created especially for EXPO'70.

From the main vestibule the "Sun Stone" – "Aztec Calendar" – shines forth at the head of the remarkable collection of masterpieces of pre-Colombian art, baroque religious and New Spanish works of the 17th Century; all national treasures. The many images of "Mexico through Centuries" will be projected on a movie screen with original kaleidoscopic effects.

In the two outdoor stages of the pavilion, daily folk dances and concerts by famous musicians called "mariachis" fill the air with vibrant rhythms full of vitality and gaiety.

In effect, Mexico transmits by means of the rich emotion of her art, Harmony, as a principal structure of the Philosophy and Life Concept of her people.

Yukari-chan, Do you know what the future is?

Yukari-chan is a lovely 4-year-old girl. She breathes the air of the modern age and gracefully accepts the speedy changes of daily life. She's been familiar with television, high speed transportation, and moon rockets since she was born. For Yukari-chan, the future is indeed exciting. Yukari-chan doesn't know anything about the Furukawa Group yet, but it is obvious that the Furukawa Group has helped to sustain the daily life of Yukari-chan in one way or another. The Furukawa Group is challenging the future. In this way, they contribute to the daily progress of human society. To enrich and make life happier for Yukari-chan, The Group will exert more effort.

The Furukawa Group Looks to the World of Tomorrow   FURUKAWA GROUP

FURUKAWA MINING CO., LTD./THE FURUKAWA ELECTRIC CO., LTD./THE YOKOHAMA RUBBER CO., LTD./FUJI ELECTRIC CO., LTD./ FUJITSU LIMITED /THE JAPANESE GEON CO., LTD./ASAHI DENKA KOGYO K.K./NIPPON LIGHT METAL COMPANY, LTD./ASAHI MUTUAL LIFE INSURANCE CO./THE DAI-ICHI BANK, LTD./TOA PAINT CO., LTD./THE TAISEI FIRE & MARINE INSURANCE CO., LTD./THE FURUKAWA CHEMICAL INDUSTRIES CO., LTD. / FURUKAWA ALUMINUM CO., LTD. /THE FURUKAWA BATTERY CO., LTD. /FURUKAWA MAGNESIUM CO., LTD./FURUKAWA SANGYO KAISHA, LTD./NIHON NOHYAKU CO., LTD. /HAMA PLASTICS CO., LTD. /THE KANAMACHI RUBBER INDUSTRIAL CO., LTD./FUJI ELECTROCHEMICAL CO., LTD./NIKKEI ALUMINIUM COMPANY, LTD./NIKKEI SHOJI COMPANY, LTD./ THE SHIBUSAWA WAREHOUSE CO., LTD. / NIPPON FOIL MFG. CO., LTD. / TOKAI METALS CO., LTD. / FURUKAWA CASTING CO., LTD. / FUJI DIESEL CO., LTD./FURUKAWA TOKUSHU KINZOKU KOGYO CO., LTD.

Man the problem solver

Intelligence is often defined as the ability to solve problems. Man as an intelligent being makes use of accumulated knowledge, and in the process comes up against barriers which demand new approaches to problem solving.

Creative new tools aid this quest for fulfillment. Many may be seen at this exposition. We invite you to come and personally experience how some of our tools help solve man's problems.

SCANDINAVIA

Denmark • Finland • Iceland • Norway • Sweden

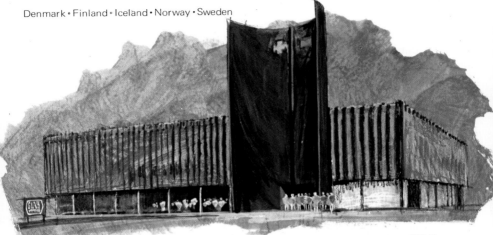

Two views of man's industrialized world — the one that could be and the one that might be — are given in their joint pavilion by the five countries of Northern Europe commonly known as Scandinavia — Denmark, Finland, Iceland, Norway and Sweden.

"Protection of environment in an industrialized society" is the theme. Man's use and misuse of his world is the subject. A challenge to care more about our future problems of living on our globe is the message.

The pavilion's exhibition hall is divided in two. One half is positive — a visualization of what our environment could be in a well-planned industrial society. The other shows what it is and might become with unbridled industry leading to increased pollution of air, water and soil, as well as noise and urban concentration, and culminating in the extreme: the total detruction of life.

More than a hundred projectors flash pictures (about 5,000 of them) in ever-varying sequences. Visitors are actually part of the exhibit: ceiling projectors flash images that don't show on the floor but on the heads and clothing of those walking about the hall. Guests are given small square fans to catch these vertical messages. Special sound effects emerge from the floor to surround the viewer. At the exit, a giant screen summarizes the great potential of our world.

The achievement of a proper environment in the modern world will require regional and global co-operation that transcends nationalistic boundaries and desires. In short, the harmony that is Expo's theme.

The Scandinavian countries have shown that this is possible. Denmark, Finland, Iceland, Norway and Sweden have for many years co-operated in many fields where it is evident that no national boundaries should exist. The pavilion is such a project. No part of the exhibition refers to any particular country in Scandinavia. All administrative, technical and artistic work has been freely shared by all five.

You may, though, obtain at an information counter data on any of the five countries. And for Scandinavian food in all its variety, there is the Royal Viking Restaurant.

DENMARK
Kingdom of Denmark

Denmark is a country on an extremely high educational and cultural level — as one would expect of the birthplace of Hans Christian Andersen, the writer of fairy tales, philosopher Soren Kierkegaard and composer Carl Nielsen.

Because of a well-developed system of social welfare, in which a third of the annual budget is set aside for social security expenditures, education is highly developed.

Denmark is also world-famed for theoretical physics and for its unique method of physical education.

Denmark occupies most of the Jutland Peninsula, and adjacent islands in the Baltic and North Seas. Including Greenland and the Faroe Islands, it is 2,277,000 square kilometers in area with a population of just under 5 million.

The climate of Denmark is mild, considering the country's latitude.

The Kingdom of Denmark is well-known for its considerable production and export of many various kinds of foodstuffs.

However, over the past decade, Denmark's economic emphasis has switched from agriculture to industry; Danish industrial products and technical know-how today enjoy a high reputation all over the world.

Denmark is also famous for its unique designs in furniture and handicrafts.

FINLAND
Republic of Finland

With an area of 130,000 square miles — a third of it in the Arctic zone — Finland is larger than Great Britain, yet contains only 4.7 million people. Most live in the southern and central parts, areas covered by vast

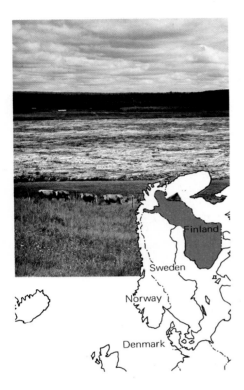

accounts for 60% of exports, the rapidly developing metal industry for the bulk of the rest. Finnish paper machines, ships, glass and textiles have made a name in the world.

The Finns live well in warm houses and many have summer cottages or saunas by the lakes. They are keen on sports; some have been world-famous. Finns have gained perhaps even more fame in music: for example, Jean Sibelius and Oskari Merikanto, the composers.

ICELAND
Republic of Iceland

forests of pine, spruce and birch and dotted by thousands of lakes. The northernmost part, Lapland, is a summer land of midnight sun.

Finland is a sovereign republic whose democracy and culture are of old Scandinavian heritage. Separation of the legislative, executive and judicial powers is strictly observed.

Finland is a member of the United Nations and presently of its Security Council. She maintains good relations with all her neighbours. Her foreign policy is one of strict neutrality and keeping outside of all international conflicts.

Foreign trade is important to Finland and the wood processing industry

Iceland is a North Atlantic island,

half the size of Japan's mainland, with fewer than 200,000 people. Yet she is a cradle of modern democracy.

A republic, Iceland has operated a democratic Parliament since 930 A.D. — over 1,000 years — and Icelanders are justly proud of their political system.

Iceland is located in the Atlantic Ocean, halfway between Greenland and Norway.

It is covered with lava plateaus from nearly 100 volcanoes. Mt. Hekla last erupted in 1947. But volcanoes bring their rewards: hot springs are used for heating whole towns. Not that it's all that cold; the average in January is -1°C, thanks to the Gulf Stream's moderating effect.

Harsh natural conditions severely limit agriculture and manufacturing and Icelanders, therefore, primarily rely on fishing. In the cod season, trawlers from all Europe swarm around Icelandic waters. Iceland caught 1,238,400 tons in 1966 and exported much of it, mainly to countries in the southern part of Europe.

No Icelander is illiterate, due to the thorough, compulsory, eight-grade school system. There are numerous libraries and an outsize number of newspapers and magazines are published. Despite participation in NATO, Iceland is completely demilitarized, with but partol boats to protect the fishermen.

NORWAY
Kingdom of Norway

Norway, with a third of its 386,000

square kilometers located in the Arctic, is a land of summertime midnight sun. But winter nights become long and dark.

Only 3.3% of the land is arable, yet farming is so developed that many of its products are exported — including 6,000 tons of cheese to Japan annually. Pulp and other forest products make up 20% of exports. Iron and pyrites are among the mineral resources. Norway's 3.8 million people consume, by far, more electricity per capita than anyone else; hydro-electric power is the basis for large industries turning out aluminum, ferro-alloys, magnesium and fertilizers.

Norway is a land of the sea. Modern

pelagic whaling originated from towns at the mouth of the Oslo Fjord. Norway's annual catch of cod, herring and sardines is the highest in Europe. And shipping is Norway's principal industry; she is one of the world's leading shipping nations.

With an extensive welfare system, fully a quarter of Norway's annual budget is used for social security, enhancing Norwegians' enterprising and energetic spirit. Examples? Henrik Ibsen, the poet and dramatist; composer Edvard Grieg; Edvard Munch, the painter; Bjornson, the patriotic poet; polar explorers Nansen and Amundsen, and Thor Heyerdahl of Kon-Tiki fame.

SWEDEN
Kingdom of Sweden

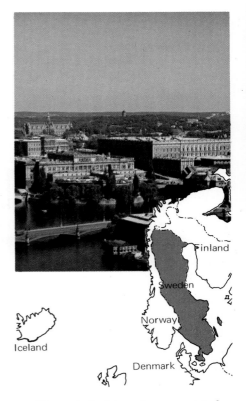

Sweden, which has 8 million inhabitants and embraces an area of almost 450,000 square kilometers, is the largest among the countries of Northern Europe.

The country abounds in forestry. Her iron ore resources are plentiful and renowned for their high quality. The forest industry boasts the world's highest volume of trees felled annually — 56 million cubic meters. Sweden also has a great number of hydro-power generation stations.

Machinery, including heavy electrical equipment, today comprises the largest industrial sector in the country.

The mechanical and electrical industries contribute more than a third to the total value added by manufacture in all Swedish industries.

These industries also account for more than 40% of Swedish exports.

Sweden is noted for its consistent foreign policy of nonalignment; she was neutral in two world wars. The living standard in the country is high, the per capita national income being the second in the world after the U.S.A. Sweden has a highly developed social welfare system, providing "cradle-to-grave" security.

Sweden has produced famous scientists, such as Carl von Linné, the "father of modern systematic botany," and Alfred Nobel, the inventor of dynamite and founder of the prize named after him.

ETHIOPIA
Empire of Ethiopia

Ethiopia presents the theme "Friendship across the Continents." Its pavilion, in the form of one cylindrical building and two traditional Ethiopian houses, or "tukuls," is partly made of bamboo woven on the site by craftsmen from the Ethiopian province of Sidamo. Inside are displayed the many facets of Ethiopian culture, development and progress.

Culture is the keynote of the exhibition hall, the largest, where five major areas of the nation are represented. As you move from one suspended platform to the next, you literally move across the face of the Empire: from obelisks and landscape of historic Axum to a replica of a Gondar castle to the interior of a typical dwelling of the southern region. A rock-hewn church nestled in a cave in the mountains of Lalibela and a whitewashed, dome-topped house of the port city of Massawa are included in this "tour of Ethiopia."

The first "tukul" is the Queen of Sheba Coffee Shop, where Ethiopian coffee, "supreme since Sheba's time," is served. Outside, additional tables and handcarved Jimma stools allow guests to sit in the shade of colorful Timkat umbrellas and chat with the beautiful young people of Ethiopia who are on hand to serve them.

The second "tukul" houses industrial and agricultural displays and areas where pavilion guests may talk with representatives from Ethiopian industrial organizations. Here also is a gift shop, offering Ethiopian handicrafts and souvenirs for sale.

Continuous showings of films and slides round out the pavilion activities and provide you with a broader knowledge of this historic Empire of Ethiopia.

The Pavilion of Ethiopia is a prominent part of the area south of the Artificial Pond. It is west of Festival Plaza and about a block from Senri Bridge Avenue.

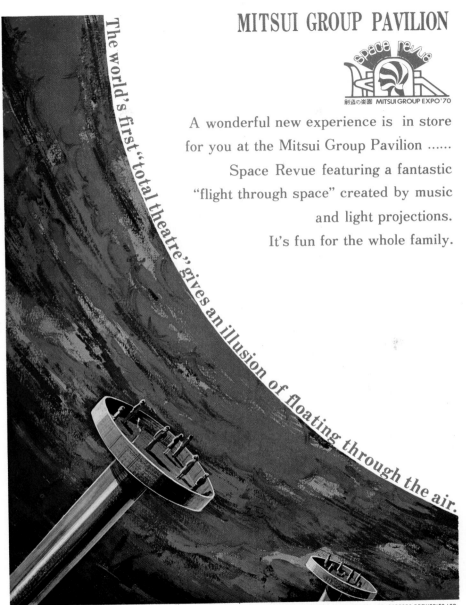

MITSUI GROUP PAVILION

A wonderful new experience is in store
for you at the Mitsui Group Pavilion ......
Space Revue featuring a fantastic
"flight through space" created by music
and light projections.
It's fun for the whole family.

93

Theme: Soul and Heart of Japan
——Man recreates Nature——

Notice to visitors:

Our Pavilion, situated to the west of Festival Plaza and in front of a station of the Moving Walkways, is close by the Canadian Pavilion. You will recognize it at once by the big triangle atop its huge inclined roof — in the traditional style of the Japanese folk house.

Points of our show:

"Cascade" 67 meters wide, will make a cool and refreshing impression on you; "Young Plaza" is where young people from all over the world can come together; at "Sun Plaza" you are put in the presence of Nature Recreated by Man, given expression through the play of artificial light and sound; in "Family Corner" you find exhibited the choice of Sanyo's electronic technology — devices such as the Ultrasonic Bath and in "Tea Room Bara (rose)" you can take refreshments and view the cool "Cascade."

94

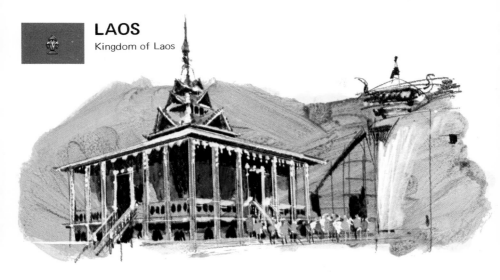

LAOS
Kingdom of Laos

Laos, a country of agricultural and handicraft industries, has long been rather isolated due to its geographical location. It is making courageous efforts, however, to catch up with modern industrialization, for the benefit of its people.

Since it is still too early to show any marked progress in this field, Laos has selected as its theme for EXPO'70: "Family and Religious Life, Culture and Economic Development".

The National Commission for the World Exposition wanted the pavilion of Laos to symbolize culture and spiritual life coupled with the dexterity of the talented Laotian artisans. For this reason, the commission chose as its model for the pavilion the Vat Sisaket Library whose elegant shape is a perfect example of 19th Century Laotian architecture.

The pavilion is an exact reproduction of the library constructed in 1818 within the precincts of the old Royal Palace on order of then ruling monarch King Anouvong.

Its 15-meter base allows an ample space of 100 square meters for display items. The exhibition hall is entered through double doors, upon one on which is carved scenes of Ramayana on both sides.

A balcony two meters wide extends around the hall. Its veranda is supported by columns linked to a balustrade. The four-sided roof is surmounted by a four-gabled, fourfold roof, the last gable of which ends with a five-floor stupa which extends over 21 meters. The wall-plates, ridges of the main roof and the gables are embossed with golden stucco ornaments created by the Vientiane Fine Arts Academy.

The Laotian Pavilion, with its beautiful exhibits, is one that will surely intrigue you. You will find it in International Place 3, just east of Saturday Plaza.

BURMA

Union of Burma

Burma's rich cultural heritage is not a thing of the past but a living presence throbbing in the hearts of its people and serving as a strong foundation for the modern advancement of the country.

"Cultural Heritage and Modern Advancement" is the theme of the Pavilion of Burma, a theme which is concordant with the main theme of EXPO'70: "Progress and Harmony for Mankind."

The theme finds beautiful and useful form in the "Royal Dragon Barge," its environs and contents. The "Royal Dragon Barge," used by ancient royalty, has twin hulls with twin dragon's heads spanned by a structure of traditional Burmese architectural design with a seven-tier spire reaching up to the sky. It is set in a man-made pond.

The panel, door-frames, eve-boards, gables, roof-walling and pinnacle of the central structure are splendid examples of wood-work in the essential Burmese manner. The parquet flooring is made of a variety of Burmese hardwood and the walls are of famous Burmese teak in its enchanting natural colour.

The Burma Pavilion is both an object of Burmese art and an exhibit of natural Burmese products.

In the Main Hall of the Royal Barge, the exhibits are displayed in a manner to blend well with the objects of art and culture. The richness of the interior decor is enhanced by the display of rubies, sapphires, jade, pearls and other precious stones, for which Burma is renowned.

The restaurant on the pavilion site is a design typical of the Burmese locale. It serves authentic Burmese food.

The Royal Dragon Barge Pavilion, capturing all the splendor of exotic Burma, is near Wednesday Plaza and south-west from the west end of the Artificial Pond.

National Pavilions

GREECE
Kingdom of Greece

Nine compact buildings, classical in form, capture at EXPO'70 the 5,000 years of continuous Hellenic civilization.

The Greek Pavilion. Based on this historical progression, the pavilion is itself a progression — on various levels to project the rough Greek terrain — through the eons: the geometric period, Cycladic civilization, Cretan-Minoan civilization, the sea as a creative power, classical Greece, Alexander the Great and his contribution to world civilization, the Byzantine period, Medieval Greece, and then contemporary Greece with its fantastic attraction to the tourist.

The pavilion is located east of Saturday Plaza, near one of the moving walks.

Though the buildings are on a small scale, in accordance with Hellenic tradition, they produce a large, unified exhibition space.

Inside, the exhibits consist of copies and original pieces of art, frescoes, vases, ceramics, sculptures, bas-relief, jewels, coins, icons, and beautiful photographs, as well as ship models to reflect Greece's great tradition of the sea and samples of contemporary handicrafts and modern-day industrial products.

In an open-air theater, patterned on an ancient prototype, folk dances and classical dramas are presented.

The pavilion philosophy is based on an abstraction of the classical form. A square module of 1.5 meters simplified construction and kept with Hellenic tradition. The floor is finished in white Pendelic marble throughout.

All is set amid landscaping of compressed earth and rocks that is based on Greek tradition. The tradition of 5,000 years. A restaurant beneath the theater serves authentic Greek delicacies, including mutton dishes. All in all, the Greek Pavilion must be rated as one of the highlights of Japan's World Exposition.

DOMINICAN REPUBLIC

The Dominican Republic occupies the eastern two-thirds of the island of Hispaniola which divides the Atlantic Ocean and the Caribbean. It has an area of 49,000 square kilometers. The country's common border with Haiti to the west extends over a length of 320 kilometers.

From east to west, the country is crossed by a central mountain chain which includes the highest peak in the Antilles, Mt. Duberge, which rises to a height of 3,175 meters. The height of this mountain forms an interesting contrast to the low level of Lake Enriquillo, 43 meters below sea level.

Located between the central and northern mountain ranges is the Cibao plain, famed for the rice, vegetables, and fruits it produces.

While situated in the tropical zone, the medium temperature in the capital city of St. Domingo is only 25 degrees centigrade, thanks to the "trade winds" blowing over from the Carib-

bean. The climate is very mild along the southern coast of the country, where the scenery is magnificent, attracting many American and European tourists. Recently, the Government has been making a special effort to develop the country's tourist industry.

Agriculture plays an essential part in the economy of the Dominican Republic. Its principal products are sugar, representing 50% of the nation's export; cocoa, coffee, bananas, and tobacco. About 50% of the land is held for farming, but only 20% is now cultivated due to geographic conditions in the west — extensive mountainous regions and semi-arid land. Realizing the great potential of this western land, the government has recently made giant strides in irrigation. New technology is helping make the region most fertile.

The Dominican Republic is in International Place 2-B, just west of the Artificial Pond.

SAUDI ARABIA
Kingdom of Saudi Arabia

Saudi Arabia is modernizing itself rapidly, and yet the processes of its modernization are in harmony with the traditions and teachings of the great religion of Islam.

The visitor to the Pavilion of Saudi Arabia must keep in mind that Islam is not only a religion – a relation between man and God – but also a way of life – governing and regulating all aspects of man's life.

The "Progress Within Harmony" concept is initially manifested in the architectural design of the Pavilion of Saudi Arabia. The design is a traditional Islamic-Arabesque style within an ultra-modern context.

As for the interior exhibit area, the one-story pavilion is divided into two sections, the General Exhibit Hall and the Religious Hall.

The General Exhibit Hall reflects the spirit of progress in the Kingdom of Saudi Arabia, a progress that has taken place within a short span of time

under the wise leadership of His Majesty, King Faisal.

The area surrounding the Symbol Zone, within the General Exhibit Hall, shows the progress accomplished in the fields of social and physical infrastructures.

The Symbol Zone is entitled "Towards Better Utilization of Natural Resources." In this section, the great efforts of the Kingdom to fully utilize its natural resources – petroleum industry, petrochemical industries, mineral industries and agriculture – are presented in a very attractive and colorful manner.

The corridor leading to the Religious Hall and the Religious Hall itself acquaint the non-Muslim visitor with the religion of Islam. The universality of Islam – the religion of over 600 million people all over the world – is presented through the display of one of Islam's Major Pillars, the Pilgrimage to Mecca.

CZECHOSLOVAKIA

Czechoslovak Socialist Republic

The Czechoslovak Socialist Republic has come to EXPO'70 with a specific aim: the communication of profound thought and the evocation of feeling through art. Mankind through the centuries has sought roads to a better future; Czechoslovaks are following the path of socialism. Their Expo exhibition is intended to philosophically describe pride, sorrow, the emotions of humanity, in four pavilion sections: Historical Introduction, Time of Joy, Time of Anguish and Hope for Mankind.

The pavilion itself is a flat, one-story structure with an intricate geometric design to its ferro-concrete roof. The design is based on the work of three young architects selected in nationwide competition. The walls are of traditional Czechoslovakian glass. The floors, covered in ceramic tile, incline gently to the building's center where, projecting upward, is discovered a cylindrical movie theater covered with beautiful glass in mosaic design.

The main single exhibits are monumental works of art created in glass, such as "The Cloud" by René Roubíček and "The Glass River" by Stanislav Libenský. The pavilion also contains a section for children to enjoy; a motion picture, in the theater, on nature and everyday life in Czechoslovakia; three restaurants serving national delicacies, and a souvenir shop offering exclusive Czechoslovak products such as glass, folk-art creations, graphic art.

Czechoslovakia also has two souvenir shops – in Friday Plaza and the International Bazaar – and presents in Expoland the "Laterna Magika" – a revolutionary entertainment discovered and developed in Czechoslovakia and based on film projection simultaneous with live acting.

The Pavilion of Czechoslovakia is found just to the west of Friday Plaza, and quite close to the West Gate.

CEYLON

Ceylon has been variously known as Lanka (Kingdom of the Lion Race), Tamba panni (land of Red earth) from which the Greeks and Romans derived the name Taprobane, Dhamma – Dvipa (land of The Doctrine), Sinhale or Sinhala Dvipa (abode of the Lion Race) from which was derived alternately the names Serendib, Celiao, Zeilan and finally Ceylon. The country is located on major trade routes between the East and West and is rich in historical tradition and culture dating back over 3,000 years.

The Ceylon pavilion is a two-storied ferro-concrete structure with an outer layer of glass, a unique innovation in design. The interior walls portray a massive fresco representing Buddhist art. On display are archaeological treasures of gold, bronze and wood, and original stone statues. Some articles date as far back as 800 years or more and have never been shown outside the country before. Famous precious

stones including the renowned giant blue sapphire are on display. Over a hundred octagon-shaped lanterns light up the pavilion.

In the center of the compound, with a pond in the background, stands a large bronze replica of a leaf of the Bo-tree. Tradition has it that Gautama Buddha attained Enlightenment after meditating under a Bo-tree. A sapling of that tree was brought to Ceylon and is today considered to be the world's oldest historical tree with a religious tradition.

A restaurant in the pavilion offers deliciously brewed, pure Ceylon tea and typical Ceylonese dishes. Visitors to the restaurant can view films illustrating the diversity and beauty of the island renowned through the ages for its scenery, its wealth in gems, its fertile land and its sacred places.

Ceylon tea, in attractive packets, is available for purchase in the restaurant.

IVORY COAST
Republic of Ivory Coast

Through these policies, Ivory Coast has become the most prosperous former French colony in Africa.

This brilliant national evolution is portrayed in the first section of the Ivory Coast Pavilion – the "Modern House," a grouping of three cylindrical buildings (ranging in height from eight to 30 meters) in shapes reminiscent of elephant tusks. This section shows the various aspects of this nation of 5 million people living on 322,000 square kilometers. And it shows the country's principal resources: coffee, cocoa and tropical woods. Indeed, Ivory Coast stands first in Africa and third in the world in the production of coffee, which represents 50% of all its exported goods.

The second section of this panorama, the "Traditional House," pictures the history of Ivory Coast and the nation's unique inheritance from the world of antiquity, through art objects, short films, photographs and a large display of the folklore and artistry handed down from the forefathers of the nation.

Still another section of this interesting exhibition, and perhaps the most important from the point of view of modern-day Ivory Coast, is dedicated to the movement for national independence. This movement was lead by Houphouet Boigny, who later became the illustrious President of this industrious Republic.

The pavilion and interior decorations were designed by architect Rinaldo Olivieri of Verona, Italy, and built by Shimizu Construction Co., Ltd.

Ivory Coast, a former French colony on the Gulf of Guinea, achieved its independence on August 7, 1960. During the past 10 years, a striking growth has taken place, a growth based on the country's political stability and on its system of actively encouraging outside investment.

Come experience ASTRORAMA...
where the world revolves around you.

Astrorama—the movie that surrounds you, that shows you your world as you've never seen it before. It's near the West Gate. Brought to you by **MIDORI-KAI** ...an association of 32 forward-looking firms.

DAIDO MUTUAL LIFE INS.
DAIHATSU KOGYO
FUJISAWA PHARMACEUTICAL
FUKUSUKE CORP.
GAKUSHU-KENKYUSHA
HITACHI ZOSEN
KANSAI PAINT
KOA FIRE & MARINE INS.

KONISHIROKU PHOTO IND.
MARUZEN OIL
MITSUBOSHI BELTING
MORISHITA JINTAN
NICHIMEN
NISSAN CONSTRUCTION
NISSHO-IWAI
NIPPON FIRE &MARINE INS.

NOMURA SECURITIES
OHBAYASHI-GUMI
OSAKA CEMENT
OSAKA SODA
SANWA BANK
TAKASHIMAYA
TEIJIN
TOKUYAMA SODA

TOYO CONSTRUCTION
TOYO RUBBER INDUSTRY
TOYO TRUST & BANKING
TOYO UMPANKI
UBE INDUSTRIES
YAMASHITA-SHINNIHON STEAMSHIP
ZENITAKA-GUMI
UNITIKA
(Alphabetical order)

MIDORI-KAI

TAKARA FOR BEAUTY

Creating interior beauty is the task of the Takara Group. Home furnishings such as sinks, stoves and enamel bathtubs - specially designed chairs for barber shops and beauty parlors contribute to interior elegance. Our chairs are installed in almost every barber shop and beauty parlor in Japan. And are exported to over 80 countries.

Takara, a worldwide enterprise, works to beautify shops and homes.

TAKARA BELMONT

TANZANIA
United Republic of Tanzania

The Tanzania Pavilion consists of four traditional-style circular houses, one lower than the others to give an impression of movement, with a central piazza surmounted by 10-meter-high, umbrella-like structures.

In keeping with the Expo theme of "Progress and Harmony for Mankind," the four halls in the pavilion portray "Nature," "People," "Culture" and "Progress." The Hall of Nature shows the fantastic paradise of wild life in Tanzania, together with animal skins; elephant tusks; Mount Kilimanjaro, Africa's highest mountain; an aquarium, and the sound of Africa's nature.

The Hall of People shows the life of the people of Tanzania in harmony with their environments, from pre-history to the Arusha Declaration. A special exhibit is a replica of a skull of the oldest man on earth; the 1,750,000-year-old Homo Zinjanthropus was discovered in the Olduvai Gorge in Northern Tanzania by Dr.

Leakey in 1959.

The Hall of Culture stresses the sub-theme "Towards a Fuller Enjoyment of Life" and concentrates on art, literature and music. Exhibited are Makonde ebony carvings, Swahili literature, modern paintings and village crafts – with the haunting rhythm of drums in the background.

The Hall of Progress gives a vision of a nation in a hurry, stressing development of natural resources, such as gemstones, and also introducing exciting agricultural developments in the country. The tourist industry and other recent developments are also introduced.

Tanzania was born in 1964 when Tanganyika and Zanzibar merged into a single nation. A youthful nation with a population of 12,170,000, it is the only country in Expo's International Place 1-A, to build its own pavilion. You'll find it to the north of Tuesday Plaza.

INDONESIA
Republic of Indonesia

Through its "close-and-open" wall space, the Pavilion of Indonesia invites the visitor to have a look inside. The pavilion, designed to bring you into a world of inner peacefulness, can be reached by two passageways. The State Emblem "Garuda" with the motto "Bhinneka Tunggal Ika" (Unity in Diversity) and the inscription "Indonesia" mark the main entrance.

The exhibition has a striking mural in the entrance way. A map in Zone 1 shows the physical distance between Japan and Indonesia, visually explaining the most efficient way for people of the two countries to visit each other. Another map features some interesting aspects of Indonesian life. Puppets in a variety of local costumes depict a "Pageant of Daily Wear." With an impressive wood relief as a backdrop, in Zone 2 there are demonstrations of seven existing branches of folkcraft — including batik, wayang, sculpture and wood carving.

Zone 3 presents "fragments from Indonesia's past," distinctly expressed by masks and traditional dress, which signify gracefulness. Photographs help the visitor understand their full meaning. Precious stones are exhibited in front of this zone and a representation of the famous "Ketjak" dance of Bali covers a whole wall. Zone 4 presents Indonesia today — its religious life, wealth of flora and fauna, education, tourism, land development, industries and cultural activities. Choice items are on display here and visitors can enjoy traditional music.

A transition between Zone 3 and 4 symbolizes the nation's awakening and its promising future. The photographs on display show the crucial moments of Indonesia's proclamation of independence.

Traditional dances and folk songs are performed daily on the pavilion's stage. The restaurant serves Indonesian cuisine in a typically Indonesian setting. Souvenirs are on sale in the pavilion's shops.

GHANA
Republic of Ghana

In consonance with the Exposition theme of "Harmony and Progress for Mankind," Ghana has selected the theme "A Richer Life through Nature" based on the beauty that surrounds us and which has found expression in Ghana's traditional art and culture. It also recognises the material benefits we derive from nature in terms of food, clothing and shelter, and raw materials which have given Ghana the basis for industrial development.

The Ghana Pavilion consists of two hexagonal steel structures located in International Place 1-A. The entrance is designed after a Ghanaian stool, a common unit of household furniture yet one of importance in the life of almost every family in the country. The traditional stool is carved in one piece from local timber, mainly "owawa." A special chief's stool, a "coronation stool," is similar, but oft-

en larger and more imposing: The famous Golden Stool of Asantehene, King of Ashanti, is indeed gold.

The stool's significance in Ghanaian life lies in the belief that the soul of a departed ancestor, if it ever returns, resides in his favorite stool. At festivals, libation is poured at the chief's Stool House, the depository of stools of departed chiefs.

Inside the pavilion, lavish use has been made of Ghana timber. The pavilion portrays the rich cultural heritage of Ghana; in addition, selected products show the efforts being made toward industrialization.

The pavilion portrays the gaiety and natural friendliness of the people and the bright vivid colours that surround them in everyday life, whether on the farm or at sea. Traditional court music and ever-popular "high life" provide traditional greetings as you enter and leave the Ghana Pavilion.

CYPRUS
Republic of Cyprus

Cyprus occupies a unique position in the development of the world's history. In both geographical and historical terms, this small but vital island justly prides itself as "the crossroads of Civilization." It is, therefore, both significant and appropriate that the Cyprus Pavilion should be situated in an International Place.

To know and appreciate the significance of Cyprus today is first to know its history and its people. The pavilion strikingly illustrates the island's development from pre-history to the present day. Displays are arranged to provide a comprehensive picture of Cyprus and its people and embrace religion, government, education, art, commerce and industry.

You are provided with a fascinating glimpse of the people who have discovered the island for themselves and stayed to establish an exciting, integrated, multi-racial society, rich in a thousand traditions and ceremonies.

This truly Mediterranean country has been enhanced, rather than encumbered, by the historical awareness it brings to the challenge of the 20th Century.

Commerce and industry thus reflect the island's appealing mixture of ancient and modern; the pavilion displays one of the world's newest airlines alongside one of its oldest producing vineyards. Minerals, citrus and shoe production are also featured to show the breadth and scope of the island's production facilities.

The island is one of fantastic growth, not least in tourism; expanding world awareness of Cyprus is reflected throughout the pavilion. And the mood of the Cyprus Pavilion, in color and form, has been carefully designed to capture the warm and sunny character of Cyprus itself.

International Place 2-B, the site of the Cyprus Pavilion, is just a block east of the west end of the Artificial Pond.

MADAGASCAR
Malagasy Republic

Theme: "Side by side to a prosperous future"

Madagascar, the home of the Malagasy Republic and the big island on the Indian Ocean whose geographical characteristics and inhabitants recall, at the same time, Africa, Asia and the South Sea Islands, should assert her place at EXPO'70 in so far as this event allows her to affirm her role as a link between Africa and Asia.

Separated from Africa as far back as the era of Genesis, Madagascar has lemurs (makis), butterflies, orchids, euphorbiaceae, fauna and flora, unique in this part of the world.

The Coelacanth, an intermediate between the fish and the amphibian, likewise live in the waters of Madagascar.

A country of fragrance and light, the Island shelters, on its eastern slope, scented plants such as vanilla, clove, ylang-ylang, coffee. And, on the other side, it glistens with precious and semi-precious stones like emerald, aquamarine, amethyst and quartz.

Stock-farming, fishing and cultivation of rice are the principal resources of the country. Also, the subsoil contains elements indispensable to heavy industries, such as graphite, chromium, nickel, and to the pioneering industries, such as mica, monozite, uranothorium and beryllium.

By nature of their geographical location and the stage of development of their economy, the Malagasy Republic and Japan have compensatory economies and can co-operate with each other, in so far as the first is an agricultural, pastoral and semi-industrialized country, while the other is highly industrialized.

The Pavilion of the Malgasy Republic is located at International Place 1-A, which is found just to the north of Tuesday Plaza and quite close to the Festival Plaza.

UGANDA

The Uganda Pavilion is easily identified amidst Expo's colorful African section for, approaching it from any direction, you can discern "U-GANDA" written in big, bold letters.

It is a fitting identification for this bold land in the heart of Africa. The triple-peaked-tent design of the Uganda Pavilion well presents the sun, soil, lakes and wildlife with which this country is gifted. Indeed, this nation includes part of the famous Lake Victoria, and through it pass waters that reach the Mediterranean as the mighty Nile.

The entrance of the Uganda Pavilion houses, besides the executive offices of the Commissioner General, an information counter and a sales kiosk. At the kiosk you may purchase curios and handicrafts in a traditional Uganda environment.

You pass on to the Hall of Uganda Tradition. Here all the glory of the country's traditional past is exhibited through music, dances, color movies and unique works of art.

In the Hall of Wild Life and Tourism, the heart of untamed Africa is shown through three-dimensional models of unique game parks. Cleverly recreated settings, including life-size animals, giving feeling of actually being present in this beautiful nation of bountiful nature.

The Hall of Modern Uganda gives you some idea, through its bright modern exhibits, of the country's major industries and of the economic and educational achievements that already play an important part in the life of Uganda.

Uganda is grouped with other African nations in International Place 1-A. To get to it, you can take the Moving Walkway from the Main Gate to Tuesday Plaza, then just walk north to cross the street.

SINGAPORE

Republic of Singapore

Among the many interesting pavilions at EXPO'70, the Singapore Pavilion stands out for its unique design and the natural beauty of its Tropical Garden — a 3,000-square-meter paradise of shrubbery and plants, including phoenix palms, bougainvillea, orchids and other tropical flora.

The main purpose of the Singapore Pavilion is to project a visual resume of life in a multiracial society amidst the verdant lushness of a small island Republic. The pavilion, 91 meters or 100 yards from Expo's West Gate, is itself a gateway, a gateway to a miniature Singapore.

The garden beauty can be seen from a panoramic viewing platform some distance away. Cascading 4.6 meters (15 feet) from this elevated promontory to gently undulating grounds, a miniature waterfall becomes a stream that spills into a large, contoured pond full of colorful tropical fish and green aquatic plants.

Amidst meandering pathways, a small menagerie of turtles, alligators in pits, and brilliantly colored tropical birds in aviaries animate the gardens.

Towering above are two huts built in the original native manner of the Malays, with crescent-shaped roofs and timber walls.

One is an aquarium with exotic fish; the other is an attap hut with a thatched roof and open walls where you can see color films on Singapore.

Inside the pavilion a way of life is reflected. An illuminated wall mural, amidst arrays of fresh orchid sprays, projects various scenes of multiracial Singapore: of the laughter, tears and sweat of the people.

The effervescent charm of 'Instant Asia' is mirrored in a huge mural by a famed Batik painter and in the smiles of the Singaporean receptionists enchanting the pavilion.

PAKISTAN
Islamic Republic of Pakistan

From time immemorial, the area now comprising the Islamic Republic of Pakistan has been the cradle of successive civilizations which flowered into bloom under the influence of Buddhist, Aryan and Muslim cultures.

These influences are amply revealed in the design of and objects displayed in the Pakistan Pavilion.

Glimpses of the Muslim influence dominate the pavilion's Moghul arches and arabesque designs. Classified into four divisions, the exhibits take the visitor from the prehistoric period to the Buddhist period, and from the Muslim period on to modern Pakistan.

The economic and industrial development of Pakistan is depicted through charts, graphs, pictures, models and replicas on display in the economic division.

The other three divisions cover the social, agricultural and industrial potentials of its people.

Exports in manufactured goods have shown steady improvement lately. These include cotton products, jute products, art silk and synthetic fabrics, leather goods, carpets and rugs, electric goods and so on.

The most picturesque section of the pavilion, however, is the handicraft corner where traditional arts and crafts of the people of Pakistan are proudly displayed. Of equal interest is a restaurant set up within the pavilion which serves Pakistani dishes that will tempt the taste buds of all visitors. The traditional cuisine is served by waiters in colorful Pakistani attire.

The Pavilion of Pakistan shares the Square of the Regional Cooperation for Development with the pavilions of Pakistan's two RCD partners, Iran and Turkey. With Saturday Plaza immediately to the west, the RCD Square embodies the spirit of unity that these three friendly nations share in their common pursuit of progress and harmony.

If it's a souvenir of Japan,

Kanebo *Silk*

of course!
Kanebo Silk is synonymous
with Japanese Silk.

Available at:
Kanebo Osaka Store
1st floor, Hankyu-Koku Bldg., 31 Kadota-cho, Kita-ku, Osaka Tel. (06) 312-5750
Kanebo Kyoto Store
Kawaramachi Shijo-agaru, Nakagyo-ku, Kyoto Tel. (075) 221-7928/9
Kanebo Tokyo Store
5-1, Ginza 3-chome, Chuo-ku, Tokyo Tel. (03) 567-0251
PRODUCTS: Nylon·Polyester·Cotton·Wool·Silk·Chemical Fiber·Resins·Cosmetics·Foods

Kanebo — THE WORLD'S UNIQUE CREATOR OF BEAUTY IN TEXTILES AND COSMETICS

GABON
Gabon Republic

Dedicating its pavilion to Dialogue and Progress, the Gabon Republic enthusiastically participates in the great international exposition which is EXPO'70. The theme emphasizes the two distinctive ideas that characterize the policy of President S.E.M. Albert Bernard Bongo. Fruitful and constructive dialogue permits everyone to participate in the forming of great decisions. Technical and economic progress is the basis for peace and prosperity. Gabon is striving to go forward in cooperation with all the peoples of the world particularly with Japan, a friendly and generous partner.

The four different rooms of its pavilion picture various aspects of Gabon today. In the first, three large screens show color slides and maps locate the Republic in the heart of Equatorial Africa.

The second room is dedicated to the forest economy and a third presents a comprehensive view of the nation's mineral resources — its petroleum, manganese and uranium — and of its agriculture and the production of electrical power.

The fourth and last area deals with the infrastructure development of the Republic.

After those sections dedicated to the economy and to social achievements, a spacious hall, devoted to tourism, presents the traditional arts and crafts of the country; by the great beauty and artistic value of its elements it proves a huge attraction to all visitors.

As a final piece of interest, a craftsman is carving, on the spot, works of art in the famous stone of M'Bigou, the village where this type of sculpture was created.

These small statues, heads, busts and masks are on sale at a special stand in the pavilion.

The Gabon Pavilion is in International Place 1-A. Pleasant surprises are in store for you.

Fuji Group Pavilion "Air Dome"

Leap into the 21st Century with Fuji Group.

Asahi Asbestos	Canon
Fuji Bank	Japan Oxygen
Katakura Industry	Kayaba Industry
Kureha Chemical Industry	Kurimoto Iron Works
Marubeni-Iida	Nichido Fire and Marine Insurance
Nihon Cement	Nippon Carbon
Nippon Kokan	Nippon Oils & Fats
Nippon Reizo	Nippon Seiko
Nishimatsu Construction	Okamoto Riken Gomu
Oki Electric	Okura Trading
Penta-Ocean Construction	Sapporo Breweries
Showa Denko	Suminoe Textile
Taisei Construction	Tekken Kensetsu
Toa Harbor Works	Toa Nenryo Kogyo
Tobishima Construction	Tokyo Tatemono
Yamatake Honeywell	Yasuda Fire and Marine Insurance
Yasuda Mutual Life Insurance	Yasuda Trust and Banking
Yodogawa Steel Works	Yokogawa Electric Works

FUJI GROUP EXPO'70 ASSOCIATION.

Is RICOH you know of a camera manufacturer?
True! Cameras are one of its main products, but at this time we want you to know that RICOH is the largest business machine manufacturer in Japan.

Its products include copying machines, offset duplicators, sensitized papers, calculating machines, DPS machines, etc. which are the daily necessities of all business offices today. RICOH shares about 70% of the total domestic market of copying machines. And, RICOH's "Ricopy" has now become synonymous with copying machine.

In 1967, we ranked 11th among all Japanese companies in terms of export growth. In your country, there are sure many users of RICOH products.

RICOH joins EXPO'70 by having a RICOH PAVILION. It's filled with many unique features inviting you to the dreamland of the future. Please visit our pavilion at EXPO'70.

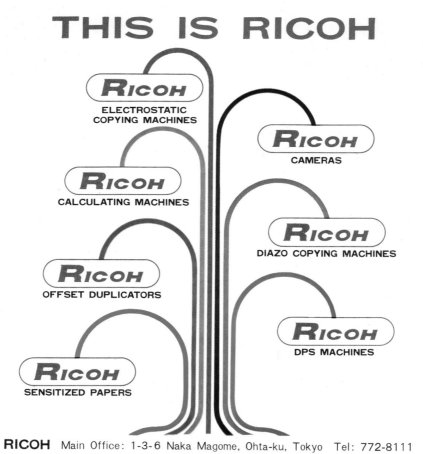

THIS IS RICOH

RICOH
ELECTROSTATIC
COPYING MACHINES

RICOH
CAMERAS

RICOH
CALCULATING MACHINES

RICOH
DIAZO COPYING MACHINES

RICOH
OFFSET DUPLICATORS

RICOH
DPS MACHINES

RICOH
SENSITIZED PAPERS

RICOH Main Office: 1-3-6 Naka Magome, Ohta-ku, Tokyo Tel: 772-8111

INDIA

The history of India is the story of a civilization which, despite many inner changes and vicissitudes, has retained its identity for 5,000 years and given birth to many religions and philosophies.

Against the background of its long and precious heritage of culture, India projects in its pavilion an image of a country pulsating with modernization. It shows India as it is today: old and new, vast and diverse, colourful in arts and crafts, rich in heritage and traditions.

The Indian Pavilion is of bold sophisticated composition on three levels, which represent different planes and dimensions of development in an isometric pattern. The basic structure is in the shape of cut cones with a truncated roof admitting continuous subdued light.

The entrance is across a series of stepped terraces flanked by mud-built walls and semi-traditional structures representing the rural base of India and its recent past. Visitors are ushered into the top level where are projected the traditions of Indian arts and crafts, resplendent in colors, richness and variety.

The middle level presents the emergence and impact of Buddhism and co-existence of religions. Selected sculptures, paintings, art pieces and crafts build an atmosphere of beauty, serenity, and harmony. The ground level offers a glimpse of India's inner dynamism, her new urges of development and progress, her efforts to harness the resources of nature and to acquire sophistication in industry and science.

Among the many interesting exhibits is a replica of the Taj Mahal. The pavilion also features the renaissance of arts in India through dances, music and other presentations.

The pavilion is just a block west of the Japanese Garden Station of the monorail.

CHILE
Republic of Chile

"Broadening the Pacific Horizons" is its pavilion theme, and Chile is determinedly looking towards the Pacific and the nations of Asia with a view to broadening its cultural and commercial relations.

This is the first exposition of this type in which Chile has participated since the Paris Exposition Universelle of 1889 – a demonstration of the importance Chile places in EXPO'70. As a further demonstration, it can be underlined that Chile was the first country in South America to apply for participation. Chile has also issued a series of postage stamps commemorating the Japan World Exposition.

The Chilean Pavilion was designed by the Chilean architects Federico Guevara, Gonzalo Asenjo and Isaac Esquenazi. Collaborating with them were consulting architect Hugo Hernandez and Engineers Ramón Undurraga and Raul Ramirez. The build-

ing is a steel cylinder resting on a reticular structure of steel piping; it has a roof of Chilean copper sheets.

Full advantage has been taken of the potentialities of the construction materials, as limited only by all the norms of stability. Thus the pavilion reflects one of the fundamental characteristics of the Chilean people: their love of simplicity, of elegance and of balance in their daily lives. This trait reveals itself in the manner in which they utilize all their resources and knowledge in a rational manner.

The pavilion is located in front of Friday Plaza. At the entrance, a moai of volcanic stone brought from Easter Island symbolizes the presence of Chile in the Pacific. The interior design presents an image of Chile in its geographic, cultural, industrial, institutional and human aspects through the media of audio-visual aids and folders in such a form that the visitor encounters an oasis of rest and tranquility.

VATICAN
Vatican City State

Participation by the Vatican City in the Japan World Exposition takes the form of co-sponsoring and actively supporting the Christian Pavilion, built by the united efforts of Catholics and Protestant Christians in Japan.

Japanese Christians felt challenged by the World Exposition to give a common witness to the saving message of Christ, and for this purpose they have pooled their resources to build the Christian Pavilion. Its main theme is "Eyes and Hands," i.e. the discovery of Man with the eyes of faith and love, and hands extended in prayer and service for Humanity, following the teaching and example of Christ.

The Vatican has helped to illustrate this theme by sending a facsimile of a precious fourth century Bible manuscript, the Vatican Greek Codex 1209, preserved in the Vatican Library. It shows the sacred sources of the Christian faith, which unites Christians of all places and all times.

The theme of the pavilion is further illustrated by three tapestries with biblical motifs, which have been lent by the Vatican. About 1515, Raphael designed the cartoons for these tapestries, which were woven in Brussels. The scene depicted on the tapestries are: 1. The Miraculous Catch of Fish, narrated in Luke 5, 1-10; 2. The Apparition of the Risen Christ at Lake Tiberias, with Christ examining Peter's love, giving him the Keys, and entrusting him with his Lambs, according to John 21, 11-17; 3. Paul preaching in Athens, proclaiming to the Athenians the "Unknown God" and the Resurrection of Christ, according to Acts, 17, 17-34.

This participation by the Vatican City in the Christian Pavilion is an important contribution to the ecumenical movement. It symbolizes also the spiritual bonds uniting Christianity in Japan with the Western Christian world and its ancient traditions.

VIET-NAM
Republic of Viet-Nam

Out of shroud of flames and blood, out of a merciless war of aggression, the EXPO'70 Pavilion of Veit-Nam emerges as a vivid picture of the past of Viet-Nam stemmed from a millenary heritage of "Culture and Harmony."

The Pavilion of Viet-Nam offers its visitors the opportunity to ponder over the inside of its modest construction and to evaluate the firm determination which has made Viet-Nam, such an old country, rank amongst young and modern nations whose cooperation in a spirit of "Freedom and Respect for Human Value" is considered as one of the prerequisite efforts for human ascension.

The architecture as well as the decoration of the stands of the Viet-Nam Pavilion are designed to convey to the visitors the very image of the people who have been expanding in a land where through geographical and historical contingencies tides of ambitions and civilizations have been confronted.

This strategic position was in fact the main cause of the many contentions, which fortunately did not affect the fundamental qualities of a people loving poetry, avid of culture and eager for progress.

That explains also how the Vietnamese people have been able to defy many foreign interferences and at the same time to cooperate with other nations in this area for progress in harmony.

This Pavilion of Viet-Nam is located in International Place 4, which is but one Moving Walkway stop to the east from Saturday Plaza.

COLOMBIA
Republic of Colombia

"The World's Largest Emerald."

"Sobriety and Harmony" are the main characteristics of the Colombian Pavilion. The triangular modulation of this Pavilion is due to architectural reasons but reflects some of Colombia's national features — the three pillars of her government system, the three main periods of her art's history, the three chains of mountains that cross her territory, the three primary colors of her flag.

The upper floor was designed as an art gallery and the ground floor as a large recreation terrace in which coffee service and musical entertainment can be enjoyed.

Outstanding features of Colombia's presentation are three main galleries housing original pieces from the Gold Museum of Colombia, only of its kind in the world; the Colonial Museum of Bogota, and the Colombian Collection of the Museum of Modern Art of New York. And, for the first time ever,

The famous legend of El Dorado originated in the highlands of Colombia. Its primitive goldsmithing stands as first in the whole American Hemisphere. The Colonial Gallery shows remarkable art pieces of the 17th and 18th Centuries, including the well known shrine of "El Santuario," of barroque influence.

Colombia has one of the most varied and productive economies in the world, owing to its exceptional geographic conditions, abundant natural resources, recent technological progress and planned economic development. Her traditional economy is based on agriculture, livestock and mining. Colombian coffee is widely known as the "the mildest coffee in the world." Even prior to World War II, the country sported a number of well-established industries: notably, textiles, foodstuffs, beverages, air transport, and building materials.

NEPAL
Kingdom of Nepal

The land where Lord Buddha was born, the Kingdom of Nepal, has fittingly drawn on the forms of a Buddhist temple for its pavilion at Expo.

Nepal, where rise the highest mountains in the world, situated between India and China, is an agricultural country with rich forests. Within its 140,000 square kilometers (56,000 square miles), 10 million people live under an indigenous system of Panchayat democracy.

The present ruler, His Majesty, King Mahendra Bir Bikram Shah Deva, has successfully introduced this democratic system which is best suited to the genius and tradition of the Nepalese people.

Nepal opened its doors to the outside world in 1950 following the revolution led by the late King Tribhuwan. Since then, many have visited the country – to see its famous cultural masterpieces, to view breathtaking sceneries and to climb its famed Himalayan peaks.

The Nepalese Pavilion, located at International Place 3, is domed and its entrance flanked by two pagoda-shaped temples. Lumbini, the birthplace of Lord Buddha, and the soaring Himalayas have been incorporated. On the front wall is a grand Himalayan panorama resplendent in color transparency photographs; other photos show cultural places and development projects the government plans to undertake in the near future.

An array of Buddhist images and Art objects, and lilting Nepalese folk music, are other attractive features of the pavilion – along with exhibits of the "mani" wheels, which the faithful turn while chanting Buddhist Sutra at the temples, and native items of interest such as musical instruments, ornaments, ethnic attire, objects of daily use, medicinal herbs, agricultural products, handicrafts. Minerals and manufactured goods are also prominent in the displays.

ECUADOR

Republic of Ecuador

Pacific coast, temperate highlands between the ranges, and tropical eastern lowlands bordering Peru.

One of Ecuador's main industries is the manufacture of Panama hats. They are made from Toquilla straw, a native plant called carludorica palmata. The name is derived from the fact that they were originally exported to world markets through Panama.

An interesting and little-known fact is that these hats are hand-woven by moonlight. The straw becomes coarse and hard if exposed to the sun. By the same token it gets soiled if woven near lamplight.

The mainstay of Ecuador's economy, however, is the banana industry. Aside from exporting large quantities of bananas it does equally well with coffee and cocoa.

Relations between Ecuador and Japan have become increasingly closer in recent years, particularly in the field of economic cooperation.

Ecuador desires to accelerate its economic development. For this reason international collaboration is necessary to attain the various goals that have been projected.

Plans are now being studied and the works are to be carried out shortly. Japan has the opportunity to be one of the principal markets for the planning and financing of these works, especially projects involving infrastructure.

The Pavilion of Ecuador is situated at International Place 2-B. That's found beneath the Aerial Cableway — a short distance from the west end of the Artificial Pond.

As its name implies, Ecuador is a South American republic astride the Equator.

Two ranges of the Andes run north and south, splitting the country into three zones, each with different climates — hot, humid lowlands on the

PERU
Republic of Peru

Peru is the third largest country in South America, following Brazil and Argentina.

The country is divided into three regions. The narrow coastal area has been made like a desert by the trade winds. The mountainous region, the plateau between the eastern and west-ern chains of the Andes Mountains, is commonly referred to as the "roof of South America." The jungle region to the east is in the upper reaches of the Amazon and accessible only by rivers and airplane.

Since 1960, Peru has averaged 6.9% in annual economic growth, the highest of all South American nations. Its manufacturing, mining and fishing industries are expanding rapidly.

About 46 per cent of its inhabitants are Indian, 43 per cent mestizo, and 11 per cent white.

The northern desert areas are hit periodically by torrential rains. And the whole coast is subject to earthquakes.

The climate varies greatly with the altitude. In the lowlands it is subtropical; above 3,000 feet it is temperate, and above 10,000 feet it is quite cold.

The Inca Empire controlled Peru and all territories from Ecuador to Bolivia, part of Chile, Colombia and Argentina for centuries before the Spanish conquistadores set foot on the land. A colony of Spain for 300 years, Peru finally attained independence in 1824.

Peru, the world's third-largest silver producer, is also a great producer of copper, zinc, lead and iron. In fishery output, Peru has no equal. Annual hauls from the Pacific, the Amazon and the Titicaca total 11 million tons. Included among the varieties of fish which abound in the waters are anchovy (for making fishmeal), bonito, tuna and grey mullet.

Peru's Pavilion, in International Place 2-A, is east of Friday Plaza.

ITALY
Italian Republic

Visitors to the Italian Pavilion "visit" the country itself — thanks to a unique film technique that gives the impression of flying over the cities in a helicopter. As you leave, you can take your own souvenir photo — against one of 10 typical Italian scenes.

The result of a nationwide contest won by two young architect brothers (Tommaso and Gilberto Valle in cooperation with engineer Sergio Brusa Pasque), the pavilion is a startling structure, a four-level steel-and-glass creation with a series of interlocking, slanting components. You enter first a section on Italy's history. A special feature: multiple television screens tracing the story of Italian explorers in Asia — from Marco Polo to the present.

"Italy Today" summarizes modern life — sports, fashion, science, culture, industry and architecture. Italy's famed crafts and arts are on parade on the second level, near a full-scale, classical Italian garden. Another section covers graphic arts, typography and calligraphy.

Vividly presenting three eras are three room interiors: a Roman villa, the hall of a Renaissance mansion and a modern living room. And two magnificent works in bronze symbolize the continuity of Italian art. The "Mercury" inside the pavilion, by Giambologna, a disciple of Michelangelo, is a masterpiece of Italian Renaissance. The other work, at the pavilion entrance, is by the sculptor Manzu, author of one of the doors of St. Peter's Cathedral.

An adjacent building, prefabricated in Italy of steel and fiberglass, contains a special exhibition of contemporary Italian industrial development. A typical Italian restaurant occupies a corner of the first floor; also, a shop there sells art books, reproductions, records, stamps and other items.

CENTRAL AFRICAN REPUBLIC

The Central African Republic is situated in the heart of the African Continent. The remarkable progresses which she has recorded in the economic and social fields since her independence in 1960 and her political stability have won her the name of "The African Switzerland."

Indeed, this harmonious development and political stability, achieved in a part of the world stricken by troubles, has been a surprise to many peoples.

The aim of the pavilion of the Central African Republic is to introduce the abundant resources of the nation to Expo visitors.

Although small, the pavilion has a huge economic and moral significance: painted in white, and in the form of a diamond (the principal export product of the country), this pavilion rises harmoniously over the dark-blue background of the International Place 1-A.

The vast range of objects and products exposed shows not only great aspirations towards the modernization of the country and the civilization of its people, but also determination to conserve certain aspects of ancient traditional arts.

This is a country that has actively striven for "Progress and Harmony for Mankind," as one can rediscover by its national creed: unity, dignity, work.

The Central African Republic expects that visitors from the entire world will discover at its pavilion the hidden treasures of this country.

The site is landscaped with a magnificent fauna, certain species of which are quite rare. And above waves the striking flag of the Republic. Four horizontal stripes — blue, white, green, yellow — are crossed by a red one; in the upper left is a gold star. The flag symbolizes the great unity of human beings: no matter their color, all are united by the same red of their blood.

National Pavilions

See Your Future Today at the MITSUBISHI PAVILION.

A glimpse of the world 50 years from now?
We've created it.
But then the Mitsubishi group has always been ahead of the times.
Come see.
The Mitsubishi Pavilion at EXPO '70.

 **MITSUBISHI**

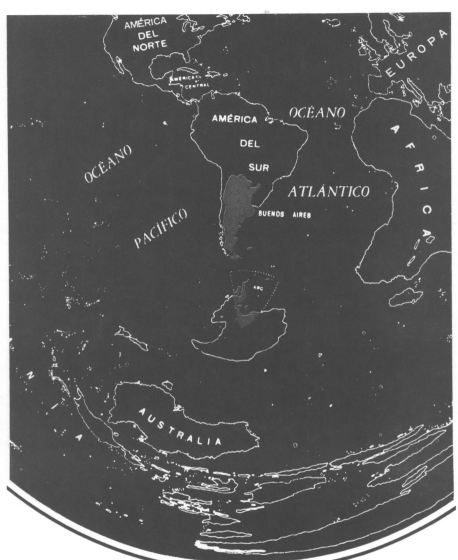

Argentina

ARGENTINA
Argentine Republic

The Argentine Pavilion is a bright, modern structure with a total floor space of 1,100 square meters and comprising three stories and one basement level. It is lively painted in primary blue, red and yellow, offering a striking contrast with the white-tiled floor. Architect Roberto Quiros designed the pavilion to express the youthful image of Argentina; his Japanese co-architect was Miss Toshiko Ezaki.

The pavilion houses on its first floor a restaurant seating 184 persons. It offers native Argentine beef dishes and a variety of wines. On its central stage, artistic Argentine performances are presented so you may dine in an atmosphere of the land of the tango.

The main exhibition hall is on the pavilions's second floor. Under the theme "Peace, Freedom and Happiness," cultural and art objects and agricultural, dairy and light industrial products testify to the highest standard of living in South America. In-

cluded are fancy articles used by gauchos herding cattle over the pampas long ago.

Outside the pavilion is a cafeteria with nine crimson chimneys. Here you may enjoy charcoal-broiled and other delicious dishes in a cozy atmosphere. Movies in an annex theater introduce the beautiful nature and life of Argentina.

Argentina is as big an agricultural and dairy country as Australia. It ranks first in the world in meat and hide exports, second in wool and corn exports and third in wheat exports.

With its great farming and cattle-raising potential, Argentina stands ready as a producer of food for the world's peoples. In addition, it has developed to a large scale industries such as food, cowhide tanning and weaving and has attained an international level in electronic technology. Yes, agriculture and industry are the mainstays by which Argentina will perform its role in the future world.

BRAZIL
Federative Republic of Brazil

Brazil is a nation built largely by a vast number of immigrants who came from all corners of the world to fulfil their long-cherished dreams. About a decade ago, the country carved a new capital, Brasilia, in a plateau hitherto thinly inhabited by man. This remarkable achievement is symbolic of the limitless energies of the many races which contribute to the development of this young nation.

Although Brazil and Japan are separated by thousands of miles, the distance has been immeasurably narrowed through the immigration of enterprising Japanese, beginning more than 60 years ago. At present, some 200,000 Japanese and 400,000 Brazilians of Japanese origin live in this country, all actively engaged in a variety of business and professions. As a token of Brazil's appreciation of Japan's cooperation in its economic development, the Brazilian Government is participating in EXPO'70.

Brazilians firmly believe in their continuous work to enlarge the civilization they have created in the tropics. They are building it at a lively tempo.

"Rhythm" has been selected as the theme of their pavilion. The exhibition is located under the cover of the pavilion, which opens in all directions, its cover just touching the ground. The ground rises in gentle undulations; the landscape fits into the architecture. Through numerous windows in the ornate roof, sunlight enhanced by artificial light is filtered into the building's spacious, partitionless interior, in representation of the openmindedness of the Brazilian people, ever ready to welcome all who desire to visit and live in their country.

As the green background of the Brazilian flag symbolizes verdant forests, Brazil takes pride in her promise of new life and in the youthful energies of her people.

NIGERIA
Federal Republic of Nigeria

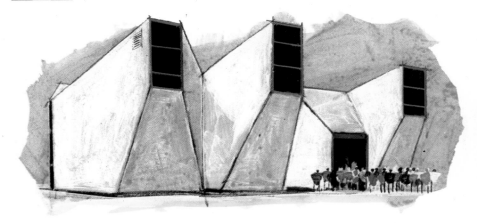

With a population of 60 million, Nigeria is the largest nation in Africa. It is on the west coast and became independent on Oct. 1, 1960.

Nigeria is primarily agricultural, with 80% of the work force in farming, fishing, forestry and the like. Chief products are peanuts, of which she is the world's largest producer; cocoa (second largest producer); palm oil, used in margarine and soap; palm kernel, used in animal feeds; timber (about 40 varieties are now exported), and cotton. Manufacturing industries are being established however and an iron and steel complex is being studied.

The main mineral resources now exploited are petroleum, gas, coal, cassiterite (containing 80% tin) and columbite. There is also lead, zinc, bauxite and iron ore.

Trade with Japan is well estab-lished, with Nigeria importing manu-factured goods and machinery and exporting peanuts, cocoa, cotton seeds and timber. Low-sulphur petroleum is likely to be Nigeria's most important export to Japan in the near future.

Nigeria is a federal nation with 12 states. The three eastern states attempted to secede in May, 1967, as "Biafra." A civil war ensued, which came to an end in January of this year with the leaders of the small remaining secessionist area proclaiming fidelity to Nigeria and declaring: "The Republic of Biafra no longer exists."

Because of her cultural and linguistic diversity, Nigeria abounds with a variety of folklore, dancing and art. But happily, this rich cultural past does not hinder progress; rather, it enhances it with self-respect and self-confidence which are so necessary for development. As the pavilion theme proclaims: "Nigeria Looks Ahead."

ABU-DHABI
Trucial State Abu Dhabi

Dotting the tip of the Arabian Peninsula, Abu Dhabi is a sheikdom seeking its way to modernity through the blessing of a prospering petroleum industry.

But the country is also rich in its history, in its Arab traditions, and the Abu Dhabi Pavilion adopts the basic design of the simple yet imposing fortresses that spotted the coastline in ancient times. These fortresses served as places of residence, gathering and worship for the sheikhs, or tribal chiefs. Though constructed simply, some have stood the ravages of man and nature to survive today as silent yet eloquent witnesses to the tenacity of the Arabs.

The pavilion is noted by its two minarets, one round and the other square and has an exhibition hall and a motion picture hall. The land and people are portrayed with films and in display alcoves around the main minaret. The theme: "Abu Dhabi — Her Past, Present and Future."

The exhibits offer an idea of the tremendous work and wide-spread improvements that have been taking place since the accession of His Highness, Sheikh Zayed Bin Sultan Al-Nehiyan, and of the manner in which oil revenues are employed for the welfare of the people.

Also, you are presented with an artist's impression of Abu Dhabi's past and of the part the sea and pearl fishing played in the picturesque life of the people.

A special feature of the exhibit is a replica of a colorful and romantic scene from the world-famous tales of the "Thousand and One Nights." Here pavilion visitors find themselves entertained in a manner that would have impressed those storied Arabs of many centuries ago.

The Abu Dhabi Pavilion is to be found facing the Pond, half a block east from Senri Bridge Avenue.

IRAN
Empire of Iran

Irán, also known as Persia, covers 628,000 square miles of the Middle East. Turkey and Iraq are on the west, the USSR and the Caspian Sea on the north, Pakistan and Afghanistan on the east and Persian Gulf on the south. The population is over 26 million, 3 million of them in the capital, Tehran.

Iran's history as one of the oldest civilizations is a blend of myth, legend and facts — from the legendary exploits of Bahram the Hunter to the actual grandeur of the Achaemnia dynasty. Iran was once famous as a vital link of the Silk Road connecting East and West. Many excellent examples of fine art and craftsmanship have been handed down as testaments to its glorious past.

The Indo-European tribes were the first settlers to come to this country. They called themselves Aryans and the name Iran is derived from the land of the Aryans, though the West called this land Persia.

Among an abundance of natural resources, oil is the country's main export, with a revenue exceeding $900 million. Most of this income is invested in Seven-Year Development Programs.

H.I.M. Reza Shah the Great, who founded the Pahlave dynasty, sensed the tremendous potential of the nation and its people, and set it on the road to full development and prosperity. His son, H.I.M. Mohammad Reza Shah Pahlavi, Shahanshah Arya Mehr, in a remarkably short period, has realized his father's dreams and goals, and transformed the country from an unproductive feudal state into a modern advanced nation. Iran is a fast developing country and has achieved in three decades progress that took others a century or more. And Iran now presents one of the best potential sites for productive enterprise in Asia.

Iran shares the RCD Pavilion with its two friendly nations, Turkey and Pakistan.

MALAYSIA

The Malaysian Pavilion has a unique architectural design based on Malay rural house and is built entirely of quality Malaysian timber. The pavilion roof carries three symbolic structures in the "minangkabau" style typical of houses in the southern region of the Malay Peninsula.

The building stands on stilts as in a Malay "kampong" (village) house and the interior is enhanced by a generous use of intricate wood carvings as well as "batek" (a hand-painted fabric) and rattan panelling.

Visitors to the pavilion first pass through an area which introduces Malaysia as a beautiful and booming nation. From there you move into the main display area which shows the progress of Malaysia and highlights the natural resources, the industrialization program and the general economic and social development of the country.

On the floor above is shown the art, culture and history of the various peo-

ples of Malaysia in a traditional and exotic Malaysian setting.

The cultural display highlights in particular the multi-racial society and the harmony between the various peoples of Malaysia. It also presents the "old" Malaysia as a direct contrast to the ultra-modern presentation in the "progress" area.

On the way out visitors can rest in a typical Malaysian garden restaurant or eat the famous Malaysian barbecued dish, "satay," while watching a stage show performed by a Malaysian troupe of 15 artists.

Malaysia's participation in EXPO'70 is highlighted by cultural performances by a troupe of about 20 artists introducing, for the first time in Japan, the folklore of Malaysia in all its color and splendor.

Malaysia's pavilion, as many-faceted as this old-yet-young country, is just west of Senri Bridge Avenue and a little south of the Pond.

THE FRAGRANCE OF JAPAN — FROM KIKKOMAN

Mellow, fullbodied, distinctively right in subtle zestiness of taste, Kikkoman perfection is the result of a guarded production process behind which are more than three centuries of experience and tradition. Kikkoman Soy Sauce is loved by gourmets all over the world because it enhances the natural flavor of food. Every drop of Kikkoman is carefully age-brewed a full 12 months. Kikkoman — the soy sauce that sets the quality standard by which all other soy sauces are to be judged. Discover the taste of Japan — the taste of Kikkoman — at the Kikkoman Aqua Restaurant and snack bars at EXPO '70.

Kikkoman
SOY SAUCE

135

From coal to the boundless potential of the chemical industries. UBE INDUSTRIES — driving force in the progress of the chemical and petrochemical industries and a better world tomorrow.

Chemicals, Petrochemicals, Cement, Machinery, Coal

UBE INDUSTRIES, LTD.

Participants in the creation of the Midori-kan "ASTRORAMA", the Chemical Pavilion, the United Nations Pavilion and others.

AFGHANISTAN
Kingdom of Afghanistan

Afghanistan is a landlocked constitutional monarchy of 15 million people occupying a mountainous area the size of Texas. For centuries it has prospered as an important link connecting the Near and Middle East, Central Asia and India — earning the name "Crossroads of Oriental and Occidental Civilization."

Alexander the Great, Marco Polo, Genghis Khan and many other renowned figures of history passed through this land. The 35-mile-long Khyber Pass is famous as a gateway linking the east and west of Eurasia. Afghanistan is a non-allied nation friendly to all; it remained neutral during two world wars.

Participation in EXPO'70 was decided when King Mohammed Zahir Shah inspected progress at the Expo site during a state visit to Japan in April, 1969. He gazed upon the many pavilions in various shapes and sizes from an observation platform and almost immediately announced willingness to participate in this first World Exposition in Asia.

"No nation in Asia could afford to overlook such a large World Exposition and the opportunities it offered to show the world's peoples their cultural heritage and the progress they are making toward mutual harmony and peace."

The Afghan exhibition is located with the Asian group at International Place 3, a block east of Saturday Plaza.

The exhibits create an image of Afghanistan as a vast mountainous country with a rich cultural heritage. Huge bazaars are held regularly in the capital of Kabul. Domestic and foreign commodities packed across the glimmering sand by caravan are actively traded and mindful of the caravans of old which crossed this main silk road from China to Europe by way of Afghanistan.

EL SALVADOR
Republic of El Salvador

Resembling Japan in many aspects, El Salvador is the most densely populated republic in Central America.

Her mountains are accented by volcanic cones and beautiful crater lakes which present magnificent views. Plains are limited to a narrow area on the Pacific coast, but she is the most intensely cultivated country in Latin America.

Thanks to the rich volcanic soil, high-quality coffee and cotton are abundant. El Salvador coffee is regarded as one of the best in the world with its pungent aroma and rich taste. Coffee and cotton constitute more than half of the total exports.

The republic has close trade and economic ties with Japan, her fourth-ranking trade partner. In 1968, El Salvador imported textile machinery, steel and automobiles valued at $14,814,000 from Japan. In turn she exported to Japan $15,950,000 worth of cotton and coffee. Also in that year Japan sent the first team of 12 young Japanese Peace Corps workers to El Salvador. The team is assisting the El Salvador Ministry of Education in the field of physical education.

Late in 1969, the Export-Import Bank of Japan started aiding in the financing of the micro-wave communication system of the Central American Common Market, of which El Salvador is the most active member.

Japanese-Salvadorean joint ventures are good examples of international cooperation in the world.

The welcome mat is always out for foreigners and the warm nature of the people is revealed in the credo, "My home is your home."

The Pavilion of El Salvador is located at International Place 2-B, in between the West Gate station of the Aerial Cableway and the western end of the Artificial Pond — or about two blocks away from Friday Plaza.

CAMBODIA

Kingdom of Cambodia

covered plain irrigated by the Mekong River and its tributaries and the Tonle Sap.

Located in the heart of South-East Asia, and a crossroads of Indian and Chinese civilizations, Cambodia has kept its individuality. The past glories of the Khmere civilization left as its own testimony such masterpieces as the famous Angkor temples, the spirit of which can still be found in modern monuments such as the Royal Palace of Phnom Penh, and in festivals and traditional dances.

The Cambodian Pavilion at EXPO'70, reflecting the traditional Khmere architecture, was designed under the direction of Cambodia's Chief of State, Prince Norodom Sihanouk, and executed by Khmere architects M.M. Uk Someth and Soum Samkol under the supervision of Commissioner General Khek Vandy. As for the materials and fittings of the pavilion, inside and outside decorations were designed after originals in Angkor Vat.

Visitors to the pavilion may view a model of Angkor Vat and also attend many artistic performances where they can admire the evolution of the "Apsaras," or the dancers of the Royal Cambodian Ballet. Classical Khmere dancing is renowned throughout the world; the dancers, richly dressed in silver-and-gold-embroidered silks, present the Indo-Khmere legends of Ramayana to traditional music.

The Cambodian Pavilion is in International Place 3. Just stroll half a block easterly from Saturday Plaza along the Moving Walkway.

Cambodia, the country of the "Khmeres," is a land where tourism is highly developed, a land possessing uncountable riches in archaeology and in art. Covering an area of 181,000 square kilomet Cambodia counts a population of 8 million people. The rural majority live on a vast, paddy-

Feminine Co., Ltd.

おしゃれな毛染め
フェミニン® ヘアカラー

Feminine® HAIR COLOR

140

MALTA

Malta achieved its independence from British rule in 1964, and is fast becoming a tourist paradise through a climate enjoyable during most of the year.

The pavilion of this newly independent nation, located at International Place 2-B, reflects the newfound spirit of freedom which pervades Malta's modern generation.

Stress is laid on the important and relevant aspects of Malta's character, history and art through the ages, under the theme "An Island of History, Progress and Harmony."

The central platform, an island in miniature, represents Malta's character as a small island in the Mediterranean.

The pavilion contains replicas of statuettes found in the Neolithic temples on the island dating as far back as 2500 B.C. A small cannon belonging to the period of the Order of St. John (1530–1798) is also on exhibition, as well as works of art by Maltese artists.

There are also handicraft specimens of gold, silver filigree, lace, glassware, costume jewelry and ceramics.

A cyclorama in the pavilion, highlighted by a shimmering cascade of falling water, serves to highlight the various objects on display carefully chosen to represent in chronological order the relevant aspects of Malta's long history, as well as its industrial and tourist development.

Particular emphasis is placed on Malta's contributions to the fields of art, archaeology and history.

To commemorate Malta's first participation in a world exposition, a medal has been reminted for exhibit in the pavilion. The original medal was struck in 1566 to commemorate the foundation of the city of Valletta by the Knights of Malta. The exhibits also include a complete set of the postage stamps issued since independence. International Place 2-B is just west of the Pond.

VENEZUELA

Republic of Venezuela

Venezuela. Oil. Industry. Abundant in petroleum and iron, Venezuela is a prime example of a country using rich natural resources to lubricate progress to a modern industrial economy. Nature plus policy.

Petroleum yields about 65% of Venezuela's public revenue and 90% of its foreign exchange. Much of the industrial and social development in this northern-most nation of South America is financed by oil income which the Government by policy reinvests to diversify the economy and to underwrite social reform.

Thus Venezuela is undergoing an intense industrial transformation. Since 1950, progress has been made at the rate of 9.5% annually. Industry is the fastest growing sector of the economy.

Food, chemical, basic-metal, beverage and textile industries are the most important in terms of value. But the spread of industrial activity is wide — automobile assembly (there are now 14 plants turning out 60,000 units a year), furniture, tires, paper and pulp, metal products, building materials.

Venezuela contains 10 million people, 2 million of them in the capital of Caracas. The nation is divided into 20 states, two territories and a Federal District within four geographic areas: the mountains, including the Andes; a coastal zone north of the mountains; plains south and east of them, and Guayana.

In this Guayana region, bordering Colombia, one can find exemplified Government economic efforts. In 1960, for example, the Venezuelan Guayana Corporation was created. Now it manages a steel mill in Matanzas and in partnership with Reynolds Metals International, an aluminum plant in Ciudad Guayana. Also, it supervises two hydroelectric plants.

Venezuela's exhibits are on display at International Place 2-A, just a block away from Friday Plaza.

One World, One Refreshment

DRINK Coca-Cola Coke

EXPO'70
EXPO'70—4—CT—6
Things go better with Coke

"COCA-COLA" AND "COKE" ARE THE REGISTERED TRADEMARKS OF THE COCA-COLA COMPANY

UNITED ARAB REPUBLIC

"The cradle of civilization" is virtually a synonym for Egypt. Over the past 8,000 years, contributions have been made by all nations and in every field toward the construction of the huge edifice of civilization.

Yet, the edifice would be very different today without Egypt. The foundations were laid there in 6000 B.C., at the dawn of history, with settlements along the River Nile. The never-ending drive over the road of progress had begun.

The UAR Pavilion is a creation of descendants of people who, Egyptologists note, had achieved high levels in various sciences by 3000 B.C. These particularly included medicine, surgery, astronomy, geometry, mathematics and pharmacology.

The early Egyptians also excelled in industries like shipbuilding, paper fabrics, metalurgy and jewelry.

Great thinkers expounded the theory of the creation of the universe.

And sociologically, Egyptians were the only peoples of ancient times to have respect for women; indeed, in many cases succession to the throne was bound to them.

The United Arab Republic has chosen for its pavilion the shape of a pyramid. This shape is a symbol of eternity and culture. The pavilion itself gives the visitor a brief review of Egypt's contributions to civilization during the Greek, Roman, Christian, Islamic and contemporary eras.

Even now Egypt still keeps pace with civilization.

Exhibits reflect endeavors constantly made to build the national wealth on two major pillars, agriculture and industry.

This drive coincides with the building of a strong basis for a society of justice, prosperity and freedom in which culture prevails and prospers.

International Place 4 is the site of the UAR Pavilion. It's toward the north end of Senri Bridge Avenue.

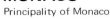

MONACO
Principality of Monaco

The Grimaldi Dynasty which rules the Principality of Monaco, one of the oldest houses of Europe, is descended from an old patrician family of Genoa. Jealous of their independence, the sovereigns who have succeeded to the throne of Monaco have sought to preserve the unity of their country in a tradition which has been perpetuated since the 11th Century and is today personified in His Highness, Prince Rainier III.

True to this tradition but also resolutely facing the future, Prince Rainier is determined to give his country the prodigious growth which will make it one of the most modern of states, through town planning and tourism and through industrial and commercial expansion.

The Monaco Pavilion is designed to illustrate this double aim. Its theme: "Tradition and Progress."

You find in this beautiful pavilion, next to portraits of outstanding figures of the Grimaldi Dynasty, diagrams picturing this ancient principality soaring towards modernization.

A special section presents the scientific achievements of Prince Albert I, one of the originators of oceanography.

A lively performance depicts cultural and social activities of Monaco, festivals and sporting events, such as the world-famous international Grand Prix auto race. Philately as a manifestation of the country is presented, too; philatelists can obtain stamps specially issued for EXPO'70.

An ever-young state, where one man's authority preserves every man's liberty, this millennial principality reflects in its harmony one of the world's oldest civilizations: the Mediterranean culture. See it in International Place 2-B, which is just north of the Aerial Cableway and just west of the Pond.

NICARAGUA

Republic of Nicaragua

The largest of the Central America Republics, Nicaragua lies between Honduras and Costa Rica, which form its northern and southern boundaries respectively, and reaches from the Caribbean Sea on the east to the Pacific Ocean on the west. Its area, which is still undetermined because of incomplete surveys, is generally put at 150,000 square kilometers or 53,398 square miles.

Nicaragua's population of more than 1,800,000 is largely agricultural and concentrated in the western third of the country, especially in the small section near the Pacific coast that extends from the city of Chinandega on the north to the city of Granada and Lake Nicaragua on the south.

The principal products of Nicaragua are: coffee, cotton, beef, lumber, gold, oil refinery products, sugar, sesame seed, corn, rice, beans, flour.

Nicaragua has advanced from a one-crop economy of coffee to a more balanced and diversified economy based principally on cotton, beef and coffee. In manufacturing, private enterprise has turned to processing one of the country's own raw materials, coffee, into soluble coffee, which has enjoyed success in the quality markets of the United States and Europe.

The capital, Managua, on the Inter-American Highway, is a frequent starting-out point for tourists. It's on Lake Xolotlan and contains the National Palace, with its government offices, as well as the Presidential Palace and National Museum. In the northwest corner of town are the human footprints of Acahualinca, reportedly the oldest traces of man in Latin America. And to the south, on the precipitous cliffs of Lake Asososca, colored hieroglyphics date to pre-Columbian times.

The Pavilion of Nicaragua, in International Place 2-B, is just to the west of the Artificial Pond.

PANAMA

Republic of Panama

Panama, if the Canal Zone is set aside, is 75,650 square kilometers (29,500 square miles) in area and mostly of high terrain. It forms the narrowest part of the strip linking North and South America.

Visited by Columbus in 1502 on his fourth voyage and explored by Balboa in 1513, Panama was the main transshipment point for Spanish treasure and supplies in colonial days. In 1821, when Central America revolted against Spain, Panama joined Colombia, which had already declared its independence. In 1903, Panama proclaimed its separation.

Panama had an estimated population of 1,372,000 in 1968, about a third of it concentrated in Panama City, the capital, and in Colon on the Atlantic coast. Colon's Free Zone is the most important center of international commerce in Latin America; it offers unrivaled geographical advantages as well as the opportunities of tax-exemption, both of which allow unequalled contact with Western Hemisphere markets.

The Panama Canal is the country's biggest economic asset. But Panama has been exploiting natural resources as part of an industrial development program under which steel mills have been built, manganese mines opened and other industrial activities taken.

About 40% of the people are engaged in agriculture, which accounts for 20% of the gross national product. The main farm products include bananas, coffee and sugar. Panama has an important food processing industry. Manufacturing is expanding; chief products are cement and furniture. The main exports include bananas, refined petroleum and marine products.

Panama exports scrap iron, turtle shell and refined petroleum to Japan in exchange for electrical appliances, drugs and so on.

The Pavilion of Panama is in International Place 2-A, just a block east of Friday Plaza.

COSTA RICA
Republic of Costa Rica

Costa Rica was discovered, and named, by Columbus in 1502. It proclaimed its independence in 1821. The backbone of Costa Rica is a chain of highlands stretching from northwest to southeast. In central Costa Rica about 12 kilometers northeast of the main crest of mountains, is a series of 11 great volcanic cones. The southern Pacific coast, formerly jungle territory, has been opened up and is traversed by the Inter-American Highway.

The population of Costa Rica was estimated at 1,707,000 in mid 1969. More than 95 per cent of the population is of European origin. The proportion of Spanish blood in Costa Rica is greater than in any other Latin American republic. The colonial period was one of poverty and neglect, but since the middle of the 19th century the country has in general enjoyed peace. Visitors to Costa Rica immediately sense the democratic atomsphere that prevails in the country. Every citizen

from the humble peasant to the educated university professor has an attitude which combines self-respect with participation in the community life. Love of the land is another dominant characteristic of the people, and in this regard, an economic system has been established which functions very satisfactorily.

The country's main products include coffee, bananas, abaca, fiber, meat, cocobeans and sugar. In the mountainous areas, such forest products as balsa, cedar, dyewood, mahogany and rosewood are produced on mountain slopes. Costa Rica's chief exports include coffee, bananas, cocobeans, beef, sugar.

Costa Ricans have the highest annual percapita income in Central America, which in 1968 was $457. They also have a high educational level. According to a survey made in 1963, about 94 per cent of the people in urban areas, and 78 per cent in agrarian areas, were literate.

URUGUAY
Oriental Republic of Uruguay

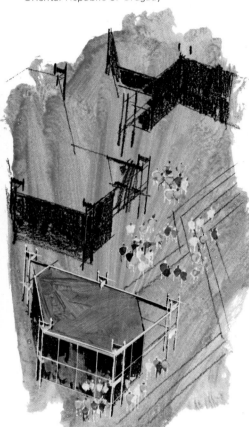

Uruguay is located in South America in the temperate zone. Its 187,000 square kilometers (72,930 square miles) are bounded by the River Plate and the Atlantic Ocean. The country consists of a succession of small hills with rounded curves; the climate is mild and temperate.

The near-3,000,000 population of Uruguay is of European origin, mostly Spanish and Italian descendants, and 1,400,000 live in the capital: Montevideo.

A highly civilized country, the Republic of Uruguay benefits from one of the world's most advanced political and social systems. All its inhabitants enjoy complete freedom and only talent, work and civic virtues count. There are no castes and privileges. The language is Spanish. The state is laic and respects all beliefs. In this country foreigners and natives are equal to the law: the first find fine hospitality as well as a generous country and soil.

The public education at all levels — primary, secondary, industrial or university — is absolutely free. Illiteracy is practically non-existent and almost all citizens benefit also from free medical assistance.

The agricultural, live-stock raising (more than 30,000,000 head) and industrial enterprises have shown in recent years an increasing index of rationalization, specialization and integration. The leading exports are meat and its derivatives, wool, leather, textiles and marbles; the major imports: raw materials, machinery, fuel and vehicles. Tourism has steadily developed in these last years and is on its way to becoming the main industry. Every year thousands of tourists enjoy Uruguay's sunny Atlantic beaches. Among its popular summer resorts, Punta del Este is known all over the world.

The Pavilion of Uruguay is located at International Place 2-A near Friday Plaza.

MAURITIUS

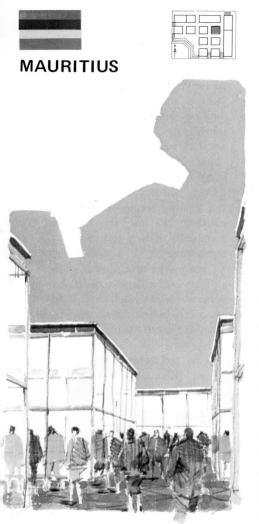

It is fitting that the theme of this pavilion should be "Harmony and Challenge," for on that 1,865 square kilometers (720 square miles) of mountain and plain — situated on the Tropic of Capricorn in the middle of the Indian Ocean, 2,015 kilometers (1,250 miles) from the east coast of the African Continent and 805 kilometers (500 miles) from Madagascar — 790,000 people live happily side by side.

The island was probably known, in early Medieval times, to Malay and Arab navigators. But the first European visitor was the Portuguese navigator, Pedro Mascarenhas. A few years later the Dutch established a settlement, which they later abandoned. Resettled by the French, the island became an important naval base and a center for corsairs. After 99 years of French administration, the island was ceded to the British, who administered it until 1968 when Mauritius gained independence.

In the design of display, a motif symbolizes Mauritius: Star and Key of the Indian Ocean and an international rendezvous. Just as the colors of the motif blend harmoniously, so do the Eastern and Western cultures, customs, religions and faiths making up this mosaic of races.

Besides featuring the sugar industry, backbone of the country and recognized as one of the most efficient in the world, the exhibit shows the potential for productive investments. This young nation with an old history takes up with determination the challenge of its economic problems.

The aim of the Mauritius Pavilion in International Place 2-B is to provide you with the opportunity to survey very easily and rapidly the economic potential of Mauritius, with emphasis upon its developing tourist industry against the background of the history, culture and traditions of the country.

This "PAVILION" welcomed 95 million visitors last year

Daimaru is the ideal "Pavilion" for shopping. Our wide range of merchandise includes the luxurious and the necessary. We've been serving people for 250 years. Let us serve you during Expo'70.

DEPARTMENT STORE

DAIMARU

OSAKA, TOKYO, KYOTO, KOBE

Branch Stores: Hakata, Shimonoseki, Kochi, Tottori, Besshi, Okamasa (Nagasaki)
Overseas: Hong Kong, Thailand

SIERRA LEONE

Sierra Leone is in the southeast corner of the West Africa bulge. Its name, meaning Mountain of the Lion, was acquired from an early Portuguese mariner named Pedro de Cintra, who fancied the mountains which rise along the coastline resembled a lion. Its Atlantic coastline is about 340 km (210 miles), and its terrain extends inland about 290 km (180 miles) between Guinea and Liberia, covering 70,000 square kilometers (27,300 square miles).

The national flag has three colors, green symbolizing land, blue for the Atlantic Ocean, and white for peace; the flag can be considered a true symbol of Sierra Leone.

Freetown, the capital, was founded in 1787 by the British government as a home for destitute freed slaves.

Their descendents, known as Creoles, number more than 50,000; the total population of Sierra Leone is 2,500,000.

Sierra Leone is usually hot, and at times, very wet. There are swamps and mangroves in the south, high savannas in the north and arid plateaus rising to some 3,000 feet.

Sierra Leone is known for its diamond production. In 1965 the country produced 1,530,000 karats of diamonds which is equal to 3.5% of the total diamond production of the world, and 64.2% of the total exports of this country. The country has reserve of rich deposits of iron ore, chromium, bauxite, and other mineral resources.

Important exports are palm kernels, piassava, ginger, cocoa, kola nuts, peanuts and rice. All are on display at the Sierra Leone Pavilion — found in International Place 1-A, a block east of Senri Bridge Avenue and near the Artificial Pond. Tuesday Plaza is across the way.

IRELAND

Ireland is one of the oldest nations and one of the youngest states in Europe. She is thus a land of contrasts, where respect for tradition co-exists with a will to progress which in recent years has brought her material advancement on a scale unparalleled in her history. This is the basic theme of the Irish Pavilion (in International Place 4), reflecting the special character of a country which, while contributing names like Yeats, Shaw, Joyce and Beckett to modern literature, still draws inspiration from the art of 2,000 years ago, where agriculture, mainly represented here by dairy products and meat, flourishes side by side with rapid and intensive industrialization, and where the quality of life together with a wealth of natural attractions and recreational facilities act each year as a magnet to millions of overseas visitors.

Bridging the gap between antiquity and modernity, the pavilion features megalithic remains, (2,000 years old and among the finest in Europe), as well as sophisticated products of a fast-expanding export industry. Agriculture, Ireland's oldest industry, remains one of her most important, but in recent years the country has made rapid and substantial progress in developing and diversifying the industrial sector of the economy and today Irish manufactured goods — from cosmetics to computers and from crystal glassware to space-satellite parts — are competing successfully, in growing volume and variety, in world markets. At the same time it illustrates Ireland's unique cultural traditions and her charms as a holiday country.

Thus the pavilion gives a significant impression of the Ireland of Yesterday and Today with the added attraction of a restaurant where the visitor may sample Irish food and drink. This pavilion, in its different aspects, conveys something of the rich variety of Irish life today.

UNITED NATIONS

The UN Pavilion is a steel frame structure the shape of which suggests a bowl carrying an imaginary globe. The pavilion is surrounded by 526 metal poles representing the peoples of the United Nations.

The basic message which the pavilion seeks to bring home to visitors concerns the size, scope and results of the UN's "peace-building" activities. These activities, designed to help spur world-wide economic and social progress, account for the vast majority of all the work done by the United Nations, by its related agencies and by the Asian Development Bank.

The Japanese Peace Bell, donated to the United Nations by the UN Association of Japan in 1954 as representing the prayers of mankind for peace, has been brought back to Japan on loan for prominent display in a belfry at the entrance to the pavilion.

Special displays include: Nobel Peace Prize scrolls and medals given to UNICEF, the UN High Commissioner for Refugees and to ILO; the Population Dome and Population Meter, illustrating the problem of population explosion; displays of "Breads of the World" and "Moneys of the World." Also: space satellites and their use for communications (telenewspaper), world weather watch and educational TV, and a special display on "Water for Development," featuring the Mekong Basin Development Project.

Other pavilion facilities include: a small theater, information desk and documentation counter, and a post office and souvenir shop where UN postage stamps and special UN-related philatelic items are on sale.

Located in a center of internationalism at Expo, the U.N. Pavilion, with the Asian Development Bank, is found beside the OECD Pavilion, to the north of the Artificial Pond and east of the Museum of Fine Arts.

ASIAN DEVELOPMENT BANK

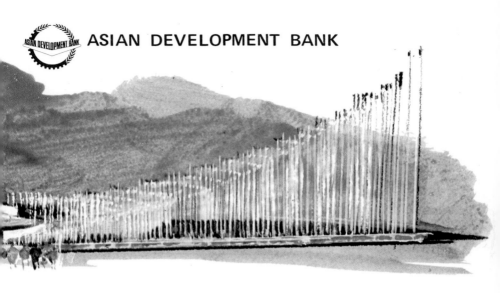

The Asian Development Bank (ADB) is an international bank established in 1966 to accelerate economic progress and cooperation among the developing countries of Asia and the Far East.

One of its primary aims is to promote investment of public and private capital for development purposes in the region. It has extended loans totaling $83,900,000 for 13 projects, including Malaysia's Penang state water supply, South Korea's Seoul-Inchon Expressway, and Ceylon's modernization of tea factories.

An additional $930,000 special loan has been extended to Indonesia for an irrigation project.

The ADB is participating in Expo together with the United Nations which was instrumental in its creation. The theme of its exhibit is "Development Through International Cooperation."

It places emphasis on its broad display of pictures depicting scenes in the varying stages of progress being made by developing nations in the Asian and Far East region.

Takeshi Watanabe, Japanese president of the bank, which has its headquarters in the Philippines, will make a personal appearance at the ADB Pavilion on Asian Development Bank Day, April 16.

The bank which commenced operation in December 1966, with an authorized capital of $1,100 million, currently has a total membership of 33 countries, 20 of which are regional nations. It is a ready helping hand to those nations which desire to walk alone, but at present are unable to operate under their own steam.

The ADB exhibit, found in the United Nations Pavilion, is located on the north side of the Artificial Pond. It is a short distance east of the Expo Hall and the Museum of Fine Arts.

STEEL PAVILION OF SOUND AND LIGHT

Japan's iron and steel industry opens the way to the future.

THE JAPAN IRON AND STEEL FEDERATION

O.E.C.D.

The Organization for Economic
Co-operation and Development

The Organization for Economic
Co-operation and Development consists
of 22 nations. This, the world's largest
grouping of industrialized, market-
economy countries, is dedicated to the
idea of "Progress and Harmony for
Mankind" through international
cooperation — for sound economic

growth, for higher standards of living,
for expansion of world trade, for solution to the problems of modern society, and for aid to developing countries.

The OECD Pavilion is about 20
meters square and 10 meters high, and
is entered from the ground level by
means of twin staircases. Pools on the
north and south sides reflect the flags
of the 22 member countries. OECD's
Special Day at Expo, April 28, celebrates the sixth anniversary of Japan's
membership.

North of the Artificial Pond and
east of the Museum of Fine Arts, the
OECD Pavilion forms a center of internationalism with the United Nations
and the Asian Development Bank.

The exhibit consists of an audio-
visual presentation of the work of the
Organization:

1. OECD Today
2. Economic Growth in OECD Member Countries
3. Problems of Modern Society
4. OECD and the Developing World

The story of economic growth, a
key part of the exhibit, graphically
illustrates the principle that international cooperation is indispensable to sus-
tained economic expansion.

"Problems of Modern Society"
demonstrates OECD's concern with
the solution of the new problems
accompanying rapid economic growth.

OECD countries account for approximately 90% of the total flow of
aid to the developing world. "OECD
and the Developing Countries" illustrates the Organization's role in this
important field.

E.C.
European Community

"Imagination for Peace" — in other words, how a new Europe, uniting and co-operating for peaceful ends, replaces the perpetual conflicts between states — this is the main theme of the European Community Pavilion.

The pavilion's concept is quite remarkable. To the building, partly underground and entirely horizontal in its lines, a vertical, 24-meter "structure of light" is integrated, while its garden roof is decorated with a large panel of painted ceramic.

The European Community consists of six countries: the Federal Republic of Germany, Belgium, France, Italy, Luxembourg and the Netherlands.

The exhibition depicts their evolution in a simple and concrete manner both as regards the main steps in European history up to World War II and the aims and achievements of the European Community since its establishment.

As soon as he enters the pavilion,

the visitor finds himself surrounded by a representation of 2,000 years of European civilization, starting with its origins in the Empires of Greece and Rome. It ends with the two World Wars and the first attempts at European unification which brought with them the setting up of the European Community.

The visitor becomes familiar with the European Community, about its entirely new way of cooperation, and about how economic frontiers are gradually disappearing.

Before leaving the pavilion, the visitor experiences an audio-visual presentation, lasting about eight minutes, which — using wholly different means of illustration — sums up the principal subjects within the exhibition. A film on a wide screen, combined with 17 series of transparences (2,000 pictures in all), forms a sort of "Ballet" which will completely absorb the visitor's attention.

TAKEDA
(1781 –)

Meet Mr. Takeda. He started our business in 1781. And yet his pioneering spirit lives on.

Today, Takeda Chemical Industries is Japan's largest pharmaceutical company.

But that's not all. Our name can be found in the four corners of the world. We are important international suppliers of vitamins and various other pharmaceuticals. This includes subsidiaries in Taiwan, the Philippines, West Germany, U.S.A. and Mexico. Plus more than 40 strategic points of service.

With our experience in fine pharmaceuticals as a foundation, we have successfully expanded our operations. From the manufacture of flavor enhancers and vitamin additives to industrial chemicals.

As we said, Takeda has been around for a long time. Making good health for all mankind our business. We intend to continue our work for another 189 years . . . at least.

TAKEDA CHEMICAL INDUSTRIES, LTD. Osaka, Japan

HONG KONG

Hong Kong Government

Twice a day the sail ceremony is held. The baker's dozen of graceful bat-winged sails — like the sails of a Chinese fishing junk — are raised and lowered upon soaring masts which top the water-surrounded pavilion of Hong Kong.

Like Hong Kong itself, the Hong Kong Pavilion combines the contemporary with the traditional. Hong Kong owes its success to two factors: one of the finest natural harbors in the world, and the dynamic drive of its 4 million people. Standing on the sea lanes to China, Hong Kong prospered as a prime entrepot center until political embargos caused that trade to dwindle. Yet, within a few short years, it has emerged as an industrial force making itself felt throughout the world's markets.

The population has boomed amazingly, from 600,000 in 1945 to more than six times that today. Many who came from China brought with them their skills and ingenuity. But Hong Kong is much more than the sum of its industrial efforts; in its New Territories it offers a glimpse of old China. There the agricultural people continue the centuries of old cultural traditions of their mainland ancestors. And East meets West in the towns, where the young lead a modern life.

The Hong Kong Pavilion shows a large slice of the community's life in all its aspects — its industry, its social progress, its festivals, its nightlife and its internationally famous Cantonese food, here served in the second of the two pavilion buildings. But above all, the pavilion shows the world the people who have made Hong Kong what it is today.

Located across from the British Pavilion, the Hong Kong Pavilion may be thrillingly viewed from above — from the western end of the Aerial Cableway. The pavilion is directly adjacent to Friday Plaza.

Territory

QUEBEC
Province of Quebec, Canada

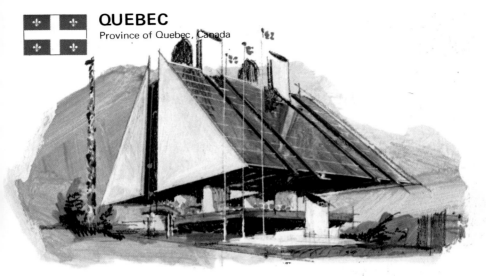

In the spirit of the theme Progress and Harmony for Mankind, the Quebec Pavilion dynamically presents the evolution, the culture and the aspirations of the people of Quebec.

The visitor will become aware of the immensity of the Quebec territory and its unique position on the world map. Because the climate of Quebec has a marked influence on her people, the four seasons of Quebec have been recreated for the visitor to give him a better understanding of the kind of man that inhabits this great land.

Quebec is one of the richest territories in the world, and the visitor will become well familiar with Quebec's immense forests, its paper industry, the seemingly inexhaustible mineral resources and its hydroelectric power stations.

Taking the stairs to the floor above, the visitor will plunge into the Quebec Carnaval, a carnaval of snow which is unique in America and which vividly demonstrates the "joie de vivre" and exuberance of the people of Quebec.

An audio-visual montage will illustrate the social as well as the personal life of the typical Quebecer.

In another section of the Quebec Pavilion, the audacious pioneers who live in the grand north of Quebec are represented by marionettes in the midst of an Eskimo village.

Walking toward the exit, one can admire tapestries produced by the most outstanding Quebec Province artists, typical Quebec jewelry, paintings or sculpture.

Quebec, host to the world during Expo 67 at Montreal, occupies 1,540,000 square kilometers (594,600 square miles) at the northeast corner of the North American continent. Its area, over four times that of Japan, forms 15% of Canadian territory, making it the largest province. There are approximately 6 million inhabitants.

BRITISH COLUMBIA

Province of British Columbia, Canada

tains of British Columbia. Soaring high into the sky, 300 Douglas fir trees symbolize the grand geography of the many richly timbered mountain ranges in the province. The trees, some over 50 meters high, make the pavilion the world's tallest wooden structure. Located inside is an unusual theater, with a special screen three meters wide and 15 meters high. Here, a 10-minute film dramatizes life in British Columbia. On one side of the pavilion, there is a small mountain, symbolizing the sources of the Province's mineral wealth, and a miniature park with replica animals in their natural setting. Two waterfalls drop to a lake surrounded by underground exhibition halls.

The pavilion entrance is graced by metal spars in the shape of a fan to express the Province's developing metal industry. The entrance hall contains a metallic sculpture showing the history of British Columbia.

A number of carved wooden doors supported by totem poles, all made by British Columbia Indians, lead to the Theme Theater within the log structure. In other halls "plastic sculptures" and constantly changing photographs demonstrate how the people of British Columbia live in harmony with their surroundings. After passing through the World-of-Water Hall, where the waterfalls drop into the lake, and the World-of-Industry Hall, a second special movie house is entered where 48 movie projectors show pictures on a dome made up of 96 screens surrounding the visitors, who then exit through the small park.

British Columbia, the most western of the Canadian provinces, has old historical ties with Japan. Vancouver, Canada's most important port on the Pacific coast, opened its door to trade with Japan a long time ago.

The British Columbia Pavilion represents the forests, lakes and moun-

ONTARIO
Province of Ontario, Canada

Canada's most populous and prosperous province features a dramatic 70 mm. color film made by Christopher Chapman, the Ontario producer-director who won a Hollywood Academy Award with his movie for Ontario's pavilion at Montreal's Expo 67.

The Ontario Pavilion, occupying a 31,000-square-foot site, is a striking blue and white structure of prefabricated steel panels and cylindrical steel posts. The two-level pavilion is a modern example of quick assembly construction techniques.

Inside, the display is entirely audio-visual. The film shows the people of the province at play and in the festive spirit, as well as some of the magnificent natural scenery, including unbelievably exciting shots of Niagara Falls.

Another exhibit is a revolutionary multi-slide presentation which greets visitors after they have entered the pavilion. It's a dazzling 12-minute sequence of rapid color photographs flashed by 26 carousel projectors. The story of Ontario's wilderness, rural to suburban to urban development, production, construction, transportation, communication, education, leisure and spiritual life is seen on a 30-meter-long (98 foot) screen. The radically different equipment from which this programmed entertainment is projected is known as the Modular Communications Vehicle, and is the first of its kind.

The film, the second part of the pavilion's exhibit, is on view in a 525-person-capacity theater. The huge screen is 27.5 meters (90 feet) by 11 meters (36 feet) and shaped in a 120-degree parabolic curve to give the impression of enveloping the audience.

Look for the Ontario Pavilion when you get off the Monorail at the Japanese Garden Station. It's west of you.

WASHINGTON STATE

State of Washington, U.S.A.

Rising from multi-level pools, the State of Washington Pavilion is designed as a reflection of the waters, forests and rich lands of this state located in the northwestern-most part of the United States mainland. The Washington theme: "The Harmony of Nature and Man."

The pavilion highlights a 12-minute color movie exposing the best in the environment and life of the State: the purity and beauty of the wilderness as preserved by man for his enjoyment and enrichment. The film shows the cities and how they influence and enrich lives and how man is developing resources from his natural environment. There are glimpses of a more tranquil past existing side-by-side with the future; and the ways that man has found to adapt, preserve, change and grow with his environment in the State of Washington. Filmed in the Dimension 150 process, the movie is projected on a single, deeply curved screen; a multi-channel stereophonic sound system produces the dramatic effect of being transported to the lakes, forests, cities and farms of the State of Washington.

The feeling of the natural woodland environment is impressively maintained throughout the pavilion itself, which features exhibit clusters on the history and settlement of the State, Pacific Northwest Indian culture, education, resources, Columbia River Basin projects, lumber and related industries, aircraft and aluminum industries, nuclear energy and so on.

The pavilion form is expressed in native western red cedar mounted on a prefabricated steel frame. Visitors enter and exit on the single level maintained throughout and guides are happy to discuss exhibit details.

Take the Moving Walkway from the Main Gate to Senri Bridge Avenue. The Washington State Pavilion is halfway up to the Artificial Pond.

164 Provinces·States·Cities

HAWAII
State of Hawaii, U.S.A.

Hawaii is the newest — the 50th — state of the United States. Its exhibit is designed to show that Hawaii is unique, that it is the heart of the Pacific, that it is the blossoming of American society at its best, uniting East and West with its racial harmony and with its enlightened view of the role of the United States in the Pacific.

The Hawaii structure is strikingly simple in its design. The building resembles a Hawaiian volcanic cinder cone with graceful curls and swirls embodied in the approaches, the entrance and attached office spaces. The low, truncated cone is 21.3 meters (70 feet) in diameter at the subterranean floor level, and about 7.6 meters (25 feet) high from floor to cone-top.

There are a variety of plantings on the grounds to soften and balance the rock-like texture of the pavilion structure. The building is air-conditioned throughout.

Audio-visual exhibits tell the story of Hawaii's people living, playing, working, building a better society — a "Pacific Community" in microcosm — a harmonious, dynamic, and productive social and cultural integration of people of Asian, Polynesian and other ethnic backgrounds, diverse but finding unity in their diversity.

The pavilion, north of Friday Plaza, has two circular exhibit areas. A movie in the larger one dramatizes the natural beauty of the islands and Hawaii's unique cosmopolitan society where people live, work and play in peace and harmony. The movie is periodically augmented by live performances of Hawaiian music and dance.

Five kiosks, utilizing the senses of sight, sound, smell, taste and touch, give a momentary experience of being in Hawaii. The second exhibit area projects Hawaii as the center of a future Pacific Community of Mankind.

ALASKA
State of Alaska, U.S.A.

Alaska was purchased by the U.S.A. from Russia in 1867 and admitted into the union of the United States as the 49th state in 1959. It occupies the northwestern part of North America, and is the largest state in the U.S.A. Because of an abundance of natural resources in fisheries, forestry, mining, oil and gas, the state possesses the potentialities of becoming one of the richest in the union.

Much of Alaska's surface area is tundra and mountain ranges with glaciers and snow-capped mountains, among which is Mt. McKinley, the highest peak in North America. The southern and south-eastern coasts are washed by the warm Japanese Current which brings the area a mild,temperate climate.

Alaska was first explored in 1741 by Vitus Bering, a Dane in the service of Russia. He was followed in later years by such noted explorers as James Cook, George Vancouver and Alexander Mckenzie.

It was sparsely populated until 1880 when gold was discovered near Juneau. Subsequent discoveries of gold in Canada's Yukon Territory, Nome and Fairbanks, added to the influx of settlers.

Today Alaska has a population of 280,000. Of this number 55,000 are Eskimos and American Indians. The Eskimos live in the north-western coastal areas and still retain some of their old customs. But, as elsewhere in the world, their living has become westernized of late.

Alaska hopes to change its image from an "ice and snow" region to that of a modern up-to-date state. It intends to do so through its unique exhibits at EXPO'70, where it is sharing part of the American Park Pavilion. This includes the tallest Indian Totem Pole in the world, belonging to the village of Kake in Alaska.

166

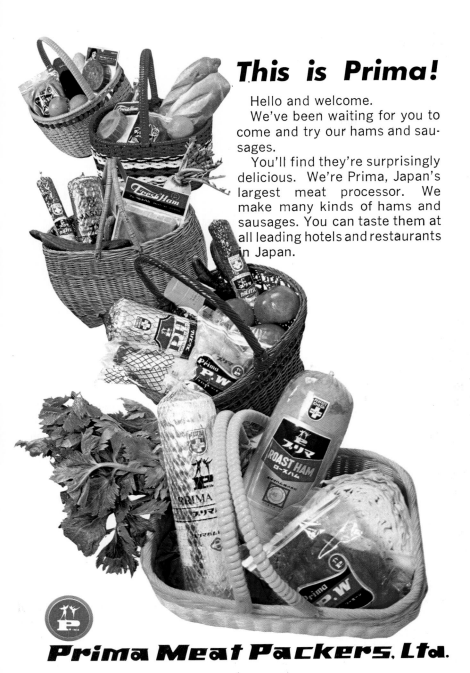

This is Prima!

Hello and welcome.

We've been waiting for you to come and try our hams and sausages.

You'll find they're surprisingly delicious. We're Prima, Japan's largest meat processor. We make many kinds of hams and sausages. You can taste them at all leading hotels and restaurants in Japan.

Prima Meat Packers, Ltd.

SAN FRANCISCO

City of San Francisco, California, U.S.A.

A cosmopolitan city of all races and cultures, San Francisco exemplifies the greatness of America.

Few visitors can ever forget their first glimpse of the Golden Gate Bridge looming out of the mist, the exotic flavor of a stroll through Chinatown, or the excitement of the colorful wharf area. These and many other attractions have inspired the wistful popular refrain, "I left my heart in San Francisco."

What sets San Francisco apart from any other city in the world, however, are the distinctive cable cars running up and down the steep streets lined with Victorian townhouses and charming shops. In 1873, San Francisco became the first city in the world to operate cable cars for public transportation. Although outmoded now by the extensive use of automobiles and rapid transit, the cable cars, still in operation, have been immortalized as a national landmark.

Honoring the sister-city relationship that has flourished for more than a decade between Osaka and America's famed "Gateway to the Orient" is the pavilion complex of the city of San Francisco.

One of the picturesque buildings serves as a "terminal" for the fleet of fabled San Francisco cable cars which transports visitors free-of-charge throughout Expoland.

Inspired by the spaciousness of parks which front the San Francisco Bay, this group of buildings offers a variety of attractions reminiscent of California's early history and of the world-renowned metropolis of San Francisco.

Included in the San Francisco Pavilion, located in the north-east sector of Expoland, are an art gallery, an exhibition of historical buildings and a cable car waiting station. There is also a restaurant serving delightful foods representative of sunny California.

LOS ANGELES
City of Los Angeles, California, U.S.A.

Los Angeles — the fastest growing city in the United States — is highly innovative, as well as highly industrialized. Ten million people live within a 60-mile radius of City Hall, center of the world's largest government complex outside of Washington, D. C. These 10 million people now earn $36 billion a year and their income is increasing by $2.5 billion annually.

What's more, Los Angeles' $46-billion "gross national product" is topped by only nine actual nations in the entire world.

Greater Los Angeles is home base to countless scientific, electronics, research, aerospace and oceanographic industries. Within its golden circle is the greatest concentration of mathematicians, scientists, engineers and skilled technicians in the nation. Its growth has been truly phenomenal, in view of the fact that a hundred years ago the entire city population was only 1,000 people. Now, nearly an equal number arrive each day to live in Greater Los Angeles.

The city's mammoth industrial development had its start during World War II. Aviation and shipbuilding began the boom, with oil refining, automotive and aerospace soon to follow. Today, these are multi-million-dollar enterprises, with Los Angeles leading the nation in many areas. Among these, of course, are the movie and television industries, which make Hollywood the film capital of the world.

The city and its diversified industries utilize one of the world's largest man-made harbors, the Port of Los Angeles, "Cargo Capital of the West." Los Angeles is also served by 22 airlines; but this is essentially a city on wheels — with a car for every 2.2 persons, highest ratio in the world. And this highly-developed five-county urbanized complex boasts the world's most extensive freeway system — presently 1,144 miles, with more being built daily.

MUNICH

City of Munich,
Federal Republic of Germany

In the turbulence and excitement that mark any world exposition, in the prolific demonstration of the unrelenting progress and progression of mankind, the Munich Pavilion establishes a mood of calm and cheerfulness and invites you to linger for a while and to rest.

The Munich House provides you the visitor to EXPO'70 and, primarily, the Japanese people with a picture of Munich, a picture of a city, founded in 1158 by Henry the Lion, of 1.28 million cheerful souls living but 60 kilometers from the Alps.

It is a picture of Munich in all its manifold variety – as a city of the arts, of culture and the joy of life, as the capital of the much-visited German tourist land of Bavaria, as a city world famous for its breweries and, by no means least, as the city where the 20th Olympic Games will be held in 1972.

Located on the northeast side of Expoland, the Munich House is entered through gardens designed as a Bavarian marketplace. In the Munich Information Center, hostesses and interpreters provide any desired information on Munich and explain a model of the Munich Olympia sports ground that is exhibited there.

The main emphasis of the Munich House is placed on the theme "Bavarian Joy in Living." A wonderful Munich restaurant brings to Osaka a breath of the world-famous Munich October Festival. Neatly fitted into the overall design of the pavilion are exhibits, presentations and documentations of all that which Munich has to offer as a focal point of international tourism, as well as of a leading industrial city.

You will leave the Munich House much relaxed and with a desire to become much better acquainted with Munich and its joyful citizens.

Provinces · States · Cities

**Enter mirrors of gold
at the Kodak Golden Picture Pavilion.**

The Pavilion glistens in the sun and
glows softly by night.

Gleaming towers of glass enclose fascinating
exhibits that speak to you in the universal
language of photography.

Ramps winding around the outside present
sweeping views to your camera.

Experts are on duty to offer advice on how
to capture memories of
your EXPO '70 visit in pictures.

So be sure to . . .
Visit Kodak's Golden Picture Pavilion.

Coparticipants: **Kodak and Nagase**

Participating Countries, International Organizations, Territory, States, Provinces and Cities at EXPO'70

Iceland
Sweden
Finland
Norway
Ireland
Denmark
United Kingdom
Netherlands
Belgium
Germany
U.S.S.R.
France
E.C.
Munich
O.E.C.D.
Czechoslovakia
Monaco
Switzerland
Italy
Bulgaria
Portugal
Turkey
Vatican
Algeria
Greece
Cyprus
Iran
Malta
Afghanistan
Pakistan
Korea
Kuwait
United Arab Republic
India
Nepal
Chir
Abu-Dhabi
Saudi Arabia
Hong Kong
Burma
Laos
Thailand
Philippines
Cambodia
Asian
Sierra
Ghana
Nigeria
Ethiopia
Ceylon
Viet-Nam
Development
Leone
Central African Republic
Bank
Ivory Coast
Uganda
Malaysia
Gabon
Singapore
Tanzania
Madagascar
Indonesia
Mauritius
Zambia

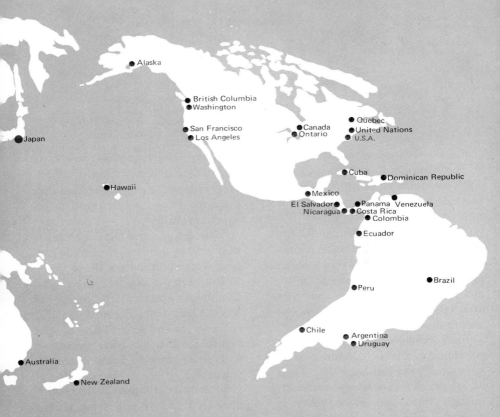

Alaska

British Columbia
Washington

Quebec
United Nations
Canada
Ontario
U.S.A.

San Francisco
Los Angeles

Japan

Cuba

Dominican Republic

Hawaii

Mexico
Panama Venezuela
El Salvador
Nicaragua Costa Rica
Colombia

Ecuador

Peru

Brazil

Chile

Argentina
Uruguay

Australia

New Zealand

AMPARK CORPORATION

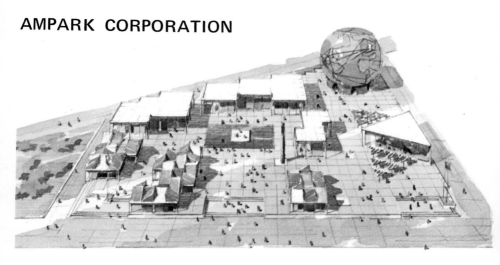

The American Park is a complex of eight structures representing many aspects of American commerce and culture.

The Park, through the theme "Reflections of America," provides a variety of experience to promote a better understanding of American life. In addition, several restaurants and cafes offer typical American foods in unusual environments.

Each exhibitor features a unique presentation. Sunkist Growers provide an exciting light and color experience, while Miles Laboratory presents, through word and image, "Joy in America." Encyclopedia Britannica has created a representative showing of American painting and Los Angeles captures on film many facets of this well-known city. The Unicot Inc. exhibit appeals especially to women, while the State of Alaska attracts the entire family in depicting its unique heritage.

Those contemplating travel to America must visit the American Express Company exhibit. The Coca-Cola Company is also a participant in the American Park.

Two unique structures rise on the west side of the Park. A giant air-supported sphere introduces the spectacular United States Travel Service exhibit featuring a pictorial panorama of America. In the Pacific Wings building you can see the actual plane Charles Lindbergh flew to bring America's message of peace to Japan almost 40 years ago.

In addition to the many exhibits, the American Park provides American entertainment on its central plaza stage.

The structural concepts and space layout were designed by Herb Rosenthal of Los Angeles, one of America's leading designers. These concepts were implemented by Barry Howard of New York, acting as the American Park's theme and exhibit design coordinator.

EASTMAN KODAK EXPOSITION COMPANY
NAGASE SANGYO KABUSHIKI KAISHA

Among the multitude of pavilions at EXPO'70, the Kodak Pavilion is the only one co-sponsored by an American company and a Japanese corporation. It identifies "Photography as a Universal Language."

A striking six-sided glass tower highlights Kodak's "Golden Picture Pavilion." The 22.5-meter-high glass tower is encircled from top to bottom by a ramp from which visitors can photograph many memorable views of the exposition.

Other major elements of the pavilion are two brightly colored towers of smaller diameter. Each tower also has six sides, painted alternately red and yellow.

Visitors may enter the pavilion at the ground level, or by the ramp that encircles the glass tower, or by a sloping bridge that pierces the glass tower at the second level.

The four-story golden glass tower is one of the main exhibit areas, and it encloses one of the wonders of EXPO'70 — The Tower of Smiling Faces — a kaleidoscope of color prints rising from the center of a water pool.

Using advanced audio-visual techniques, showcases of photography and the role it plays in this age of space exploration and expanding technology are shown in four other exhibit areas in the pavilion, but with recognition of man's family and enjoyment of life.

These other exhibit areas are respectively titled "Photography is a Tool," "Photography is to Remember," "Photography is Fun" and "Photography is a Universal Eye," where photography is acknowledged as a fine art.

The Kodak Pavilion also provides a photographic information center to assist visitors with their photographic questions. The pavilion is on the south side of the Pond, almost directly across the Moving Walkway from Monday Plaza.

JAPANESE
PRIVATE
PAVILIONS

Index of Pavilions

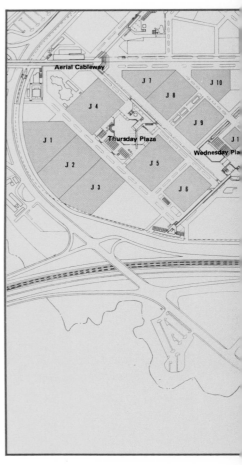

Pavilions on this page are listed in alphabetical order.

Descriptions of pavilions are arranged in order of dates contracts were signed.

Japanese Private Pavilions

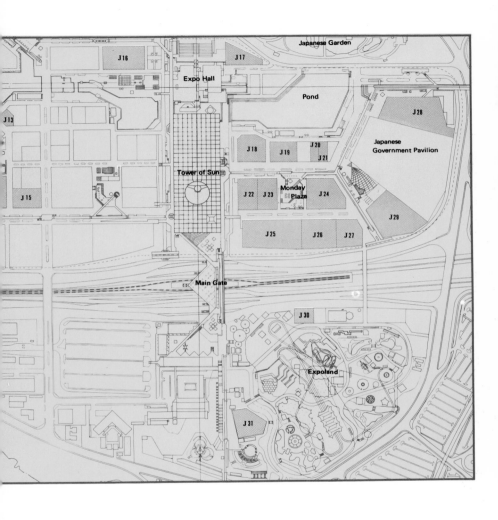

Japanese Private Pavilions

LOCAL GOVERNMENTS' Pavilion

Producer: Yoshihiko Okamoto
Architect: Takeji Tsukamoto

Japan's local self-governing bodies — from prefectures to towns to villages — have all joined together to present the Local Autonomy Pavilion. Here is a quick tour of Japan with remarkable thoroughness.

"Local Governments Forging Ahead — Japan Stands on the Threshold of a New Era" is the theme of the three-structure pavilion.

Hall No.1 is entered through a morning glory-shaped "tunnel of light." On the first floor are displays about local self-government. Guide corners give visitors an idea of the scenery and products of each area. On the second floor, the history of local government from its beginnings to the present day is shown. On the fourth floor, 53 cylindrical screens flash pictures of all the prefectures and Okinawa and show the various activities of governing bodies throughout Japan.

Moving down a gently sloped passage, visitors see what Japanese towns and villages will look like in 20 years' time.

Guests are then lifted slowly up and around the circular building and into Hall No.2 — an immense single-story structure. A 25-minute "air ship" takes you on a trip over the entire country. The model of Japan is on a scale of 1:30,000 and the air ship "floats" 10 meters above the floor — creating an illusion for seeing Japan from an altitude of 30,000 meters. Films projected on the walls as the ship makes its trip point out details and facts about the country's eight regional blocs.

Hall No.3 is devoted to rest and entertainment. Here a round stage resounds with folk dance performances and traditional entertainment programs from various parts of Japan. Restaurants and stores in the area offer food and other products from each area of the country. Visitors can watch local color on stage as they sample local flavors from the small stores.

RAINBOW TOWER

Producer: Zenzo Matsuyama
Architect: Kiyoshi Seike

Save your visit to the Rainbow Tower until you're a little tired. For here's a pavilion designed to relieve that weary feeling.

Sponsored by the Japan Monopoly Corporation (maker of Japanese cigarettes) the 70-meter-tall conical building has silvery walls. Water sprays from the top of the tower to create an artificial rainbow. The silver walls become red at twilight and then at night lights turn the structure into another kind of rainbow.

"Peace of Mind" is the theme, in keeping with one of the EXPO'70 subthemes: "Toward fuller enjoyment of life."

On the first floor is the "Forum of Rest" which features special music by Japanese composer Ikuma Dan.

After that a round elevator — holding 150 people — lifts you to see a special "smoke" show. This presentation combines smoke, light and sound. It occurs on a gigantic wall, designed to create for visitors a unique environment and experience.

Next — viewed from seats in a semi-circular space — comes a film projected on a large three-faceted screen that appears from out of the floor. Japan's four seasons and its traditional arts are the subjects of the film. This, however, is a special film that seeks to "blend the viewer" with the action on the film.

From the movie you may visit the "Plaza of Rest" and the "Plaza of Recreation." Both are located on the first floor.

Modern man, the planners say, has lost some of his sensitivity due to the rapid advance of science and technology. So the Rainbow Tower is to serve to isolate the viewer — for a short time — from the modern world. Some may find a visit a chance for a bit of meditation and self-reflection. Others may welcome the quiet and peace. No matter what it means to you, a visit here is sure to be a welcome change of pace during a hard day of Expo-ing!

TELECOMMUNICATION Pavilion

Producers:
Kazuhiko Honjyo
Tsubasa Asano
Architect:
Building Engineering Bureau of NTT

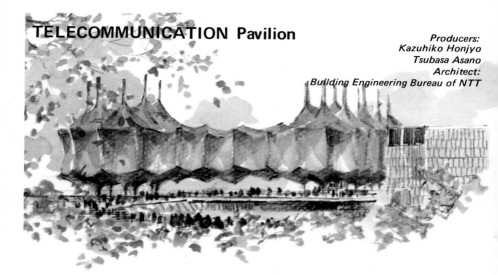

Here the visitor not only learns about communications but has a chance to communicate with people all over the world.

Communications start even while waiting to visit the pavilion. In the entrance area — under a sculpture-like yellow tent supported by steel beams — the latest news from throughout the world will be presented. Escalators then take visitors into the pavilion.

The beginning of human communication is a baby's cries and sounds ... and on screens in the first section visitors will see babies from throughout the world as they begin communication. There's a chance to talk with people from many countries as they appear on the screens.

Next comes the triangular Eidophor hall — each side is 40 meters long. An Eidophor — a huge television screen — is at each of the three corners. Pictures shown on the screens are all live telecasts from Tokyo, Kyoto and Japan's southern-most part, Tanegashima island. The live telecasts will continue for the entire 183-day exposition period.

In the general exhibition hall, the telecommunications industry will present a wide array of new ideas. Push-button video telephones for international use. "Music" composed by a telephone switchboard. The world's first picture telephone, laser operated and featuring color and great clarity, is on display.

"Man and Communication" is the theme of the three-part pavilion.

The Nippon Telegraph and Telephone Public Corporation and the Kokusai Denshin Denwa Co., Ltd. are co-sponsors of the pavilion, in co-operation with the Japanese Ministry of Postal Services and the Japan Broadcasting Corporation (NHK). Kokusai Denshin Denwa handles Japanese international telephone service, satellite communications and telex service.

GAS Pavilion

Producer: Dentsu Advertising Ltd.
Architect: Ohbayashi-Gumi

*"Laugh and the world
laughs with you ..."*

"World of Laughter" — the pavilion of the Japan Gas Association (201 companies from across Japan) — is next to Wednesday Plaza.

Outside the pavilion is unique — a flying saucer or a funny face with an open mouth, determined by your imagination.

Inside the highlight is the largest work ever done by the famed Spanish-born artist Joan Miro — a 5 by 12 meter mural in ceramic specially produced for EXPO'70.

Visitors first enter a large hall to see "The Story of Laughter," a 20 minute movie. A giant screen on the floor and one that comes down from above the audience plus two walls on both sides of the hall are used to project the film.

Seated face to face with your fellow visitors on the other side of the screen, you can watch their laughing faces while following the action projected all around.

As the movie ends you enter the following room and wander around admiring a striking Miro frescoe entitled "Innocent Laughter," which is enhanced by an amazing setting of water and light before an unusual musical background. In that room you can then enjoy a film dedicated to all the different kinds of laughter.

The Gas Pavilion is, naturally enough, powered totally by gas — even the movie projectors! New gas appliances are installed in the pavilion's restaurant (accommodating 90), where visitors can see the Miro mural through the glass wall.

Through the Pavilion the sponsors hope to " ... restore laughter to a world which needs it more acutely today then ever before."

Pavilion of WACOAL·RICCAR

Producers: Hisao Domoto (Artist)
Toshi Ichiyanagi (Music Composer), TEAC
Architects: Ren Suzuki
Shota Majima,
Ren Architects & Associates

"Love"

That's the theme of the joint pavilion built by Wacoal Inc. and Riccar Sewing Machine Co., Ltd.

If you're lucky, you'll see "love" in action — for twice a week a wedding is held in the pavilion. Brides and bridegrooms will come from Japan and from other countries.

Unique wedding ceremonies — many reflecting the customs of the country of the bride and groom — will be held.

Free movement and an exchange of friendship are the goal of the sponsors. So there are no fences around the exhibition hall — you just go in wherever you like, through gently sloping corridors.

There is the "Space of Rest" — softly lighted and with soothing back-ground music.

Then there's the "Space of Love." Love from ancient times to the present day is traced — with a movie that is projected on an eight-faceted screen. The movie also examines the various types of love — such as romantic, brotherly, national, etc.

Art works related to the theme will also be on display

The pavilion's designer may have received his inspiration from a balancing toy. The pavilion itself is round and white. The roof is a 30-meter disc, supported by a single pillar. The 30-ton roof is balanced by a weight that is hung at the center. Don't worry — it's earthquake proof!

Through the pavilion of love the sponsors hope to emphasize that only the progress of a world filled with love can truly bring peace and happiness to all mankind. This pavilion, the site of Expo weddings, is adjacent to Wednesday Plaza.

This is how it all began.
Before we did our part of the Symbol Zone.
Before we built 18 pavilions.
Plus hotels, highways, stations and
power plants to back it all up.
A special welcome.
We hope you like the way
it all turned out.

Japan's internationally award-winning
construction company...founded 1892

OHBAYASHI-GUMI, LTD.
Osaka/Tokyo

Leading
department stores
in the Orient

MITSUKOSHI

Main Store: Nihombashi. *Branch Stores in Tokyo:* Shinjuku, Ginza, Ikebukuro. *Local Branch Stores:* Osaka, Kobe, Hirakata, Takamatsu, Matsuyama, Sendai, Sapporo.

Electric Power Pavilion — ELECTRIUM

Producer: Masakazu Kotani
Architects: Junzo Sakakura
Yutaka Murata

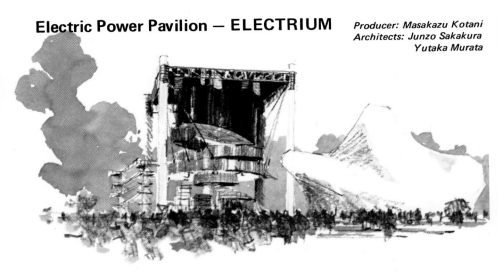

Night is not the only time to see the Electric Power Pavilion. It is an awesome structure always. But at night, the brightly lit surface radiates a multitude of colors with the effect of a huge and glorious electric lamp.

This "lamp," this pavilion also known as the Electrium, is a 1,200-ton structure suspended by 16 steel cables from four 43-meter-high columns.

The visitor is first taken by elevators to the 500-seat Aerial Theater on the highest level to see "Hunter of the Sun."

Projected on five screens, this movie shows man's dependence on the sun's energy; it traces man's gradual harnessing of various power sources — beginning with the taming of fire and climaxing with the development of nuclear power reactors.

On the lower level are engrossing displays centering on the Electrium theme — "Man and Energy."

After leaving the main structure of the pavilion, the visitor is led to a 400-seat Floating Theater where magicians reveal new and fascinating aspects of electricity. A tent supported by three huge air-beam arches, this structure is constructed to revolve in a man-made pond during the performances.

The Electrium, the Electric Power Pavilion, is the result of the combined efforts of the members of the Federation of Electric Power Companies of Japan.

The pavilion and its various features were designed and constructed with the aim of improving the image of the electric power industry as well as to reinforce the public's familiarity, understanding, and confidence in the industry.

The pavilion can accommodate 1,800 visitors at a time, and the viewing interval for the complete program is 50 minutes.

The SUMITOMO Pavilion

Producer: Masakazu Kotani
Architect: Sachio Otani

In the western corner of the Expo site, as if floating in the air, is a world of fantasy. The Sumitomo Pavilion.

What is more universal than fairy tales?

Hardly anything, reasoned the Sumitomo group of companies, and that's the subject they chose for their modernistic pavilion at EXPO'70.

"Familiar Fairy-Tales of the World" is the theme of the pavilion.

If you're with children, this is certainly a "don't-miss" exhibition.

But the pavilion offers a great deal for adults, too. Here is a selection of fairy tales and legends from around the world (including Japan, of course) and a chance to learn a great deal about the differences (and similarities) of cultures through folk tales.

The pavilion itself is made up of nine "flying saucers" — six containing exhibitions. Through the transparent saucers you can get a bird's-eye view of the big fair.

On the ground is a 250-seat theater. Here old and new combine to bring to life an old Japanese legend.

A rear-screened motion picture is used — along with "live" performances by the Takeda Marionettes — an Osaka institution since the 16th century.

Inside the saucers, about fifty different legends and fairy tales come to life in different ways — utilizing a whole realm of new electronic techniques.

There's also an opportunity to "talk" with famous characters from Hans Christian Andersen's and Wilhelm Karl Grim's fairy tales.

Through this soaring, floating pavilion structure, the Sumitomo group seeks to convey to you the visitor a world of hope, of love, and of beauty. Isn't this what fairy tales are all about? This world is located in Expo's west end. Just take the Moving Walkway to Thursday Plaza and you are there — in the Sumitomo happiness world.

TAKARA BEAUTILION

Producer & Architect:
Noriaki Kurokawa

Beauty knows no bounds nor differences of generations.

The pursuit of beauty, the Takara group of companies feel, is very much in keeping with the Expo themes.

So they have chosen "Joy of Being Beautiful" as the theme of their pavilion . . . and named it the Beautilion.

Outside, the pavilion presents a new kind of modern beauty in an architectural style utilizing steel pipe units. The units, fabricated in factories, were assembled into the pavilion in only one week.

There is a symbol tower made up of plastic capsules. It contains symbols of man's past and progress.

Visitors enter the pavilion area across a flower-filled elevated garden.

In the subterranean theater, guests are seated — 48 at a time — on special flower petal-shaped chairs. The chairs gradually elevate for about two meters and begin to revolve. Above, a view of sky appears — and spectators are taken on a simulated trip beyond time and into outer space. Twelve screens are used, along with laser beams, film projection and special sound effects.

Visitors are then invited to an area of the future — where ideas for the kitchens, barber shops, beauty shops, etc. of the next age are shown.

On the second floor are 24 special capsules, each equipped with special gadgets. Women, for example, can "try on" different fashions, hair colors, hair styles just by the push of a button.

On the third floor is a revolving stage where beauty pageants and fashion shows will be held.

Throughout the pavillion, background music especially composed for the Takara Beautilion is heard.

The sponsors have also kept the weary Expo visitor in mind — for comfortable seats and resting places are scattered throughout the exhibition.

STEEL Pavilion

General Producer & Architect:
Kunio Maekawa

Japan Iron and Steel Federation has created for Expo visitors a "Song of Iron" or "Consonance." It's sure to be a song that is new to everyone.

The main hall of the pavilion can accommodate about 1,000 in an amphitheater-like arrangement around a round stage. The stage itself can be elevated or rotated. On the walls and ceiling of the hall there are 1,300 sound boxes, comprising a dozen sound systems.

Electronic music to be performed in the hall utilizes those speakers to create a unique sound experience — with sound moving, twisting, overlapping and becoming quite alive. The music is under the direction of Toru Takemitsu whose composition "November Steps" was commissioned by the New York Philharmonic Orchestra.

Various programs will be held here.

— Modern music composed by Takemitsu and the Greek musician Iannis Xenakis.

— Traditional Japanese music performed by famed artists, many of whom have been designated "Human National Treasures."

— Modern music programs by the Japan Philharmonic Orchestra.

— And performances of "musical sculptures."

In a large foyer leading to the hall are displayed musical sculptures which are creations of France's François Baschet and his brother Bernard. The metal/glass/loudspeaker constructions gained wide attention when they were displayed during the Mexico City Olympic Games.

The sculptors and their assistant, Alain Villeminot, worked for three months in Osaka to create 17 works. Visitors can actually "play" the sculptures: hammering metal rods, running moistened fingers along glass tubes, pulling a bow against a steel plate.

A feature of the pavilion is a large, stainless steel pendulum that moves with the action of earth's gravity.

FUJI GROUP Pavilion

Producer: Hiroshi Kawazoe
Architect: Yutaka Murata
Taisei Construction Co., Ltd.

Directly adjacent to Thursday Plaza stands a novel "building."

"Message to the 21st Century" is the theme of the Fuji Group Pavilion. The modernistic message starts with the building itself — for here is the world's largest pneumatic structure.

Sixteen "vinylon" tubes, each four meters in diameter and 80 meters long, are joined to create the pavilion.

The resulting shape is somewhat like a covered wagon. The resulting space is huge — the pavilion could contain a 10-story building. Several years of research went into the creation of the structure that may have applications in the future in space, in undersea work and in tomorrow's cities.

Worried about Japan's famed typhoons? The pavilion, by a change of internal air pressure, can withstand winds up to 214 kilometers (133 miles) per hour!

Here's a pavilion that's easy on the feet. Enter by a gently-sloping bridge that crosses an artificial pond and step onto a huge turntable. The slowly revolving platform circles the interior of the pavilion once every 20 minutes.

As the platform revolves, visitors go from complete darkness into what the sponsors call a "total experience." This blends film, light, sound, and mobiles into a synchronized, computerized presentation.

On a huge screen a 210-mm film is projected by newly developed equipment. At the same time, twenty-eight special projectors flash pictures on ceilings and all interior walls. The objective is to have a feeling of being transported to different and new worlds.

After the turntable ride, move to the first floor via moving walks to see the machinery that produced the show upstairs.

The Fuji Group is made up of 36 leading Japanese companies.

Pavilion TEXTILES

Producer: Mitsuru Kudo
Contractors and Architects: Ohbayashi-Gumi
& Takenaka Komuten Co., Ltd.

One of the first Japanese private pavilions to be completed at EXPO'70, the Pavilion Textiles represents a massive co-ordination effort.

It is sponsored by the Expo Textiles Association, which was created for the occasion by three textile organizations (Japan Cotton Spinners, Wool Spinners and Chemical Fiber Associations) and some 30 textile-related associations.

"Textiles Enrich Human Life" is the theme of this pavilion.

The pavilion is actually more in praise of women than men, however.

"Space Projection" — a new idea in movie effects — is the highlight of the exhibition.

Ten film projections and eight slide projectors are used. Six of the film projectors are rear-screen. The screen in this case is the interior wall of the pavilion's dome.

The dome itself is decorated with sculptures of women's heads, limbs and torsos. At one point, moving beams of light play on them, giving an illusion of movement.

The movie is about women, too. Well, about one woman. The title is "Ako" — a popular girl's name in Japan. The movie itself was shot on location throughout Japan during the spring and summer of last year.

Also in the exhibition hall are seven sections of special displays that are concerned with the modern world of textiles.

The sponsors of the Pavilion Textiles aim to enhance not only the image of textiles but also that of this exciting industry itself.

Through unique presentations, you realize the long history of textiles; the richness of materials; the diversity of their uses; textiles' personal relationship to the life of every man and woman. And the colors, designs, fashion and feel through which textiles appeal so much.

SUNTORY Pavilion

Producer: Takao Yamazaki
Architect: Yasui Architect Office

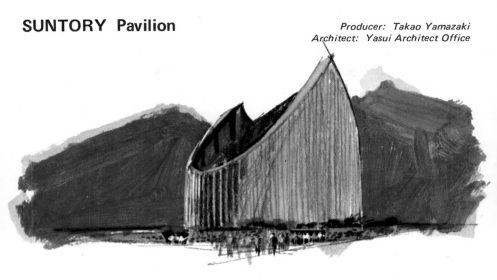

Suntory Limited is Japan's leading distiller.

The prime ingredient in making whisky is good water. In Japan, wherever one finds water, one finds bamboo.

So it's natural that the Suntory Pavilion looks like a bamboo stalk cut aslant . . . and that the theme of the exhibit is "Water of Life."

The relationship of man and water is shown in many ways throughout the pavilion — but the most dramatic presentation is a movie shown in a four-story movie theater on a 6-sectioned mammoth screen.

The film shows water as an integral part of nature, as friend (and adversary) of man. And it traces festivals throughout the world that man uses to offer thanks for harvests made possible by water.

Japanese festivals are well repre-

sented in the film — including the "Awa-odori" dance of Shikoku, the snow festival of Hokkaido and the devil's drum festival of Sado Island.

Spectators will literally be surrounded by the movie for it is projected above, beneath and in front of them at the same time.

In addition to the movie, there is a special three-dimensional display in front of the pavilion. "Mikiguchi" is its name — and it was inspired by a bamboo ornament that was used on auspicious occasions in ancient Japan.

In the basement there is a special attraction in a small winding stream. The stream is made more dramatic by unique lighting effects. In ancient times, poets played a water game — writing the first half of a poem and floating it on a stream to a friend who would complete it. This old custom inspired the Suntory stream.

The Suntory Pavilion is right next to Wednesday Plaza.

KUBOTA Pavilion

Producer: Dentsu Advertising Ltd.
Architect: Osaka Architecture
& Engineering Firm Inc.

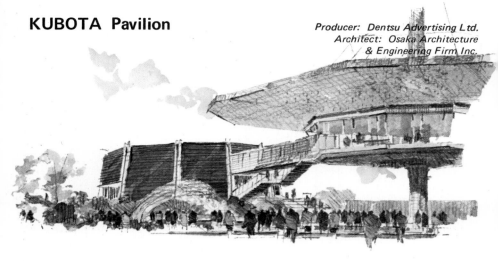

Purposeful in its thrusting tower, exciting in its suspended Skyroom, honest in its theater of the harvest, the Kubota Pavilion offers a glimpse into human productivity and consequent human needs.

In the industrial pursuit of economic gain, the beauties of nature, the quiet and peace of the suburbs, fall victim. "What will we leave the children of the future?" Posing this question in the corridor outside the circular theater, the pavilion — hopefully along with its visitors — seeks a meaningful answer.

Beneath the Skyroom, a glittering display of "A Bountiful Harvest" is emphasized by a colorful array of lights: efforts must be made to harmonize production growth with preservation of the dwindling beauties of nature. Every 'affluent society,' just as every primitive one, requires pure air,

clear water and wide-open spaces.

We are reminded in the multi-screen theater — with scenes of rice production the world over, from Thailand to Italy to Egypt to Japan to the U.S.A. — of the farmer's endless sweat and toil which is relieved only by the sweet joys of harvest time.

The preservation and restoration of nature beauties, the plight of the laborer, the real meaning of living as a human being — relaxed contemplation is offered in the Skyroom. Pleasant music from a dozen speakers accompanies a view of pond, waterfall and fountain outside. '0-nigiri,' rice formed into little balls, and drinks are served.

Will mankind create a more plentiful and more beautiful place to live for those who come after us?

The Kubota Pavilion is directly adjacent to Monday Plaza, east of the Tower of the Sun, and just a short stroll north and west from the Main Gate.

Matsuzakaya ... Five Permanent Exposition Sites.

Matsuzakaya is one of Japan's mammoth department stores. Five stores, actually, and we're often called "The Store That Has Everything."

We have a store in EXPO City, Osaka. And another in Nagoya. There is a Matsuzakaya in Shizuoka. Tokyo is big enough to rate two: one on the Ginza, main street of Tokyo and Japan, the other in the busy shopping district, Ueno.

Matsuzakaya is the place to go for your souvenirs of Japan and for any other incidental shopping while you're here. You will find nothing but the best at Matsuzakaya. As one of Japan's mammoth department stores we have a reputation to uphold. We've been upholding it for 359 years. Pay a visit to Matsuzakaya. Any of our five.

The Symbol Flower of Matsuzakaya

Closed Mondays.

Matsuzakaya
DEPARTMENT STORE

MITSUI GROUP Pavilion

Producer: Katsuhiro Yamaguchi
Architect: Takamitsu Azuma

"The Creative Paradise" is the theme of the pavilion sponsored by the Mitsui group of companies.

This building is quite a creation in itself — a cylindrical structure with a dome which stands beside a 50-meter symbol tower that is rather tusk-shaped.

Pneumatic tents are provided for those waiting to enter the pavilion. (The 32 staves encircling the building represent the number of Mitsui companies.)

A pipe-like tunnel runs around the building. Visitors move into it and stroll its 400-meter length. The interior walls are made of mirrors and the tunnel is full of colorful lights.

Then an escalator takes the guests into the dome.

Here there are three discs — six meters in diameter — that take visitors on a "trip into outer space and the world of creation."

The discs (there's seating space for 240) move up and down and slowly rotate during the trip.

A large number of projectors, electronic equipment (including 1,700 speakers) and special effects create for the guest the sensation of traveling through space. One of the highlights of the trip will be viewing the earth as though from a space vehicle.

It is not a long trip. You will be "back" to the earth in six minutes, ready to walk through the "Tunnel of Bubbles" which is made of synthetic resin tubes.

The hostesses dressed in crimson colored uniforms are called "Paradise Girls."

If, after your trip, you've developed an appetite, there's a 100-seat restaurant in the pavilion — located in a round building near to a pretty pond.

The Mitsui Group Pavilion is right next to Thursday Plaza, and quite close to Wednesday Plaza.

TOSHIBA IHI Pavilion

Producer: *Shinya Izumi*
Architect: *Noriaki Kurokawa*

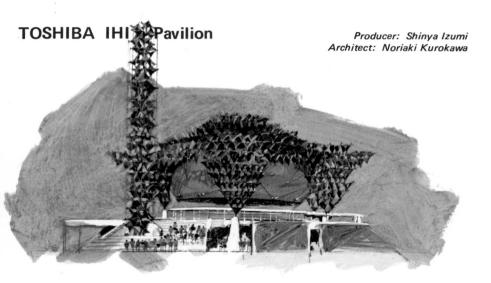

Computers helped design and build the pavilion sponsored jointly by Tokyo Shibaura Electric Co. (Toshiba) and Ishikawajima-Harima Heavy Industries Ltd.

The result is intended to symbolize a "forest of the future". The exterior is composed of 1,500 metal tetra-shaped units welded together into a striking framework. Suspended within the framework is the 500-seat Global Vision Theater. Next to this is a landmark tower, also made of tetra units, that is lighted at night for a sculptural effect.

"Light for Man" is the theme of the pavilion. The sponsors explain that the pavilion is dedicated to the hope that man holds for the future and that "light" means intelligence and technical achievement.

A spacious reception area welcomes visitors waiting to see the main exhibit. The waiting area is air conditioned and background music is played at all times.

To reach the Global Visition Theater, visitors step onto a rotary platform. The platform can seat 500 at one time. The platform then rises up and into the 360-degree theater ... and, so everyone can appreciate the scope of the presentation, the platform revolves from time to time.

The twenty-minute film is a documentary on youths of the world whose common task is to build the future of mankind. Film crews toured the world in producing the movie.

At the end of the film, the platform descends. Visitors are led to an underground "park" through entrances beneath the platform. The underground area is called the "Plaza of Water and Light." Sound and light effects highlight the displays and the passageways to the Plaza.

The Toshiba IHI Pavilion is found immediately to the southwest of Wednesday Plaza.

PEPSI Pavilion
(World without Boundary)

Architect: Takenaka Komuten Co., Ltd.

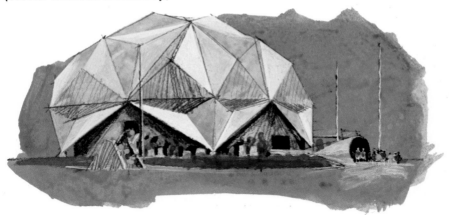

Enter the Pepsi Pavilion and you enter an involvement in sights and sounds and 'feels" you have never experienced before. You are a participant, not an observer, in a technological environment.

Even before you step onto the broad fore-plaza, you encounter a unique sight — the white, domed pavilion surrounded by a cloud of mysterious fog or, at night, by a wall of light. On the plaza you may suddenly meet one of seven man-sized, dome-shaped 'floats' which emit wonderful sounds, and change direction immediately you touch it.

You enter a shiny tunnel and receive a small handset from a silver-suited hostess. Each handset picks up audio signals from amplifiers buried in the floor as you tour the pavilion.

Now you come to the Clam Room, so called by shape. The floor at the entrance is soft; you sink gently to the first sounds from the handset. It's dark. But light comes from several sources; a laser beam is split into red, yellow, green and blue, then split again by prismatic devices activated by sounds.

Climbing stairs, you enter a large, domed room, a world you've never experienced before. A 90-foot, spherical mirror captures overhead your image, upside down. The floor is in either sections, each of a different material: you step onto a grassy segment and immediately hear lawn movers, birds, crickets, even a golfer teeing off; then an asphalt area sounds of traffic, children playing on the street, a fire truck.

You move thus around the room to a little rise and look down at people taking their time, doing their own thing, being involved. You have added to your life a new and personal experience. You'll find the Pepsi Pavilion in the southwestern part of Expoland.

JAPAN
FOLK CRAFTS MUSEUM

Producer:
Japan Folk Crafts Museum Foundation,
Tokyo
Architect:
Ohbayashi-Gumi

Traditional Japanese design is world famous. The country's folkcraft shows that the fame is justified.

"Beauty in Daily Life" is the theme of the exhibition, contained in a modern building that reflects a classical Japanese home in design.

True Japanese folkcraft is the product of an anonymous artist — who, in fact, does not regard himself as an artist. Rather he is creating objects for everyday use and needs, usually following methods handed down from father to son for generations. His products are often not for sale — but are intended for use by him and his family. There is a great naturalness in Japanese folkcraft (synthetic materials are never used.) Unassuming as it is, however, each folk art item — from tea cup to toy — possesses great beauty of design, coloration, simplicity that is in keeping with Japanese taste.

On display are about 500 works collected from all over Japan — from Hokkaido in the north to Okinawa in the south. Exhibits are changed several times during the exposition period.

There is a section of antique folkcraft, reflecting Japanese life of other eras. A modern section shows how folkcraft designs and techniques can be passed on into present-day life. Another section is of recent works by artists who follow faithfully the old traditions in producing their art.

Part of material on display is on loan from the Japan Folk Crafts Museum Foundation in Tokyo . . . the remainder has been collected specifically for EXPO'70.

At the close of EXPO'70, the pavilion will become a permanent museum. It will be donated by the seventeen sponsoring firms to the Osaka Prefectural Government.

The Japan Folk Crafts Museum is located diagonally opposite the Expo Museum of Fine Arts.

200   Japanese Private Pavilions

FURUKAWA Pavilion

Producer:
Furukawa Pavilion Committee, EXPO'70
Architect:
The Shimizu Construction Co., Ltd.

The 29 member companies of the Furukawa Group went back over 1200 years for inspiration for their pavilion "Dream, Ancient and Modern."

The 86-meter tall pavilion is a re-creation of a seven-story pagoda that once stood in the compound of Nara's Todaiji Temple. Here is indeed a dream of ancient Japan for the original pagoda was constructed in 730 A.D. The pavilion was constructed as a faithful reproduction. Techniques unused for centuries were employed in building it. But there was one big difference. The original took more than 10 years to build – this one was built in only a year!

The top floor is an observation tower which you can reach by two elevators. Towering 23.6 meters above the top is a Sorin ring, a Buddhist symbol.

Outside we're in yesterday – but inside it's strictly tomorrow. Electronics of every kind work to create an unique experience.

The pavilion is divided into three areas: Theme Space, Electronics Experiment Theater and Computer Music Hall. The total exhibition is called "Computopia."

In the first area visitors learn the background of modern electronic technology and its place in modern living.

In the theater there are applications of electronics to tomorrow's world. Individual identification by voices – particularly helpful in a cashless society. (Demonstrated at a cashless shopping corner.) A crane hanging from the ceiling moves according to vocal commands. Women get new fashions designed just for them by stylish computers – and all for free.

In the music hall you'll find an "electronic composer" at his electronic organ. Feed him a short combination of improvised sound and he'll compose music right on the spot – and play it for you, while his "synchronized" friends dance for you.

HITACHI GROUP Pavilion

Producer:
Tokyu Advertising Agency, Inc.
(Total Planner: Katsuo Takahashi)
Architects:
Tohnichi Construction Consultant Co., Ltd.
Ohbayashi-Gumi, Ltd.

Ever want to fly a flying saucer?

Here's your chance — at the Hitachi Group Pavilion.

"Search — Invitation to the Unknown" is the theme of the flying-saucer shaped pavilion.

Go to the "sky lobby" on the top of the pavilion by a 40-meter-long escalator. Then down to the space craft landing area on a giant double-decker elevator (capacity: 260 persons) that goes through the core of the building.

Take your place in one of 16 cockpits (each holding eight passengers). You may be chosen to be the "co-pilot" of your craft.

For the next 10 minutes, you'll experience a remarkable new flying sensation — thanks to a remarkable computer. You "fly" to the destination of your choice in a simulated flight marked by its realism.

And where do you go after that?

Well, you'll get a chance to see what took you on your "trip" — the computers and other equipment that created the feeling of flight.

Other features of the pavilion include a lounge on top with a transparent canopy where more conventional scenery may be viewed.

A huge four meter by three meter color television screen is also on display — a laser beam system, the largest of its type in the world.

Various programs — including scenes of the Exposition — will be telecast.

"Harmonizing science and humanity," say the sponsors, is the basic concept underlying the Hitachi exhibition.

The Hitachi Pavilion is located near the West Gate station of the Aerial Cableway, and just north of Thursday Plaza.

MIDORI-KAN (Astrorama)

Producer: Yoshiro Ohbayashi

Movies, the Midori-kai companies feel, are to be seen and to be part of. That's the principle behind this large, domed "Astrorama" — a coined word combining astro and drama.

To create this experience, there first came years of research into cameras, projectors, lenses, light, film and sound. And then into the unique design of the pavilion itself.

Inside, the visitor is totally surrounded by film images and sounds; he is, in fact, a part of it himself. Images cover the whole interior surface. So, in one sequence for example, a submarine scene can be seen on all sides.

"Astrorama — Multi-dimensional World" is the theme of the exhibition. It is housed in a dome 31 meters high by 46 meters in diameter and made of panels of glass fiber-reinforced plastics highlighted by bright colors. The interior projective space, greater than 12 Cinerama screens in area, involves 190,000 pieces of tape, each 40 mm in width.

The upper part of the structure was built of pre-cast concrete sections that provide a sound-proof area for the Astrorama, yet can be quickly assembled or disassembled.

Five cameras — each set specially in a unit with a fish-eye lens — are used in projecting the spectacular.

Also on display, in the Entrance Hall which runs halfway around the base section of the building, are works of the modern fine arts. Visitors can rest here before the film presentation begins and listen to background music especially composed for the Midori-kan Astrorama.

You'll find this dome shaped pavilion right in front of Thursday Plaza in the western part of the exhibition area.

IBM Pavilion

Producer: Herb Rosenthal
Architect: James Pulliam

Theme: Man, The Problem Solver

Man has been solving problems since civilization began. By rubbing sticks together he found he could make fire. The rise and fall of a lid on a kettle of boiling water led to the steam engine. He then harnessed electricity and went on to invent radio and television.

Today it is the computer. Civilization has progressed to the point where man's knowledge is so great and the routines of his society so complex that he has had to find ways to store his information for instant retrieval and devise machinery to perform his complex routines to help him solve his problems.

The IBM Pavilion gives you an opportunity to test for yourself some of the ways today's computers can be used. A host will speak your birthdate into a computer and it will respond, also by voice, with facts and highlights of that time.

On visual display screens ladies can choose their fashion ensembles and the computer will evaluate their selections. Or you can choose a cartoon and let the computer complete the story. Select a vacation spot and the computer will show you pictures of the area, prepare your itinerary and calculate your expenses. Golfers can boom their drives down a simulated fairway and know exactly where the ball landed. Would-be astronauts can blast off for the moon and be told whether they achieved a correct orbit.

In a 500-seat theater, a motion picture by the Oscar-winning team of John and Faith Hubiey, set to music by Quincy Jones, shows the many stages, from primitive times to the present, by which man learned to solve his problems.

The IBM Pavilion is found immediatly to the east of the Tower of the Sun.

EXPO'70
3-PT-9
4-ST-5

Ito Ham / Morinaga
Restaurant "Grand Roue"

Have you ever had a meal in a Ferris-wheel gondola? The Morinaga Group and Ito Ham, Japan's biggest producer of quality ham, serve swinging snacks at EXPO '70! *Ito Ham on Wednesday Plaza — Morinaga on Thursday Plaza.* Ride in one of the 29 gondolas and enjoy the view from 100 feets above the EXPO site while enjoying a delicious snack sandwiches or spaghetti. Each gondola seats four—so bring your friends.

WEDNESDAY PLAZA	THURSDAY PLAZA
Japan's biggest producer of quality ham.	Quality products for every household.

ITO HAM PROVISIONS CO., LTD.

MORINAGA CONFECTIONARY CO., LTD.
MORINAGA MILK INDUSTRY CO., LTD.

Morishita's Shiga plant

SPECIALISTS SERVING SPECIALISTS

Morishita Pharmaceutical Co., Ltd. serves society by serving the medical profession. We develop and supply the finest drugs to hospitals and to doctors.
"Moriamin" a pre-post operative medicine, "Biftenon" for poor digestion and "Inosie" used in helping patients with heart trouble, are among our leading products. Morishita can be depended on to make the drugs that will make a healthier society.

Morishita Pharmaceutical Co., Ltd.

Head Office: 29, 4-chome, Doshomachi, Higashi-ku
Osaka, Japan.   Post cord 541

MITSUBISHI Pavilion

Producer: *Tomoyuki Tanaka*
Architect: *Mitsubishi Estate Co., Ltd.*

The Mitsubishi Pavilion provides a glimpse of the Japan of tomorrow as envisioned by one of the country's largest industrial and financial groups. It is a prescription of how harmony can be achieved between science and nature.

The theme of the pavilion is "The Nature of Japan and the Dreams of the Japanese." In the first of five sections, you are enveloped by raging storms, floods and volcanic eruptions. This nature-gone-wild experience is created by a "Hori-Mirror-Screen," a joint development of Mitsubishi and the technical labs of the Toho movie studios. As an extension of this three-dimensional sensation, a blue sky suddenly unfolds and you see the earth revolving as you "fly through space."

Next you pass through a transparent tube-tunnel into a futuristic world weather control station to get a first-hand view of man taming some future typhoon spawned in the South Seas. Then comes a trip on moving sidewalks, called "travators," to the bottom of the sea and a marvelous underwater city.

The fourth section is designed around science's idea of Japan of the 21st Century. Displays include a living module; you can look through the windows of this "home of tomorrow" and view the fantastic scenes of a new Japan.

In the final area, you may participate in the future yourself. In a huge recreation hall, many unique devices allow you to create your own vision of the future. And thanks to the various conveyors and moving sidewalks, you have toured this entire pavilion in half an hour.

The Mitsubishi Pavilion is located near the Main Gate, and just south of Monday Plaza.

RICOH Pavilion

Producer: Iwao Yamamoto
Architect: Shoji Hayashi

There should be no trouble in finding the Ricoh Pavilion — it's the one that is centered by a huge balloon, 25 meters in diameter. Determined by temperature and winds, it floats at varying heights — up to 55 meters in the air.

Mark this pavilion down for two visits — during the day to go inside and another at night to watch the balloon. For at night the huge balloon becomes a unique screen. Projectors and electronic devices inside it create an ever-changing vision of color and light — from fireworks to abstract designs.

During the day, looking up at the balloon, you'll find a huge eye — an eye that you and those around you are reflected in. For the theme of the Ricoh Pavilion is "Enlighten through EXPO'70" — and the eye, say the sponsors, is "the better eye of mankind."

The balloon is what the sponsors call "Float Vision" and the pavilion also features "Space Vision" and "Intro Vision."

"Space Vision" is viewed by taking a moving conveyer around the exterior wall of the cylindrical main building. Screened images appear on the wall surface — images that vary according to your position.

"Space Vision" is visible even during the daytime, thanks to special equipment. The conveyer, by the way, is air-conditioned.

"Intro Vision" is on the inside of the exhibition hall.

Go in and you're surrounded by a large, quiet space and a feeling of timelessness. There is a unique sound system producing very unique sound that goes with a light image show projected on the interior walls. Special chairs — that can turn with the occupant in any direction — feed another sound sensation.

AUTOMOBILE Pavilion

Producer & Architect: Kunio Maekawa

Music "played" on automobile engines?

In this automotive age, it had to happen sooner or later — and now you can hear it at the Automobile Pavilion.

About 60 engines zoom around the pavilion on special rails — and the sound is transmitted by speakers.

The creation of the engine music relies on the Doppler effect — the apparent change in frequency and wave length of sound when the distance between the source and the receiver is changing.

And in keeping with all of this, the theme of the pavilion is "World of Rhythm." The exhibition is sponsored by 14 automotive companies of the Japan Automobile Manufacturers Association.

In the pavilion's theater a multi-screen movie called "240 Hours a Day" is shown. Basically humorous, the film relates what happens when a pill is developed that lets people do everything ten times faster than before. The movie lasts about 25 minutes.

On top of all that, there is a computerized miniature driving circuit, complete with remote-controlled two-seat mini cars. The circuit symbolizes an ideal traffic pattern for a future city, as envisioned by the sponsors of the pavilion. Children are given a chance to ride in the cars and find out what it might be like to "drive" when they are adults.

The Automobile Pavilion has two cone-shaped buildings cut aslant on top, which let sunlight come through in the daytime. At night colored beams of light are projected from the openings.

The pavilion is located near West Gate of the Expo site, across from Thursday Plaza.

SANYO Pavilion

Producer:
Sanyo Planning Executive Committee
Architect:
Takenaka-Komuten

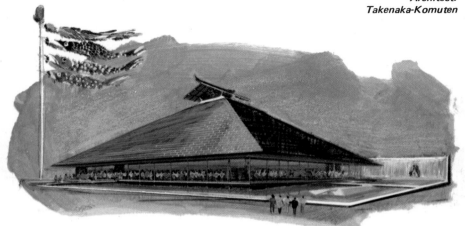

Red leaves fall; snow covers white.
Yet under all, waits green spring . . .

A chance to live through a whole year in just a few minutes will be yours at the "House of Health" — the Sanyo Pavilion. The pavilion is easy to find — for over it fly colorful, giant carp, the kind that many Japanese homes display on the annual Children's Day.

The "instant year" is an attraction in Sun Plaza where a miniature sun shines 18 meters above ground. In "spring", the plaza is covered with greenery, birds sing and the sun is bright. Gradually it becomes summer with showers, thunder, and beautiful rainbows. Tree leaves fall during "autumn" and during the "winter" snowdrifts collect in the plaza.

Sanyo Electric Group, the sponsor, is trying to show the way that man can live in harmony with electronics and how man's technology can produce a better life.

Appliances of the future are on display. A home "capsule" unit that produces perfect living conditions is also shown — light, atmosphere and other aspects are automatically controlled. There are also capsules designed for specialized use by various members of a family. A "universal" TV set is also on display — it offers entertainment, serves as a telephone communication system and even works as a calculating machine.

Near the pavilion is the "Pond of Peace" — the water came from all over the world. Some brought by a Japanese expedition to the Antarctic, the rest in co-operation with the Postal Friendship Society, a pen pal group with members in 84 countries. Around the pavilion is a flowing stream, fed by a cataract in the northern part of the Expo site. Japanese events such as a floating lantern festival and the rinsing of dyed fabrics (a scene of Kyoto's Kamo River) are re-created here.

FUJIPAN Robot Pavilion

Producer: Osamu Tezuka
Architect: Noboru Igarashi

A fantasy land for children or a view of the future for adults?

That's up to the visitor to the Fujipan Robot Pavilion to decide.

Since the sponsor, a baking company of Nagoya, has chosen the theme "Children's Dreams", the idea must be that of fantasy. Or is it?

Outside the pavilion looks like a sliced loaf of bread. (Or, according to some, a strange worm!)

When you approach the pavilion, you'll be welcomed by a robot. (Unless it's raining, in which case he stays inside.) As you leave, another robot bids you farewell by stamping a memento of your visit.

Inside the building it's really "robot land"! The Forest of Robots gives a comprehensive history of robots, with sound and light creating special effects. Robot mechanism and applications are also explained here.

The Town of Robots gives you a chance to have fun with robots . . . and a chance to decide if robots are human-like or if humans are robot-like. In the theater robots are busy singing, dancing, making music, juggling and playing. There's a Polaroid cameraman robot taking instant souvenir pictures. The largest one here is over 2.5 meters (eight feet) tall.

Finally, robots are seen making robots in the Future of Robots section. Robot-making capsules are the main attraction of this section. It will give you a chance to imagine what is in store for robots and for man who will use them.

Harmony is important between man and man — but it's equally important between man and machine. Fujipan Robot Pavilion should give you some ideas about both kinds of harmony.

The pavilion is suitably located at the northern end of Expoland.

The MORMON Pavilion

Architect: Masao Shiina

The Church of Jesus Christ of Latter-Day Saints, the Mormon Church, feels the EXPO'70 theme of "Progress and Harmony for Mankind" cannot be fully achieved without spir-ituality. With this in mind, the Mormon Pavilion features the theme "Man's Search for Happiness."

On approaching the pavilion, the visitor sees a four-meter-high statue of the Angel Moroni atop a steeple. This statue is a replica of the one on the 117-year-old Salt Lake City temple in Utah, headquarters of the Church. Mormons believe Moroni was sent by the Lord in 1823 to reveal in New York State to the Prophet Joseph Smith a book of golden leaf. This Book of Mormon, inscribed with ancient writings believed to have been a form of Egyptian hieroglyphics, was transcribed by the Prophet Joseph Smith. Mormons testify that it was only through the inspiration of the Lord that a 23-year-old could make such a translation. This Book of Mormon can be purchased for 180 yen (50 cents) at the pavilion.

The visitor entering the Mormon Pavilion is greeted by a four-meter-high statue of the Savior, Jesus Christ, carved from Italian marble by the world-famous sculptors of Milan, Italy. Upstairs, guides explain life-sized mural paintings and color transparencies showing the writings of the Book of Mormon and the restoration of the Gospel of Jesus Christ to "every kindred, tongue and people" in these, the Latter Days.

To climax the exhibit, a 12-minute film on "Man's Search for Happiness" answers: Where did I come from? Why am I here on earth? Where am I going after I die? Visitors are invited to ponder thoughtfully the answers given by the Mormon Church.

Every great city has one great hotel Osaka has The Plaza

Osaka, where one can enjoy the heritage of a cultural past and the excitement of a business center, is old Japan's great city. In close attendance are the ancient capitals of Kyoto and Nara and the fabled Inland Sea. All within 30 minutes from The Plaza—the great new hotel that puts the heart of old Japan right on your doorstep.

Osaka
THE HEART OF JAPAN

THE PLAZA HOTEL, INC.

Future Space

The architecture of Expo '70 plans for the future-
creating space in which men can live, work and play.
Takenaka builds for the future-developing lift-up
methods, air and suspension frame structures.
Enjoy the forward-looking results in the 28 Pavilions we have constructed at Expo '70.

TAKENAKA KOMUTEN CO., LTD.

214

LIVELIHOOD INDUSTRY Pavilion

Producer: Ryuichi Hamaguchi
Architect: Tsutomu Ikuta

Daily living, to all too many in the modern world, is a boring, humdrum existence. A drag.

"Day in, Day out" is not a humdrum affair when brought to you as the theme of the Livelihood Industry Pavilion. It dazzles not only the eyes but the taste buds as well.

To one side of the pavilion, the Honey House portrays in five parts the rhythm of man's existence from morning to night. Through a magnified flower garden and a series of intricate dances, the visitor savors the joys of "The Morning Family." This is followed by "The Working People" wherein the conveniences of modern equipment, bright working conditions and businessmen's wear are displayed.

The day rolls on and children come to the fore. In "The Happy Family," animated dolls perform and take a short trip together. An inner garden is constructed entirely of candy.

"The Pleasures of the Family," with its dependence on water and fire, on comfortable household furniture, leads to the day's close and a fantastic display of lights portraying "The People Who Dream."

Then there's the pavilion's hexagonal theater. Viewers slowly revolve to face four stages presenting Japan's seasons in a year-long trip of just 24 minutes. Spring: the birth and growth of life shown by an intricated system of lights. Summer: festivals, the season of love and youthful energy seen on three large screens with dynamic sound. Autumn: the comic portrayal by large paper dolls of a man and woman getting married and setting up their own Home Sweet Home. Winter: the cycle is complete and the mysteries of new life are unfolded.

The never-ending circle of birth and life and the intimacy of nature and humanity is the message of this section of the Livelihood Industry Pavilion.

MATSUSHITA Pavilion

Producer: *Shuji Naega*
Architect: *Isoya Yoshida*

As a great architect once said of simplicity: "Less is more."

Japan's Tempyo period (729 – 794 A.D.) produced a unique style of architecture . . . one of great elegance yet dramatic simplicity. There are two examples of the style that can be seen. Hiroshima prefecture's Itsukushima Shrine. And for Expo visitors, the Matsushita Pavilion.

"Tradition and Development" is the theme of the pavilion. Its sponsor is Japan's largest electronic and electric home appliance maker.

The structure rests on a pond near Thursday Plaza, surrounded by 10,000 bamboos planted to create a perfect traditional Japanese setting.

Equally traditional is the Japanese tea ceremony that visitors may attend if they wish.

Inside the pavilion the EXPO'70 Time Capsule and its contents are on display. The capsule is a joint project of Matsushita Electric and the Mainichi Newspapers. Globe-shaped, it is made of a special steel developed especially for this use.

The capsule will contain 2,068 items. At the end of EXPO'70 it will be buried in the grounds of the Osaka castle, to be opened in 6970 A.D. – 5000 years from now.

Expo's gift to men of the future covers a wide range of scientific, cultural and artistic objects chosen after a year's study by a special committee and a technical group made up of leaders in many fields.

All of the items that will tell man of the future what man of today is like are on display in the pavilion along with the capsule itself.

After thinking so far into the future, visitors can return to the past as they leave the pavilion – to stroll in the 100-meter-long bamboo groves.

The Matsushita Pavilion is located in front of Thursday Plaza.

CHEMICAL Pavilion

Producer:
EXPO'70 Committee
Japan Chemical Industry Association
Architect:
The Shimizu Construction Co., Ltd.

Look east from Festival Plaza and you'll see, just across the way, a rare natural phenomenon.

In the garden of the Chemical Pavilion are three huge gingko trees. The gingko is a living fossil, perhaps the oldest living plant, a plant that hails from prehistoric days.

Inside the hexagonal pavilion, however, it's a new, exciting world. The building design represents a molecule. The building materials are of chemical composition.

"Chemistry and Human Life" is the theme chosen by the Japan Chemical Industry Association, which represents various firms. The endless possibilities of chemistry for man's world is the idea of the exhibition.

In the Chemical Fantasy Hall there is a sound and light presentation. Two ceiling screens swirl with color, backed by electronic music. A curved multiple screen is used in the animation theater where a humorous program is seen. It's fun, yet quite educational at the same time.

And you'll get such a kick out of a "do-it-yourself" experiment corner, packed with thrills and surprises – all harnessed to various chemical reactions. Better leave the details unsaid here to save you the fun of seeing (or doing) it for yourself.

A theme display is found in the center of the pavilion's lobby – "Waterfall of Chemistry." The waterfall is 9 meters high, 28 meters wide. Various chemical equipment – test tubes, flasks, etc. – are symbolized in the waterfall . . . and molecule-shaped bubbles pop out of the fall as well.

And in the garden outside, you'll find those gingko trees. They're real, by the way, and more than 30 meters tall.

A restaurant joins the pavilion here – with a view of the chemical garden, the Artificial Pond and the Japanese Garden.

CHRISTIAN Pavilion

Producers: Shusaku Endo
Shumon Miura
Hiroo Sakata
Architect: Akira Inadomi

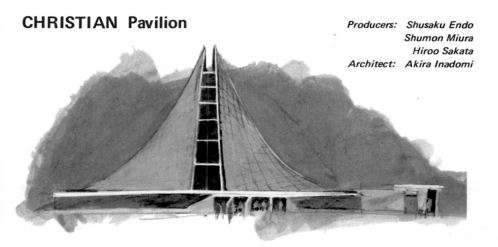

This is the first joint venture in unity by the Catholic and Protestant Churches in Japan; as such, it enjoys the cooperation of the Vatican.

Under the theme "Eyes and Hands: The Discovery of Humanity," the Christian Pavilion provides the eyes at EXPO'70 to discover the lost condition of man in the midst of industrial growth, and the hands to serve him.

From the noise and dazzle of the surroundings, visitors pass through a zig-zag corridor recalling the catacombs to the lower-floor exhibition area. Together with historical commemorative objects, here are found tapestries by Rapheal from the Vatican and other art treasures, as well as panel photographs portraying the sorrows of Japanese life usually overlooked in a prosperous society and other panels concerning world peace, justice, hunger and poverty. The exhibits awaken us to our common task of serving humanity.

The upper floor, fittingly termed "Holy Space," is a multi-purpose hall, surrounded by religious symbols, which signifies this secular world in the light of the Gospel. This is an area where you may, in a silence thankfully apart from the noise and bustle of the exposition, recover your identity as a responsible person.

This is also the place for a dynamic exhibition. Here prayers for peace are lifted up daily and ecumenical services are held every Sunday. One-act plays especially written for the Christian Pavilion are performed, and concerts and organ contests are featured on a bamboo-pipe organ. There is also a "plaza" where participants are free to carry on their own planned or informal activities. What a wonderful witness it will be if this new venture toward the discovery of humanity reaches out into the entire world from the five exits symbolizing the "hands" that serve.

SENKO will revive a fantastic world representing the acme of Oriental-beauties, filling your room with a fragrant odor and luring you into an illusion of ancient, colorful Japan.

SPECIAL EVENTS AND ENTERTAINMENT

National And Special Days

National Days, held by participating countries and Special Days, by the international organizations, the territory, provinces, states and cities, throughout the period of the Japan World Exposition, are designed to celebrate their participation in EXPO'70 and to contribute to a deeper understanding of their culture, life, customs and manners as well as to the promotion of international goodwill.

Many Heads of State of participating countries and representatives of international organizations, the territory, provinces, states, and cities have been invited to the Japan World Exposition as honored guests on their respective National and Special Days —

these invitations being issued either by the Japanese Government or jointly by the Commissioner General of the Japanese Government for the EXPO'70 and the President of the Association for the EXPO'70. National and Special Day celebrations are held at the Festival Plaza and accompanied by colorful events. Following each ceremony the parties of honored guests visit the pavilion of Japan, their own and other pavilions.

It is natural that participants should lay great emphasis on the ceremonies and special events being held on their own Days. These ceremonies and events are expected to draw great interest from general visitors.

Guest House

The Guest House is used by the Japanese hosts for receptions honoring heads of state and distinguished guests from abroad as well as by the sponsors of National and Special Days.

Standing in the vast Japanese Garden on the north side of the Expo site,

the Guest House has the traditional exterior of a Japanese shrine. But the interior is western to help foreign visitors to feel at home.

Here, guests can absorb the serenity of the Japanese Garden while commanding a view of the whole Expo site across the way.

Schedule for National and Special Days

DATE	PROGRAM
Mar. 18 (Wed.)	Colombia Day
19 (Thur.)	Hong Kong Day
20 (Fri.)	Costa Rica Day
23 (Mon.)	Mexico Day
25 (Wed.)	European Community Day
26 (Thur.)	Chile Day
27 (Fri.)	Iran Day
30 (Mon.)	Nepal Day
Apr. 1 (Wed.)	Netherlands Day
2 (Thur.)	San Francisco Day
3 (Fri.)	Czechoslovakia Day
6 (Mon.)	Finland Day
7 (Tues.)	Mauritius Day
8 (Wed.)	Italy Day
10 (Fri.)	U.S.S.R. Day
13 (Mon.)	United Nations Day
15 (Wed.)	Belgium Day
16 (Thur.)	Asian Development Bank Day
17 (Fri.)	Burma Day
20 (Mon.)	France Day
22 (Wed.)	British Day
24 (Fri.)	Switzerland Day
27 (Mon.)	Denmark Day
28 (Tues.)	O.E.C.D. Day
30 (Thur.)	Japanese Local Governments Day
May 1 (Fri.)	Dominican Republic Day
4 (Mon.)	India Day
6 (Wed.)	Norway Day
7 (Thur.)	Washington State Day
8 (Fri.)	Australia Day
11 (Mon.)	Afghanistan Day
12 (Tues.)	Alaska Day
13 (Wed.)	Germany Day
14 (Thur.)	Munich Day
15 (Fri.)	Sweden Day
18 (Mon.)	Korea Day
20 (Wed.)	Bulgaria Day
22 (Fri.)	Ivory Coast Day
25 (Mon.)	Ethiopia Day
27 (Wed.)	Canada Day
28 (Thur.)	British Columbia Day
29 (Fri.)	Malta Day
June 1 (Mon.)	Algeria Day
3 (Wed.)	Uganda Day

DATE	PROGRAM
5 (Fri.)	Nicaragua Day
8 (Mon.)	Saudi Arabia Day
9 (Tues.)	Los Angeles Day
10 (Wed.)	Turkey Day
12 (Fri.)	Gabon Day
15 (Mon.)	Tanzania Day
17 (Wed.)	Brazil Day
19 (Fri.)	Ceylon Day
22 (Mon.)	Philippines Day
24 (Wed.)	Nigeria Day
25 (Thur.)	Quebec Day
26 (Fri.)	Argentina Day, United Nations Day (Charter Day)
29 (Mon.)	Japan Day
July 1 (Wed.)	Kuwait Day
3 (Fri.)	United States Day
6 (Mon.)	Zambia Day
8 (Wed.)	New Zealand Day
10 (Fri.)	China Day
15 (Wed.)	United Arab Republic Day
16 (Thur.)	Ontario Day
17 (Fri.)	Venezuela Day
20 (Mon.)	Uruguay Day
22 (Wed.)	Madagascar Day
24 (Fri.)	Cuba Day
27 (Mon.)	Pakistan Day
29 (Wed.)	Singapore Day
31 (Fri.)	Holy See Day
Aug. 3 (Mon.)	Central African Republic Day
5 (Wed.)	El Salvador Day
7 (Fri.)	Ecuador Day
10 (Mon.)	Viet-Nam Day
12 (Wed.)	Thailand Day
14 (Fri.)	Laos Day
17 (Mon.)	Cambodia Day
18 (Tues.)	Hawaii Day
19 (Wed.)	Ghana Day
21 (Fri.)	Indonesia Day
24 (Mon.)	Portugal Day
26 (Wed.)	Abu Dhabi Day
28 (Fri.)	Peru Day
31 (Mon.)	Malaysia Day
Sept. 4 (Fri.)	Panama Day
9 (Wed.)	Greece Day

— As of February 5, 1970 —

Special Events at Festival Plaza

DATE		TIME	PROGRAM
March	15—22	6:30—8:30 p.m.	**HERE COMES EXPO'70 (A)** Parade of Japanese Drums Parade and acrobatic motorcycle riding by policemen of the World (280 policemen from 70 countries will perform.) "Awa Odori" dance Carnival in Rio Exchange of Musical Greetings by Canadian and Japanese student bands
	24—30	6:30—8:30 p.m.	**HERE COMES EXPO'70 (B)** Computer Music Cartoons on the electric sign board Parade of Flags — 300 marchers Drill Corps Performance by 300 primary school students World Singing Contest "Awa Odori" dance, Hula dance
	29	3:00—4:00 p.m. 6:00—8:00 p.m.	Musical Drama "The Emperor's New Clothes" based on the story by Hans Christian Andersen
April	2—6	6:30—8:30 p.m.	**FLOWER FESTIVAL** **OF THE WORLD (A)** Orchestra Ballet "The Waltz of the Flowers" by Tchaikovsky Kimono Show with the Koto providing a musical background Sacred Flower Palanquin Czech Folk Song Group and Bagpipe Band from Scotland Latin music Tulip dance (Netherlands) Chinese dance French chanson Hawaiian hula dance Flower Arrangement Exhibition (Ikebana) Miss EXPO'70 Parade, Finale—Visitors sing in chorus
	8—12	6:30—8:30 p.m.	**FLOWER FESTIVAL OF THE WORLD (B)** Flower shops of the world Ballet "The Waltz of the Flowers" Koto Music "Sakura" Japanese dance "Sakura" Parade of Flower Floats from each country, and fashion show Flower Game
	14—19	6:30—8:30 p.m.	**YOU AND I** Belgium's traditional "Omegangu Festival, You and I" Japanese Festival "Kaga Hyakumangoku"

Bagpipe Band from Scotland

DATE	TIME	PROGRAM
21—23	6:30—8:30 p.m.	**GRAND BALLET** "Progress and Harmony" with a troupe of 750 dancers
25—26	6:30—8:30 p.m.	**SPACE CARTOON FESTIVAL** Popular Japanese cartoonists, Ryuichi Yokoyama, Isao Kojima, Fuyuhiko Okabe, Sampei Satoh will draw fluorescent pictures on the floor of the plaza.
April 28—May 5	1:00—2:00 p.m. 3:00—4:00 p.m. 6:30—8:30 p.m.	**CHILDREN'S FESTIVAL** Children's Drum and Bugle Corps TV Stars Performance
May 7—11	7:00—9:00 p.m.	**WALTZING MATILDA SHOW** Naval Band Popular songs Kangaroo Dance and others
15—16	7:00—9:00 p.m.	**MISS INTERNATIONAL WORLD CONTEST** Beauty contest/Beauty Parade Fashion show and others
18—20	7:00—9:00 p.m.	**KOREAN NIGHT FESTIVAL** "Kankansuore" Korean Dance
21—26	7:00—9:00 p.m.	**FANTASY IN LIGHT AND SOUND**
27—31	7:00—9:00 p.m.	**MUSICAL RIDE SHOW** Parade of 36 Royal Canadian Mounted Police Folk Dances and Gymnastics by Estein Dancers Feux Follets Folk Dances and Songs Music by the 22nd Royal Regiment Band
June 2—7	1:00—2:00 p.m. 3:00—4:00 p.m. 7:00—9:00 p.m.	**MARKETS OF THE WORLD** Each country will display and sell various products. Wandering Monkey Show, Gypsy Fortune Telling, Merry-Go-Round, Wandering Musicians, and many others
19—20	7:00—9:00 p.m.	**MISS UNIVERSE PARADE** Parade/Fashion Show/And others
22—27	7:00—9:00 p.m.	**DANCING '70** Classical Japanese Dances Original Japanese Dances, depicting "The history of Japan" and "Japan and the World" EXPO'70 Marching Songs with guests' singing and dancing
July 1—3	7:00—9:00 p.m.	**JAPANESE FESTIVAL (1)** Songs and dances of famous Japanese festivals
5—7	7:00—9:00 p.m.	**JAPANESE FESTIVAL (2)** "Awa Odori" and other Japanese festivals
8—9	7:00—9:00 p.m.	**KIWI IN THE SUN** New Zealand Folk Events featuring the songs and dances by Maori tribes Lumber Cutting Contest Sheep Shearing Contest

The Musical Ride of the Royal Canadian Mounted Police (May 27/31)

DATE		TIME	PROGRAM
July	11–20	7:00–9:00 p.m.	**HOLIDAY ON ICE** American Holiday on Ice troupe
	21–23	1:00–2:00 p.m. 3:00–4:00 p.m. 7:00–9:00 p.m.	**YOUTH FESTIVAL** The University of California Band British Sword Dance Mass Games with 2,000 participants
	24–26	7:00–9:00 p.m.	**JAPANESE FESTIVAL (3)** Songs and dances of Japanese festivals, including the famous "Tanabata" festival
	28–30	6:30–8:30 p.m.	**JAPANESE FESTIVAL (4)** Songs and dances of Japanese festivals
August	1–6	7:00–9:00 p.m.	**SLOVAK FOLK DANCE FESTIVAL** Slovak Folk Artists Ensemble of Czechoslovakia Folk dances of the World
	8–10	6:30–8:30 p.m.	**JAPANESE FESTIVAL (5)** Songs and dances of Japanese festivals including the "Gion Festival" of Kyoto
	12–19	6:30–8:30 p.m.	**ASIAN FESTIVAL** Folk dances and costume parades by groups from Cambodia, the Philippines, Indonesia, Laos, Thailand and China Thai Elephant Parade
	12–21	1:00–2:00 p.m. 3:00–4:00 p.m.	**ELEPHANT FESTIVAL** Ballet: Thai National Dancing Troupe Parade of Military Elephants Elephant contest and Gymnastics Elephant race Tug-of-War — people vs. elephants
August	20–22	6:30–8:30 p.m.	**JAPANESE FESTIVAL (6)** Songs and dances of Japanese festivals
	24–29	7:00–9:00 p.m.	**NAMBAN FESTIVAL** featuring Portuguese singer Amalia Rodriguez
August September	31– 2	7:00–9:00 p.m.	**CONCRETE FINE ARTS FESTIVAL** Avant-garde Art Group will present a fine arts show
	7–12	7:00–9:00 p.m.	**GOOD-BYE EXPO'70** Brass Bands/400 Member Chorus Fireworks Show from Each Country World Singing Contest — orchestras and Jazz Bands, singing contest between famous entertainers and pavilion hostesses Good-Bye Expo — Parades of the Countries, Greeting by robots "Should Old Acquaintance Be Forgot"

— confirmed as of press date —

Special Events & Entertainment

Thai Classic Dance (August 12/18)　　　"Nebuta" Festival of Aomori (July 24/26)

"Tanabata" Summer Festival of Sendai (July 24/26)

Special Events & Entertainment

The earliest known light ray gun.

That's the label the archaeologists might pin on our 1.5" TV when they open our Time Capsule in 6969. Baffled by the long-dead language, they'll have to imagine what their ancestors did with the strange, primitive objects buried in the sphere.

And if the TV throws them, imagine what they'll make of the lipstick alongside it. A kind of warpaint, perhaps? You can see the Time Capsule in the Matsushita Pavilion here at Expo '70. When Expo's over it will disappear for 5,000 years.

When it reappears, who knows what brave new worlds people will be living in. Our guess is that electronics will be even more important in the future than they are today.

As Japan's largest electronics company, we are proud of the way our pace-setting electronic products—the world's smallest IC TV is just one—are making work lighter and leisure more rewarding, here and now, for millions of people around the world.

MATSUSHITA ELECTRIC /NATIONAL/PANASONIC®

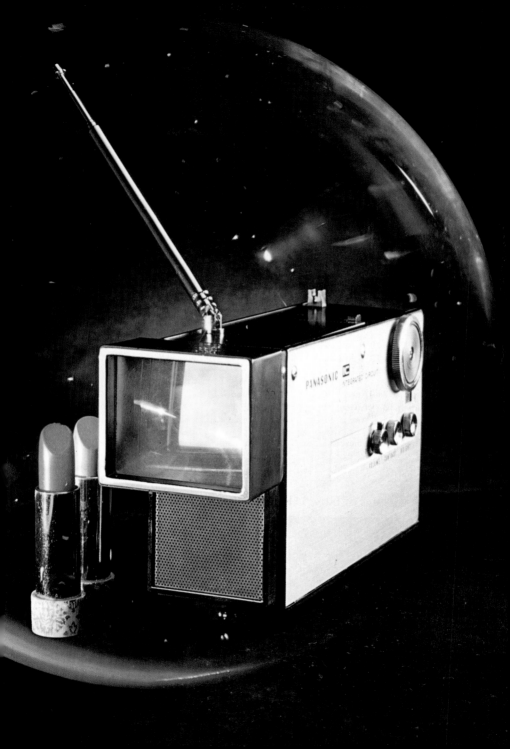

Entertainment at Expo Hall

DATE	PROGRAM
March 15 — March 19	Sammy Davis, Jr. Show
March 23 — April 3	EXPO'70 T.V. Festival
April 4—April 5	Sergio Mendes & Brazil'66 at EXPO'70
April 8 — April 14	San Remo Festival EXPO'70
April 26 — May 6	Japan DISC Festival EXPO'70
May 9	All-Japan Popular Song Festival
May 11 — May 14	Andy Williams Show
May 19 — May 22	Gilbert Bécaud Show
May 27 — June 12	"Anne of Green Gables" (Musical from Canada)
June 16 — June 25	The National Northern Russian Choir
July 3	Stanley Black Pops Concert
July 4 — July 7	Mary Hopkin Show
July 9 — July 12	Chanson Festival
July 13 — July 15	Ensemble Vocal Francais: Les Swingle Singers
July 18 — July 23	Cuban Carnival
July 25 — July 29	Family Variety Show
August 6	Melodies of Yester Years
August 7 — August 10	Fifth Dimension
August 18 — August 19	Jazz Festival
August 22 — August 25	International Pop Music Carnival
September 3 — September 9	Variety of Japanese Traditional Art
September 12	Farewell EXPO'70

— confirmed at press date —

Musical Play "Anne of Green Gables"

Special Events & Entertainment

Canadian authoress, Lucy Montgomery, wrote the famous musical play, "Anne of Green Gables." The play tells about the adolescence of a sensitive red-haired girl named Anne. This two-hour play was first acclaimed at Expo67 in Montreal. It will be the first musical from Canada to be presented in Japan.

North Russian Folk Chorus

A little town near Moscow is the birthplace of this folksong group. The troupe was founded in 1926 by a woman teacher named Antonina Korochirova. Some years later a dancing team was added to the troupe. The group won the All Russian Chorus Contest in 1944.

In 1967, they won first place in the Concours celebrating the 50th Anniversary of the Russian Revolution. They have a long list of awards to their credit. The present conductor is an Honored Artist of the USSR, Nina Meshiko. This will be the first visit of this Russian Chorus to Japan.

Pop Stars from London

Mary Hopkin, the famous London pop star, whose first record, "Those Were the Days," sold 3 million copies in its first month, will be one of the featured singers. She began her career five years ago at the age of 15. The famous model Twiggy introduced her to the Beatles, and her musical career was launched. She is one of the most popular young singers in Britain today.

Chanson Festival

The Ishii Musical Group holds the Chanson Festival every year in Tokyo. This year, to honor EXPO'70, the festival will be held in Osaka. The guest of honor will be Dalida, the international chanteuse from France.

Dalida, who was born in Italy, won a beauty contest in Egypt at the age of 19, and later began her singing career in Paris. In 1956, she became famous with her song, "Bambina." Her international fame stems from the fact that she sings in English, French, Italian, German, Greek and Japanese.

Swingle Singers

The Swingle Singers are famous for their unique blend of classical music with a jazz beat. Japan had a chance to hear them two years ago and they were immensely popular. Led by Ward Swingle, an American, the chorus consists of three men and four women from France. They sing the music of Bach, Handel and Mozart, in an instrumental style, to a jazz beat.

Look for Hitachi Zosen at the Midori-kan "Astrorama".

Shaping Big Ideas...
...That's Hitachi Zosen

Big ideas take shape thanks to Hitachi Zosen's advanced technology, know-how, skill and follow-through. For instance, mammoth tankers. Hitachi Zosen specializes in building the best. Our construction of these giants and other ships places us among Shipbuilding's Big 3. For instance, heavy industrial equipment, steel structures and plants. Hitachi Zosen not only designs and builds them all over the world, but provides on-site consultation and training. We delight in tackling big problems and solving them down to the tiniest detail. If you've got any big ideas, bring them to Hitachi Zosen. And watch them take shape.

Products: Ships—*ranging from hydrofoils to mammoth tankers.* **Machinery**—*chemical equipment, steel making machines, presses, food processing equipment, plastic making machines, B & W diesel engines, turbine engines, boilers, etc.* **Plants**—*fertilizer plants, sugar plants, pulp mills, paper mills, petrochemical plants, etc.* **Steel Structures**—*bridges, steel skeletons, water gates, penstocks, etc.* **Oceanic Structures**

HITACHI ZOSEN
HITACHI SHIPBUILDING & ENGINEERING CO., LTD.

Tokyo/Osaka, Japan
Overseas Offices: London, New York, Oslo, Duesseldorf, Hong Kong

235

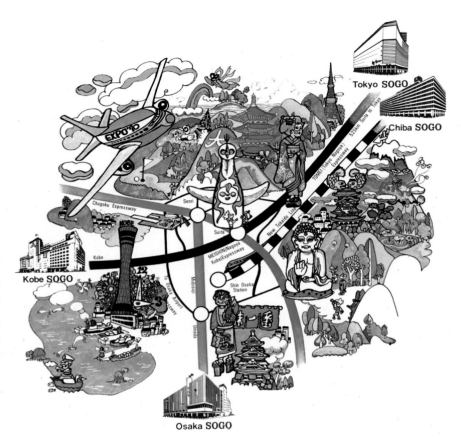

Tokyo SOGO

Chiba SOGO

Kobe SOGO

Osaka SOGO

SOGO DEPARTMENT STORES SHOPPING PALACES ALONG THE PACIFIC SEABOARD

SOGO
Department Stores

OSAKA·KOBE·TOKYO·CHIBA

Entertainment on Floating Stage

DATE	PROGRAM
March 15 — March 22	EXPO Mates Show ("The School Mates" will sing and dance with professional entertainers from various countries.)
March 28 — April 5	Musical Contest between American and Japanese Universities (Brigham Young University Band, winner of the American Competition, vs. Japanese university bands)
April 11 — April 16	Italian Show (The latest Italian fashions displayed on colorful gondolas)
April 23	Cardiff Choir of Wales
May 1 — May 24	South American Steel Band Show (Dynamic music played on steel drums popular in Trinidad in the Caribbean)
June 16 — June 25	Philippine Folk Dances (Philippine dancers will portray their country's history.)
July 1 — July 8	Canadian Band (A 30-member semiprofessional musical group featuring guitars and banjos)
July 8 — July 18	International Baton Twirling Contest
July 25 — August 24	Polynesian Water Show (The dances and music of Polynesia)
August 30/31 September 5/6 September 12/13	Expo Mates Show

— confirmed as of press date —

Steel Drum Players at Trinidad Festival

Entertainment in Amphitheater

Admission free

DATE	PROGRAM

MORNING PROGRAM

March 15—17	**THE SPIRIT OF YOUTH**
	An exchange of musical greetings by youth groups
March 28—April 12	**YOUTH GATHERING**
May 2, 3, 5/May and June, every Saturday and Sunday/July 25—August 31	

AFTERNOON PROGRAM

March 15—20	Band Concert
	Junior high school students from Canada and others
March 22	Gathering of Policemen and Children of the World
March 23—26	Chicago Fire Fighters' Band (U.S.A.), and others
March 27—30	Asian Boys' and Girls' Chorus Festival
March 31—April 2	Band Concert New Westminster Band (Canada), and others
April 3—12	Children's Drama Festival, by youths from all over Japan
April 13—15	All Japan Student Band Fair
April 17—19	Youths of the World (Children's Games of the World)
April 20—22	Stuffed Toys Contest
April 23—29	Band Concert Mussel Shoals High School Band (U.S.A.)
April 30—May 14	Puppet Drama Festival Australia's Marionettes
May 15—21	Baton Twirling Tournament
May 22—26	Japanese Music Recital by players of Japanese instruments
May 27—June 3	"Soft Breeze" Chorus from Canada, and others
June 4—8	Magic Show All Japan Amateur Magicians' Group
June 9—13	Maryland University Glee Club (U.S.A.), and others
June 15—17	Dog Show
June 18—24	Houston Girls' High School Chorus, and others
June 25—July 1	Youth Jazz Festival American-Japanese Jazz Contest
July 2—8	Band Concert (Young musicians from the U.S.A.)
July 9—15	Choral Concert St. Patrick's Choir (U.S.A.), and others
July 18—23	Youth Music Festival Australia's Youth Symphony Orchestra
July 25—30	Band Concert Purdue University Band (U.S.A.), and others
August 1—7	Band Concert North Vancouver High School Band (Canada)
August 8—13	Children's Folk Dance Festival (dances of various countries)
August 14—16	Band Concert Peoria Park Band (U.S.A.)
August 17—23	Children's Ballet Festival (U.S.—Japan)
	American and Japanese children's ballet
August 24—30	Band Concert Collingwood High School Band (Canada)
September 1—6	Band Concert Okanagan Summer School Band (Canada)
September 7—9	Tony Grant's Children's Show
	Songs and dances by the Children's Theater Group (U.S.A.)

EVENING PROGRAM

March 15—31	Film Festival (films on the culture of each country)
August 24—September 6	International Short Film Festival
September 11—12	The Builders of the Future
	Featuring outstanding groups who performed
	in the Afternoon Program at the Amphitheater

— confirmed as of press date —

Special Events & Entertainment

Houston Girl's High School Chorus

Canada's Collingwood High School Band

Entertainment in the Plazas

Visitors can enjoy many events, too, in the Plazas as they rest between pavilion tours. A pleasant time is offered by the presentation of fine music and of stage performances while you relax under one of the beautiful trees.

Located in the southwestern part of the Expo site, by Westside Boulevard, Thursday Plaza is a center of such entertainment. Visitors, aided by excellent loudspeakers and lighting, can enjoy music and other performances played on the open-air stage. Various events designed to capture the special characteristics of the peoples being honored each National Day are presented. So are college and high school brass bands, humorous playlets, the comic antics of clowns and walking stuffed dolls.

You can enjoy this variety of entertainment and music from a semicircular tier of seats before the stage or while resting anywhere in the plaza. Music is selected as balm for your Expo-excited nerves, to aid you in relaxing away from the crowds for a moment, and also to delight your lunch time.

A variety of entertainment is given in Wednesday and Friday Plazas as well. In addition, many parades start from the plazas and march on to others, sometimes in conjunction with concerts there.

Expo Clowns — Dolls

At the Expo site, a group of gaily dressed clowns will be on the move to create a joyful atmosphere, to pose for souvenir pictures with visitors, and to protect children from danger.

Wimpey the clown, dressed in shabby clothes, wearing a top hat and travelling on a unicycle, will perform tricks and acrobatic stunts. He will be on hand throughout the Exposition.

Stuffed dolls, animals and monsters will contribute to the gay spirit at the Exposition. They will be located at different spots on the grounds. Visitors will be able to see them until the middle of May.

Special Events & Entertainment

Earth Shaking Flavor

Earthquakes occur only in certain parts of the world. But AJI-NO-MOTO® is shaken (and poured) to enhance dining around the globe. It has been for the past 61 years. In fact, today, 40% of the annual output of AJI-NO-MOTO® (80,000 tons) is marked for world-wide distribution. In Europe, in the United States, in Central America, in South America, in Australia and, especially, in Southeast Asia(where AJI-NO-MOTO® is so popular that it is accepted as a home product).
AJI-NO-MOTO®. . . the flavor that has world-wide favor.

AJINOMOTO CO., INC.

Why don't you try this delicious taste yourself, now, at the AJI-NO-MOTO EXPO'70 restaurant. Photo: Orion Press

241

Performances at Festival Hall

	DATE	PROGRAM
March	15	**OPENING CONCERT** NHK Symphony Orchestra conducted by Hiroyuki Iwaki Dvorák "Symphony No. 9 From The New World" Toshiro Mayuzumi "Court Dance and Music" Akira Miyoshi "Prelude to the Festival"
	16–22	**DEUTSCH OPER BERLIN** Berlin Orchestra conducted by Lorin Maazel and Bruno Maderna to play Wagner's "Lohengrin" Schönberg "Moses und Aron" Brahms "German Requiem"
April	1–10	**FIRST JAPAN INTERNATIONAL FILM FESTIVAL**
	14–20	**ORCHESTRE DE PARIS** Orchestre de Paris conducted by George Prêtre and Serge Baudo Piano soloist: Alexis Weissenberg/Mahler "Symphony No.1" Prokofiev "Piano Concerto" and others
	18	**ALEXIS WEISSENBERG PIANO RECITAL** Ravel "Le Tombeau de Couperin"/Rachmaninoff "Prélude" Schumann "Five Pieces from Symphonic Etudes"
	24, 25	**SWISS DAY "EVENING CONCERT"** Yomiuri Nippon Symphony Orchestra conducted by Charles Dutoit Soprano soloist; Lisa della Casa/ Flute soloist: Aurèle Nicolet Honegger "Symphony No.3, Liturigique" Othmar Schöck "Songs" Frank Martin "Ballade for Flute & Strings"
	27, 29	**MUSICAL DRAMA "DAS RHEINGOLD"** Yomiuri Nippon Symphony Orchestra conducted by Hiroshi Wakasugi and the Nikikai Opera Group Wagner "Das Rheingold"
May	1–2, 4–6	**MARCEL MARCEAU PLAYHOUSE**
	3	**EXPO'70 NOH PLAY** Cast: Manzo Nomura, Manzaburo Umewaka and others Noh: "Sumidagawa" and others. Kyogen: "Kusabira" and others
	8–14	**BERLIN PHILHARMONIC ORCHESTRA** conducted by Herbert von Karajan Beethoven "Symphony No.3" to "No.7" and "No.9".
	15–18	**CLEVELAND ORCHESTRA** conducted by George Szell and Pierre Boulez Violin soloist: Daniel Majeske / Piano soloist: Gary Graffman Mozart "Symphony No.40" / Sibelius "Symphony No.2" Bartok "Violin Concerto" and others
	24–29	**NATIONAL BALLET OF CANADA** Osaka Philharmonic Symphony Orchestra Prokofiev "Romeo and Juliet" Hindemith "Theme & 4 Variations, Four Temperaments" and three modern ballets
June	4	**YOMIURI NIPPON SYMPHONY ORCHESTRA** conducted by Hiroshi Wakasugi
	6, 7	**PAILLARD CHAMBER ORCHESTRA** conducted by Jean-François Paillard
	12	**NIPPON PHILHARMONIC SYMPHONY ORCHESTRA** conducted by Seiji Ozawa

Special Events & Entertainment

DATE	PROGRAM
19, 21	**PICCOLO TEATRO MUSICALE ROME CHAMBER OPERA** conducted by Renato Fasano/Paisiello "Barbiere di Seviglia" Cimarosa "Il Maestro di Cappella" Rossini "La Cambile di Matrimonio"
22	**VIRTUOSI DI ROMA** conducted by Renato Fasano
24	**NHK SYMPHONY ORCHESTRA** conducted by Hiroyuki Iwaki/Violin soloist: Yoshio Unno Toru Takemitsu "Textures"/Tchaikovsky "Symphony No.5" Mozart "Violin Concerto No.3"
25–27	**MONTREAL SYMPHONY ORCHESTRA** conducted by Franz-Paul Decker Alto soloist: Maureen Forrester / Piano soloist: Philippe Entremont Piano soloist: Philippe Entremont Mozart "Symphony No.41: Jupiter" / Wagner "Wesendonck Songs"
29, 30	**OPERA "YUZURU"** Osaka Philharmonic Orchestra conducted by Ikuma Dan Cast: Kyoko Itoh, Yoshinobu Kuribayashi, Tadashi Miyamoto and others
July 1–5	**LENINGRAD PHILHARMONIC ORCHESTRA** conducted by Eugene Mravinsky and Arvin Jansons
8	**OPERA "JIGOKUHEN"** Osaka Philharmonic Orchestra conducted by Takashi Asahina Performance by "Togensha" troupe of Koto players Cast: Sakae Himoto and the Kansai Opera Troupe
20	**OSAKA PHILHARMONIC ORCHESTRA** conducted by Takashi Asahina/Violin soloist: Hisako Tsuji Khachturian "Violin Concerto" and others
August 6–11	**NEW PHILHARMONIA ORCHESTRA** conducted by Sir John Barbirolli and Edward Downes Alto soloist: Jeanet Baker/Piano soloist: John Ogdon Rawthorne "Street Corner" Ravel " Piano Concerto in G Major" and others
16–26	**BOLSHOI THEATRE** Mussorgsky "Boris Godounov" conducted by Rozhdestvensky and Khaikin Tchaikovsky "Eugen Onegin" conducted by Rostropovich and Khaikin Borodin "Prince Igor" conducted by Yuri Simonov Tchaikovsky "The Queen of Spades" conducted by Rozhdestvensky and Khaikin Soloist: Petrov, Sokolov, Eisen Vishnevskaya, Arkhipova
August 29 thru September 1	**NEW YORK PHILHARMONIC ORCHESTRA** conducted by Leonard Bernstein and Seiji Ozawa Mahler "Symphony No.9" / Beethoven "Symphony No.4" / "No.5"
September 3, 5	**RICHTER PIANO RECITAL**
7, 8	**ENGLISH CHAMBER ORCHESTRA** conducted by Reymond Leppard / Tenor soloist: Rober Tear Haydn "Symphony No.34" / Bach "Brandenburg Concerto No.3"
12	**FAREWELL CONCERT** NHK Symphony Orchestra conducted by Takashi Asahina Beethoven "Symphony No.9"

— confirmed as of press date —

Artists at Festival Hall

Svialoslav Richter

Svialoslav Richter, born in 1915, ranks as not only the supreme pianist of the Soviet Union but of the world as well. In 1945 he won the All-Soviet Music Contest. In 1950, he was awarded the Stalin Prize, and a decade later he won in Western Europe the highest in praise. Difficulties until now in inviting him to Japan have led to ever-greater anticipation; his passionate performance will leave a deep impression.

Berlin Opera

Born of Berlin Municipal Opera, which was established in 1912 and had its theater destroyed by World War II, "Berlin Opera" came back in 1961 when its theatre was rebuilt. It has eclipsed in stature the German State Opera, which found itself in East Berlin at war's end. Berlin Opera features the comprehensive harmony of music, direction and stage setting, not just the star singers.

Cleveland Orchestra

Cleveland Orchestra, established in 1918, is representative of the better orchestras in the U.S.A. Strict training by conductor George Szell since 1946 has allowed it to boast the highest in performance. Pierre Boulez is famed as an avant-garde composer of excellent compositions. His recent activities as a conductor have been equally distinguished.

Berlin Philharmonic Orchestra

This orchestra, established in 1882, is one of Europe's best. Conductors Bülow, Nikisch and Wilhelm Furtwängler led to the zenith of prosperity the orchestra has enjoyed under Herbert von Karajan since 1955. Although noted for its Beethoven, and contrary to the traditional and local character of Vienna Philharmonic, Berlin Phil-

harmonic features a modern and international atmosphere.

National Paris Orchestra, Alexis Weissenberg conducting

This oldest representative orchestra of France was organized in 1828 as the Paris Conservatoire Orchestra. It developed under Charles Munch and Cluytens until it was dissolved three years ago on the death of the latter. It was reorganized shortly thereafter under its present name. Weissenberg is a Bulgarian pianist who took Japan by storm last year.

New York Philharmonic Orchestra

This orchestra, now 128 years old, is the oldest in the U.S.A. It had grown under many famed conductors, including Arturo Toscanini, until Leonard Bernstein took over in 1957 as the first born in the United States. He made it one of the world's leading orchestras in ability and popularity. The "November Steps" is a composition by Toru Takemitsu commissioned by the orchestra for EXPO'70.

The Bolshoi Opera of Moscow

The Bolshoi Opera of Moscow, founded in 1780, is officially called the "Great Lenin Prize Soviet Academy Theater". It is headquartered in a theater rebuilt in 1857 after destruction by fire. The opera consists of many outstanding soloists, as well as an orchestra, chorus and ballet troupe. A training institution is also attached.

The program is principally of Soviet music. "Eugene Onegin" is sure to draw keen interest.

Leningrad Philharmonic Orchestra

Organized in 1772 by a group of nobles and given its present name after the Revolution, this orchestra, oldest in Russia, has introduced many works by such Soviet composers as Dimitri Shostakovich and Aram Khachaturian. It reflects the west-European tradition of Leningrad and Mravinsky, conductor since 1938, is considered representative of this age.

New Philharmonia Orchestra

This orchestra achieved great success under conductor Herbert von Karajan and now has become one of the most popular in England by featuring such great conductors as Sir John Barbirolli whose conducted works, it has been said, have a feeling of "the taste of wine." The other conductor for this visit, Edward Downes, is the regular conductor of Britain's Royal Opera Theater.

National Ballet of Canada

This ballet troupe enjoyed great popularity at Montreal's Expo 67. Though young, born in 1951, it gives refined performances from classic to modern. In the modern style, "Romeo and Juliet," "Wolf" and "Theme & 4 Variations, Four Temperaments," directed by Cranko, Balanchine and Petie, are considered among the best. Performers include Celia Franca, founder of the troupe.

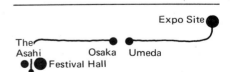

20 minutes by foot from Osaka and Umeda stations.

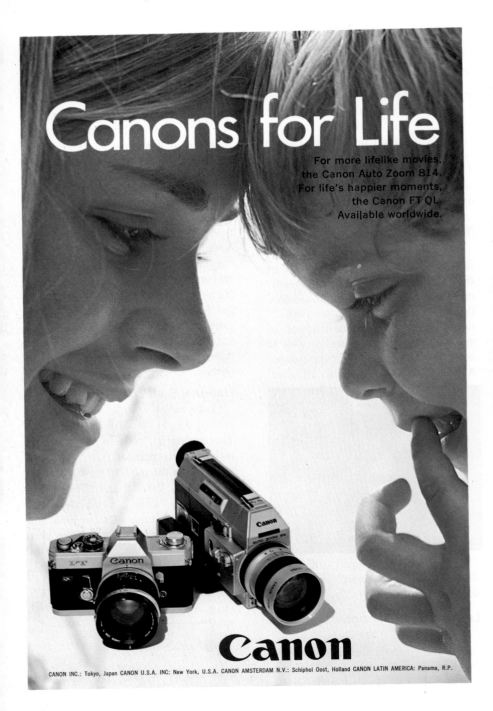

Canons for Life

For more lifelike movies,
the Canon Auto Zoom 814.
For life's happier moments,
the Canon FT QL.
Available worldwide.

Canon

CANON INC.: Tokyo, Japan CANON U.S.A. INC: New York, U.S.A. CANON AMSTERDAM N.V.: Schiphol Oost, Holland CANON LATIN AMERICA: Panama, R.P.

SERVICES
RESTAURANTS
SHOPPING

Service Facilities Map

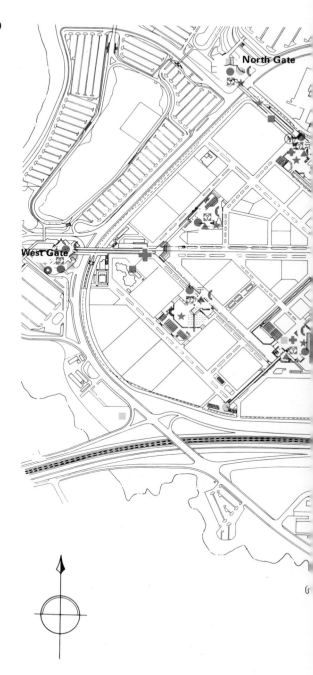

- Information Booth
- Lending Service
- Coin Locker
- Cloak Room
- Bank
- Exchange
- Guard Headquarters
- Guard Box
- Police Facilities
- Post Office
- Telegram and Telephone Center
- Photo Station
- Aid Station for the Handicapped
- Clinic
- First Aid Station
- Lost Children Center

North Gate

West Gate

Services・Restaurants・Shopping

Japanese Garden

Aid Station for
the Handicapped

East Gate

Pond

Grand
Roof

Japanese
Pavilion

Main Gate

Lost Children Center

Expoland

Guard Headquarters

Central Clinic

South Gate

Problems? Don't worry!

There's help aplenty at EXPO'70 — ready to make your visit more pleasant. For example, in the picture, from left to right:

Expo "Angel" . . . Lender of baby carriages and umbrellas. Navy blue, two-piece uniform and white tie.

Expo "Flower" . . . ticket taker and moving walk guide. Red uniform.

Expo "Sister" . . . guide girl in Expoland. Beige uniform.

Expo "Hostess" . . . interpreter for dignitaries and foreign visitors, and guide for Japanese visitors. Navy blue uniform.

Caretaker for lost children. Green uniform.

All are ready to help you in any way possible. (Note that summer uni-

forms are shown on the left, winter uniforms on the right.)

In addition, you'll find policemen about the grounds and some 1,200 special Expo Guard Corps members.

Not feeling well?

Basic dental and medical treatment is available free at these spots: Central Clinic (next to Expo Telephone Office), the dental clinic, the east or west clinic and first aid stations located in Monday, Tuesday, Wednesday and Saturday Plazas, the Symbol Area and Expoland.

If hospitalization is required, ambulances are on stand-by. Medical costs in such a case, however, are of course the responsibility of the visitor.

For fire or other emergencies, there are 100 emergency phones throughout the site that can be used to reach Guard Corps Headquarters.

Hold Japan longer
in real color...

in FUJICOLOR

Envision the silent beauty of Japan in the real color of Fujicolor. Your prints and slides will always remain fresh, vivid, natural and crisp as the day you took them. Anywhere, anytime.

And, now is a good time for you to discover the Fuji Film EXPO '70 big hit exhibit—a motion picture you can "feel". Where? In the Mitsui Pavilion (between the U.S.A. and Russian exhibits). Please come, or as we say in Japanese, "Dōzo"...

FUJICA SINGLE-8 P300

FUJICA SINGLE-8 P1

FUJICA COMPACT S

FUJI PHOTO FILM CO., LTD.
Tokyo, Japan

FUJICOLOR N100
(35mm)
FUJICOLOR R100
(35mm)

Integrated Information Communicating System

The latest in integrated information communicating systems provides Expo visitors with accurate and quick information ranging from entertainment programs to the whereabouts of missing children. The heart of the system is a huge operation control center complete with an array of electronic computers. All information handled here is available to visitors through such means as loudspeakers, electric sign boards, traffic signals, teleprinters, telex and telephones.

The system is considered a model for a city of the future, a rare attempt to handle and transmit information through a variety of devices linked to electronic computers.

Some of the features are explained below:

Information on Parking Areas

Loop coils laid underground at the entrances and exits of each parking area are designed to detect the number of passing vehicles. This information is transmitted to an electronic computer which then automatically operates vehicle-guiding boards.

Drivers are asked to follow the outer loop road clockwise and proceed in the direction indicated by the arrow on each vehicle-guiding board so that he may reach a parking area which still has space to accommodate more vehicles.

Information on Congestion at EXPO Site

An electronic computer receives data on the flow of visitors from pavilions, 50 closed-circuit TV cameras placed throughout the Expo site, 100 guard boxes equipped with dial cards for automatic reporting, all entrances and exits, the moving walks, and so on.

COMPUTER ⇒ **Information on Congestion**

場内案内図と混雑状況

As shown above, 18 information boards around the Expo site inform visitors of traffic conditions at some 140 points. The movement of visitors to each pavilion is shown by an information board in white and red. When it shows two whites, visitors may expect to enter the pavilion within about 20 minutes. White and red, they will have to wait a little longer. Two reds, and they won't be able to enter it for a considerably long time.

Information on Lost Children and Articles

If you find a lost child, take him or her immediately to the closest information office. The guard there will record with a central computer — by means of a keyboard printer — details of the child's dress and physical characteristics.

When your child is located, you can identify him through a conversation by TV-telephone and then go to retrieve him. This system can also be used to find lost articles.

Lost Children's Tags and Lost Children's Center

Every effort is made to ensure the quick and safe return of lost children to their parents. When you bring your child to Expo, obtain a lost child's tag near the entrance. Tags are also available free of charge at all information booths.

The tag carries a serial number of six figures. Pin it to your child and keep the duplicate yourself.

If you lose your child, don't try to look for him yourself but go immedi-

ately to the closest information booth. The computer will seek your child on your behalf according to the serial number of the tag you pinned on him.

If you should fail to immediately report the matter, your child will be sent by car to the lost children's center in Expoland. He will be well taken care of there by a hostess, a licenced nursery governess.

Rendezvous Information Service

When you visit Expo with other members of your family, get a family

card at any one of 13 service stations. The card carries a serial number — your family number. If you are later separated from the others, pick up a push-button telephone in a nearby information booth. You will hear the voice of an electronic computer: "This is the rendezvous information service. Please press your family number." When you punch the number, the computer will say: "Please press the place and time you want to get together with your family." Thus you can register the information. Your family can similarly inquire about you and register the place and time for a rendezvous. This electronic message system does away with the usual—noisy—loudspeaker service.

(The words from the computer are in Japanese, so ask the bilingual attendant to arrange your rendezvous for you.)

Miscellaneous Information Services Relating to EXPO'70

An electronic computer is continuously memorizing a variety of information on exhibits, entertainment programs, the schedules of state guests and commissioners general and meetings relating to EXPO'70, and so forth. It will answer all kinds of queries. Please dial 06-876-1970 whenever you have a question about EXPO'70.

Another Expo information service concerns the control of city water and sewage systems. A computer, containing data on such things as the weather, the temperature and the number of visitors, automatically controls the performance of both the water system and the sewage system at the site.

Transportation Facilities

Monorail

Japan's first automatically driven train. Tours the 4.3 kilometers (2.7 miles) of the site in 15 minutes, at 2-1/2 minute intervals. There are six of the four-car trains, painted in blue and white. They are free. Stops are: Central Station, Expoland, East Gate, the Japanese Garden, North Gate, West Gate and Wednesday Plaza.

Family Car

70 electric cars are available for intra-Expo transportation. Each holds five passengers plus driver. Cost for car and driver is ¥200 for ten minutes.

Aerial Cableway

Adults ¥200; children ¥100. For an aerial view of Expo. Twenty-two 15-passenger gondolas travel at a height of 30 meters (98 feet). The trip takes 7-1/2 minutes. The gondolas rotate during the trip for a particularly good view.

Moving Walks

Moving walkways — pedestrian "conveyor belts" to carry you in air-conditioned comfort, ease and safety — interlace Expo from each of the gates and the Symbol Area. Travelling in transparent tunnels, the Moving Walks give a wonderful, elevated view of all the pavilions. And they move you along at 2.4 kilometers (1.5 miles) per hour — just right for the safety of youngsters and the elderly.

Parking

Six lots with a total capacity of 20,000 cars have been provided. Road signs throughout the area direct drivers to the lots. Three lots for up to 1,500 tour buses have also been provided. Gasoline stations are located at the North and West Parking Lots.

Bus Shuttle

24 buses shuttle between the parking areas (South, West and North) and each entrance of Expo.

ON LAND OR SEA—
IN THE ATMOSPHERE OR IN SPACE...

Toshiba plays an all-important role
on the world stage of progress

It used to take more than 53 days . . . Now you can travel the 350 miles from Tokyo to Osaka in 3 hours and 10 minutes — in safety and comfort, because the fastest train in the world is powered by TOSHIBA.

And in aviation? TOSHIBA equipment at the busy Tokyo International Airport, for example, assures you of safe air travel.

In communications? The dramatic Apollo 11 event was relayed to Europe instantaneously through TOSHIBA's achievements in communications.

In other fields? Among many other things, TOSHIBA is involved in the building of nuclear-powered commercial ocean liners as well as in progress on the bottom of the sea to create pastures and parks.

WHEREVER YOU GO—WHEREVER YOU LOOK— TOSHIBA TECHNOLOGY FOR THE PROGRESS OF MANKIND.

TOKYO SHIBAURA ELECTRIC CO., LTD.

DO NOT MISS TOSHIBA IHI'S GLOBAL VISION AT EXPO '70

Expo Site Facilities

Expo Plazas

EXPO'70 is built around a series of seven plazas, each named for a day of the week. Linked by moving walkways, all plazas lead to the Symbol Area and to the Main Gate.

Each plaza is a center of service facilities such as information counters, restaurants, shops and rest rooms. They can serve as meeting spots — or just places in which to rest and relax. The plazas will also feature various outdoor shows from time to time.

Gates

There are five gates at Expo ... the Main Gate plus one at each point of the compass: North, South, East and West.

The Main Gate is in front of the Symbol Area. Here is the Main Gate Station of the Kita-Osaka Electric Railways. The West Gate is at the sta-

tion of the Senriyama Line of the Hankyu Electric Railways.

A parking area is located outside each of the gates.

No vehicle is allowed to enter the site itself. One exception is at the East entrance where vehicles of the physically handicapped are allowed to enter and go to the Aid Station — the starting point of their tour.

Press Center

A three-story building, next to and west of the Expo Association Headquarters. This is the news center for Expo — and open to reporters and cameramen from all over the world.

The center is equipped with typewriters for various languages, TV studios, an international communication center, a press interview room with simultaneous interpretation equipment and other facilities.

The Expo Association Headquarters

The Japan Association for the 1970 World Exposition is housed in a large building on the south slope of the Symbol Area. The design, by a young Japanese architect, was chosen in a nationwide contest.

The officials and staff of the Expo Association have their offices here and from the top floor the entire exhibition area can be seen.

Guard Headquarters

Located in the south of the site opposite the Expo Telephone Office are police and fire headquarters as well as the Expo Guard Corps H.Q.

The Headquarters is linked to five guard offices and 29 guard stations. The Emergency Control Center receives emergency calls. (Dial 110 or 119 from any of the site's 7,000 telephones, 100 emergency phones or use one of the 50 alarms.) 50 remote control TV's also direct patrols throughout the site.

Expo Postal Services

The main post office is on the first floor of the Association Headquarters Annex. Open from 8 a.m. to 8 p.m. There are four branch offices throughout the site. Outgoing mail receives a special commemorative cancellation. There are 19 post boxes (in all plazas, at main entrances, around the artifi-

cial pond), ten of them with stamp vending machines.

Telephone Services

There are 465 red indoor telephones at the site and the same number of blue outdoor telephones. Telephone and telegraph service stations are located at all Expo entrances, in the plazas and in Expoland. There are international telephone and telegraph service stations in Sunday and Wednesday Plazas.

Banks and Money Exchanges

Offices of the Daiwa, Sanwa,

Sumitomo, Fuji and Tokyo Banks are located at various spots at Expo to handle the needs of visitors: the last two and the Hypothec Bank of Japan handle foreign exchange.

Miscellaneous

Customs House: next door to the post office.

Food Inspection Center: located at the Expo Guard Headquarters. 15 inspectors supervise all food served at the site.

Expo Time

Official time for the Exposition is determined by an atomic clock, located in the Time Center of the International Bazaar Plaza. Contained in a capsule supported by three pillars, 20 meters high, this clock has an accuracy of plus or minus one second over several thousand years. This master clock controls 110 clocks located throughout the site.

A solar-battery clock is located on large steps leading to the Symbol Area.

In the Press Center there is a digital clock that gives the time for spots throughout the world.

Steel Sculptures

In September of last year, 13 top-ranking sculptors from around the world were invited to Osaka for a four-month symposium.

"Discontinuity: the Generation Gap," the theme, was designed to explore the difficulties and aspirations of young people today. The results of that symposium, representing the artists' interpretation of an aspect of "Progress and Harmony," are exhibit-

ed around the Artifical Pond. Other modern sculptures throughout the Expo site also present opportunities for reflection.

Service Facilities

Travel Information Center

Main Gate basement. Here information on all domestic and international transportation is available. All tickets can be purchased here. Hotel reservations can also be made here as well as arrangements for sightseeing in Osaka, Kyoto and Kobe.

Lodging Information Center

In the same office as the Travel Information Center. Handles arrangements and reservations for youth hostels, people's hostels, hotels and inns. The center also offers accommodation assistance in Shinto shrines, temples and other facilities as well as in private Japanese homes.

Lending Services

At all gates and plazas. Staffed by the Expo "Angels."

400 wheel chairs for the handicapped, 1,400 strollers for babies and 10,000 umbrellas in case of a sudden shower are available here.

Aid Station for the Handicapped

On the west side, East Gate Station of the monorail. Vehicles carrying the handicapped may enter into the site here and park at two indoor and outdoor rest areas. 70,000 copies of a special guide book are available to help those using wheel chairs to see Expo better. There are 10,000 copies in embossed type (braille) for the blind. Twenty staffers are at the aid station to assist the handicapped.

Photo Station

For photographic advice and other service, including camera repair. Location is shown at photo equipment shops throughout the site.

Cloak Rooms and Coin Lockers

At all Gates. Fees are charged for this service.

Expo Picture Signs

This way

Information Booth

Smoking Room

No Smoking

Don't touch

Keep off!

First Aid Post

Lost Children

Lost and Found

Toilet (Gentlemen)

Toilet (Ladies)

Stroller

Physically Handicapped

Guard

Telephone

International Telegraph and Telephone

Mail

Umbrella

Locker

Cloakroom

Exchange

Restaurant

Shop

Escalator

Stairway

Monorail

Railway

Bus

Taxi

Motorcycle

Filling Station

V.I.P. Entrance

Press Entrance

Entrance for Security Personnel

Electric Equipment

The Lion Group at work for your health and beauty

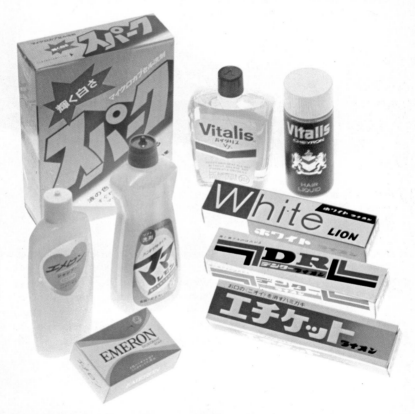

THE LION DENTIFRICE CO., LTD. THE LION FAT & OIL CO., LTD.

What would EXPO '70 be like without electrical power? ...

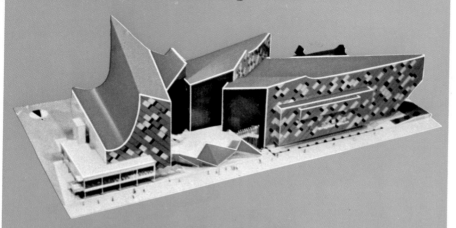

. . . a city without electricity. And, you would have to climb, push, strain, freeze and perspire. But, because we make whirling gadgets (generators) which make electricity, EXPO '70 is plugged into the future. Your future. On earth, underwater, in space stations or wherever your great, great, great grand-children decide to live. We'll be ready for them. With our sky-high elevators, escalators, electric-eye doors, wall television, air-conditioners and atomic power generating equipment for space-age heavy industry. Because, we are advanced and ever advancing. For you.

ADVANCED AND EVER ADVANCING
MITSUBISHI ELECTRIC
Head Office: Mitsubishi Denki Bldg., Marunouchi, Tokyo.

Restaurants and Concessions

Enjoying the culinary delicacies of the world ranks as one of the supreme pleasures of the Japan World Exposition. A multitude of restaurants and snack bars offer the best dishes from around the planet, including delicious Japanese foods prepared by skillful cooks sought throughout the country.

Many governments sent their most expert chefs to Japan well in advance of Expo so they would be prepared to serve their national foods away from home. Some countries, like the Republic of Korea, Czechoslovakia and India, are operating their own restaurants, placing great emphasis on their distinctive dishes. Look around. You'll find European dishes — French, Italian, Belgian, British — and Korean and Chinese foods, Indian curry, and dishes from the United States, the Soviet Union, Greece, the Philippines, Malaysia, Argentina and on and on. The delicacies of the world wide. Especially in the International Bazaar, famed restaurants from many nations prepare the particular dishes they pride themselves on. Pavilion restaurants welcome you, too, with both plain and fancy food and national atmosphere.

Among the Expo menu novelties, you'll find "Space Course," "Apollo Curry and Rice," "Apollo Lunch" and "Atom Lunch" — reflecting in food the triumphs in science. Expo "sushi" and "kamameshi" (seasoned boiled rice served in a small pot) will reward your curiosity, as will rice balls in Japanese, Western and other styles. And don't forget the hamburgers and hot dogs. Or "Festival Soba Noodles" when you're in a Japanese mood.

Meals are made even more pleasant by restaurant decor reflecting national character. You feel as though you were dining there, in that country whose food you are eating. And then you can follow that meal in Europe with coffee in the United States or tea in Ceylon.

Experimentation is obviously no alien to Expo and no exception is made in the field of food, either. Try the original "Drink for Eating" if you want to break with the past.

The "Underwater Restaurant," located on the bottom of the Artificial Pond near the Festival Plaza, is another one of those ideas unique to Expo. While dining, you enjoy the expansive scene in the pond through a large glass wall. Fish swim in large aquariums — each containing 100 tons of water — located to two sides. This restaurant, with its advances in construction technique, may be a first step toward the long-dreamed-of creation of an underwater city.

In contrast to the underwater restaurant, "Gondola Snack Bars" let you

enjoy the Expo splendor from above. These snack bars are located at five spots in various plazas and Expoland. A four-seat gondola carries you into the sky as you munch lunch and drink drinks prepared in the kitchen below. Dinner or tea time above the Expo bustle, viewing the distant hills, is indeed a pleasure.

How about, after your meal, a little shopping for souvenirs and specialities from around the world? Numerous shops stand ready for you at various Expo spots — at the plazas, gates, monorail stations, Expoland and elsewhere. The International Bazaar is a global shopping center where specialities and delicacies of countries all over the planet are sold at shops row on row.

For your convenience, these shops are grouped by the nature of their wares: foodstuffs are in one area; confections, Expo souvenirs, new products in others. Many domestic dealers are gathered at Expo and you can select special items produced in whatever country, or even Japanese prefecture, that interests you. Particular care has been taken to exclude any expensive or shoddy goods. Only articles of assured quality are offered.

Light shoes, simple rainwear, clothing, sunshades, beverages and more, displaying ideas making them especially appropriate for use at Expo, are also available in the shops. And if you do not wish to buy today, enjoy yourself window-shopping anyhow; you're welcome.

Guide to Restaurants

W: Western-style food
J: Japanese-style food S: Self-service
C: Chinese-style food T: Table-service

* ¥200–300   ** ¥300–400   *** ¥400–500

Area	Name of Restaurant or Company	Type	No. of Seats	Price	Special Menu	Service
East Gate	Sports Service Corp.	W	87	*		S
	Snow Brand Milk Products Co., Ltd.	W	87	*	Sandwiches Hamburgers ¥200	S
	Demekin Confectionery Co.	J	87	*	Apollo 12 ¥100 Rice Cake	S
West Gate	Motel Tanba	WJC	292	***	Roast beef on boiled rice (with soy-paste soup) ¥300	S
South Gate	Hegemann Harris	J	58	*		S
	Kikkoman Snack	W	58	*		S
North Gate	Letheby Christopher	J	87	*		S
	Five Ten	W	87	*	Table d'hote Cutlet ¥200	S
Sunday Plaza	Letheby Christopher	J	39	*		S
	Station Parlour	W	60	*	Curry and Rice Hot Dog Ice Cream	S
	Five Ten	W	39	*	Table d'hote Cutlet ¥200	S
	Biwako Valley	WJ	136	**		S
(Gondola Snack Bar)	Biwako Valley	W	170	**		S
(South)	Hakuho	C	118	**	Expo Lunch	S
	Asahi Restaurant	W	147	**	Hamburg Steak ¥300	S
	Kuidaore	J	244	**	Festival Lunch ¥300	S
	Ito Ham Provisions Co., Ltd.	Snack		*	Hot Dog ¥70	S

Area	Name of Restaurant or Company	Type	No. of Seats	Price	Special Menu	Service
Monday Plaza	Juso Restaurant Coop. Assn.	J	110	**		S
	Meijiya Snack	CW	125	**	Lunch	S
	Bobo Hut	W	40	*	Doughnuts and soft drinks	S
	Yoshidaya	C	70	*	"Fuji" Lunch ¥300	S
	Suntory Restaurant	WJC	285	***	Expo Lunch with Wine ¥500	T
	Suntory Corner	Snack		*		
Tuesday Plaza	La Compagnie des Attractions de Montréal Limited (Canada)	W	248	***	Salmon steak, BBQ chicken Canadian Beer	T
	Suntory (Japanese-style Snack)	J	68	*	Special table d'hote ¥200	S
	Gin Tanpo	W	65	*	Western-style Lunch ¥400	S
	Sarashina Restaurant	C	81	*	Miyajima Lunch ¥300	S
	Alte Liebe	W	120	**	Hamburger ¥300	S
	ROK (Government-Operated)	W	209	**		S
Wednesday Plaza	Australia	W			Hamburg steak, Lamb chop Beef Cutlet	T
	Nippon Ham Co., Ltd.	W	144	**	Hamburger ¥250 Fried Rice ¥300	T
	Portugal	W	122	**	Port Wine	S
	Kinki Coca-Cola	W	50	*		S
	Minoko	W	80	*	"Apollo" Lunch ¥200	S
	J.D.C.D. Enterprise	W	46	*	HamburgerSandwich Chicken	S
	Suntory Restaurant	WJC	256	***	Expo Lunch with Wine ¥500	T
	Minoko	C	80	*	"Shumai" Lunch ¥200	S
	Gin Tanpo	W	52	**	Western-style Lunch ¥400	S

Services • Restaurants • Shopping

Area	Name of Restaurant or Company	Type	No. of Seats	Price	Special Menu		Service
Wednesday Plaza	Asahi Beer Restaurant	W	52	**	Hot Dog	¥150	S
	Kuidaore	C	120	**	Festival Lunch	¥300	S
(Gondola Snack Bar)	Ito Ham Gondola Snack Bar	W	206	**	Hot Dog	¥70	S
Thursday Plaza	Sanders Affiliated	WJC	256	**			T
	J.D.C.D. Enterprise	C	39	*	Lunch, Lobster Ball Mongolian Burger		S
	Bodo Hut Ltd.	W	39	*	Doughnuts, Beverages		S
	Cafe Terrace Nichirei	W	150	**	Hamburg Steak	¥250	S
	Suntory Snack	W	45	*	Lunch	¥200	S
	Kyodaru	J	50	*	EXPO"Sushi"	¥200	S
(Gondola Snack Bar)	Morinaga Candy Store	W	224	**	Space Course	¥250	S
	Kirin Lemon Service	Snack		*			
Friday Plaza	Kyodaru	J	49	*	EXPO"Sushi"	¥200	S
	House Carelina	W	50	*	Curry and Rice	¥150	S
	Nippon Ham Co., Ltd.	W	49	*	Hamburger	¥250	S
	Suntory Restaurant	WJC	230	***	Expo Lunch with Wine	¥500	T
	Czechoslovakia (Government-Operated)	W	148	**			S
Saturday Plaza	Motel Tanba	J	39	*	Beef and Noodles	¥180	S
	Asahi Beer Restaurant	W	52	*	Hot Dog	¥150	S
	Gyokurinen Green Corner	C	39	*	Green Soft Ice Cream Chinese Noodles		S

272

Area	Name of Restaurant or Company	Type	No. of Seats	Price	Special Menu	Service
	Tad's Enterprise	WJC	238	**	Tad's Steak	T
	Greece	W	160	**	Sirloin steak, Pork chop	S
	Kobe-Ya	W	172	**	Hamburger ¥150	S
	U.S.S.R.	W	240	**		S
Tower Plaza	Kikkoman Snack	C	50	*		S
	Minoko	C	50	*	Chinese Lunch	S
	House Carelina	W	50	*	Curry and Rice ¥150	T
	La Compagnie des Attractions de Montréal Limited (Canada)	W	50	*	Chicken Burger Pizza Burger Ice Cream	S
	New Victoria	W	50	*	Hamburger, Curry and Rice	
	Eins Chain "Furusato"	W	50	*		S
	Yama	Snack		*	American Hot Dog ¥70	
	Nitto Tea Stall	Snack		**	American Sandwich ¥300	
Pond A	Suntory Snack	(Snack W)	49	*	Lunch ¥200	S
	New Tokushima	W	50	*	Naruto Steak, Hamburger Curry and Rice	S
	Kuidaore	J	270	**	Festival Lunch ¥300	S
Pond B	Restaurant Meiyoken	W	39	*	Table d'hote Croquette ¥350	S
	Beefburger Ranch	C	39	*	Beef burger Beef Dog	S
	Hankyu K.K.	J	146	**	Cutlet and curry on rice Table d'hote cutlet, Noodles	S
Pond C	Kintetsu Restaurant	W	150	**	Croquette ¥200	T
	Asuka	J	150	**	"Unagi" ¥500 Beef Cutlet on rice ¥250	T
	Asuka	J	100	*	Tempura Noodle ¥150	T
	Asuka	Snack		*		
	Juheim Confect	Snack		*	Barbecue Frankfurt ¥100	
	Morinaga Candy Store	Snack		*	American Hot Dog ¥70 Hamburger ¥80	

Harmonize Science and Beauty with Hitachi

To the naked eye, Hitachi electronic appliances are unobtrusive.
But, in truth, they are more sensitive, more compact,
more powerful, more reliable and longer lasting
than others in their price range.
For example, all transistor color TV is rather new in the world.
But, Hitachi has it today. Of course.
Hitachi is Japan's leading manufacturer and 10th in
the world outside of the U.S.A. (Fortune Magazine 1969 survey).
Plus, research and development in not-one-but-three
research laboratories by more than 5,000 scientists,
is your Hitachi quality guarantee.
What could be more beautiful than that?

CWA-200
All Transistor Solid State Portable Color TV

TRQ-777
Auto-reverse Stereo Tape Recorder

Representatives in: New York / Chicago / San Francisco / Los Angeles / Dallas / Indianapolis /
Buenos Aires / London / Düsseldorf / Hamburg / Beirut / Johannesburg / New Delhi / Calcutta /

KS-1810
FM/AM, Solid State Portable Radio

Honolulu / Montreal / Mexico City / Panama / Caracas / Rio de Janeiro / São Paulo /
Bangkok / Singapore / Sydney / Taipei / Hong Kong

Area	Name of Restaurant or Company	Type	No. of Seats	Price	Special Menu	Service
Pond D	Kikkoman Snack	J	39	*		S
	Kirin Beer Restaurant	W	60	*	Special Hamburger ¥100	S
Pond E	Mimyu	J	88		"Sukiyaki of Noodles" ¥800	T
	Kyodaru	J	80	¥200 −500	"Sushi" Edo-Style "Matsu" ¥500	T
	Nippon Restaurant Society	J	80	¥800 −2,000	Japanese Dishes	T
	Nippon Ham Co., Ltd.	Snack		**	Hamburger ¥140 Fried chicken ¥200	
Festival Plaza	Morinaga Candy Store	J	80	*	Expo Boiled Rice Beef and Rice ¥200	S
	Ito Ham Snack	W	40	*	Hot Dog ¥70	S
	House Carelina	W	40	*	Curry and Rice ¥150	S
	Kirin Beer Restaurant	W	30	*	Hot Dog Stick ¥70	S
	Nippon Ham Co., Ltd.	W	40	*	Hamburger ¥250	S
	Waraku	J	40	*	Sushi	S
	Miraku	J	80	*	Sushi	S
	Demekin Seika	J	40	*		
	La Compagnie des Attractions de Montréal Limited	W	40	*	Cheese Burger, Pizza Burger, Ice Cream	S
	Hana	W	40	*	Curry and Rice Sandwiches Soft Drinks	S
	Yamaguchi	J	40	*	Expo "Sushi" ¥250	S
	Kyoto Shin-Hamamura	C	50	*	"Shin-Hamamura" Lunch ¥380	S
	Hiroya	C	39	*		S
	Eins Chain "Furusato"	W	40	*	Curry and Rice	S
	Beefburger Ranch	W	40	*	Beef Burger Beef Dog	S
	Shinshu "Marufuku"	J	50	*	Expo Boiled Rice "Kamameshi" ¥300	S

Area	Name of Restaurant or Company	Type	No. of Seats	Price	Special Menu	Service
Symbol Zone North Plaza	Kuidaore	J	80	*	Expo Sushi ¥200	S
	Nippon-Ichi Restaurant	J	250	**	Expo Boiled Rice "Kamameshi" ¥300	S
	Sariporo	C	60	*	Sapporo Miso Noodles ¥150	S
	Asahi Beer Restaurant	W	50	*	Hot Dog ¥150	S
	Meiji Milk Products	Snack		*		
	Yama	Snack		*	American Hot Dog ¥70	
	Prima Snack	Snack		*	Hamburger ¥100 Fried Chicken ¥100	
Central Gate Theme Exhibits Area	Kyodaru	J	50	*	Expo "Sushi" ¥200	S
	Kobe-Ya	W	50	*	Hot Sandwich ¥100	S
	Sasebo Kujyukushima Kanko Hotel	W	75	**	Nagasaki Noodles ¥250	S
	Hokke Club	J	200	**	"Domburi" ¥250	S
	Tod's Enterprise	C	200	**	Sweet Vinegared Pork, Chicken Fried Rice	S
	Kuidaore	W	255	**	Festival Lunch ¥300	S
	Suntory Restaurant	WJC	255	***	Expo Lunch with wine ¥500	T
	Fujipan Shop	Snack & Bread	10	*		
Underwater Restaurant	Expo Underwater Restaurant	W	150	***		T
International Bazaar	Philippines	W	100		Philippian Beer, Chicken Food	T
	Greece	W	100		Sandwich, Beef Stew, Beverages	T
	Malaysia	W	100		Malaysian Fry, Malaysian Dish, Fruits	T

Area	Name of Restaurant or Company	Type	No. of Seats	Price	Special Menu	Service
Internatio-nal Bazaar	Canada	W	100		Expo Canadian Service Lunch ¥500 Canadian Beer	T
	China	W	100		Mongolian Barbeque, Pork Noodles, Fruits	T
	Belgium	W	100			T
	Washington State	W	100		Roasted Turkey, Western American Beer	T
	British Columbia	W	100			T
	India (Government-Operated)	W	100			T
Expoland	Letheby & Christopher	W	150	**		S
	Osaka-Ya	J	33	*	Noodles	S
	Nippon Danshoku K.K. "Apollo"	W	50	*	"Apollo" Curry and Rice ¥120	S
	Kokusai Kanko Ryokan "Rinkoan"	J	150	**	Roast Eel, "Yakitori" ¥200–400	S
	Minoko	W	50	*	"Apollo" Lunch ¥200	S
	Yama	J	50	*	"Nishiki" Lunch ¥250	S
	Suntory	WJC	300	***	Expo Lunch with Wine ¥500	T
	Bobo Hut	W	50	*	Doughnuts, Beverages	S
	Hatsukame	J	50	*	Roast Eel on Boiled Rice ¥300	S
	Tokyo "Zuien"	C	150	**	Chinese Lunch ¥400	T
	La Compagnie des Attractions de Montréal Limited (Canada)	W	50	*	Cheese Burger, Pizza Burger Ice Cream	S
	Drive-In Kadoma	W	50	*	Children Lunch ¥200 Curry and Rice ¥120	S
	Wako	W	150	**	Pork Cutlet ¥300	S
	Suntory Snack	W	50	*	Lunch ¥200	S
	Suntory Snack	W	50	*	Lunch ¥200	S
	Suntory Snack	W	50	*	Lunch ¥200	S
	Suntory Snack	J	50	*	Lunch ¥200	S

Area	Name of Restaurant or Company	Type	No. of Seats	Price	Special Menu		Service
Expoland	Sushimasu	J	50	*	Osaka Sushi		S
	Sannoya	J	50	*	Sushi	¥200	S
	Yodoman	J	58	*	Noodles	¥100	S
	Meiji Milk Products	W	50	*			S
	Kinki Coca-Cola	W	58	*			S
	Kinki Coca-Cola	C	58	*			S
(Glass Castle)	House Carelina	W	150	**	Curry and Rice	¥200	T
(Gondola Snack Bars)	Yakult Tower — Sogo Department Store	W	150	**	Atom Lunch	¥300	S
	Shiro	Snack		*	Hot Dog	¥80	
	Asahi Beer Stand	Snack		*	Hot Dog	¥150	
	Meiji Milk Products	Snack		*			
	Shiro	Snack		*	Hot Dog	¥80	
	Nakamuraya	Snack					
Monorail West Station	Shiro	Snack		*	Hot Dog	¥80	
	Kintetsu-Kanko	Snack		*			
	Snow Brand Milk Products	Snack		*	Sandwich, Hamburger		
	Prima Snack	Snack		*	Hamburger ¥100 Fried Chicken ¥100		
Monorail Japanese Garden Station	Suntory Corner	Snack		*			
Monorail Wednesday Plaza Station	"Kaga" Sushi	Snack		*	Inarizushi ¥150 Hyakumangoku Noodle ¥130		
	Snow Brand Milk Products	Snack		*	Sandwich, Hamburger		
Museum of Fine Arts	Mitsukoshi	J	300	***	Sushi, Tempura, Sukiyaki		
	Mitsukoshi	W	300	***			
West Excursion Rest Area	Yama	Snack					
	Hatsukame	Snack					

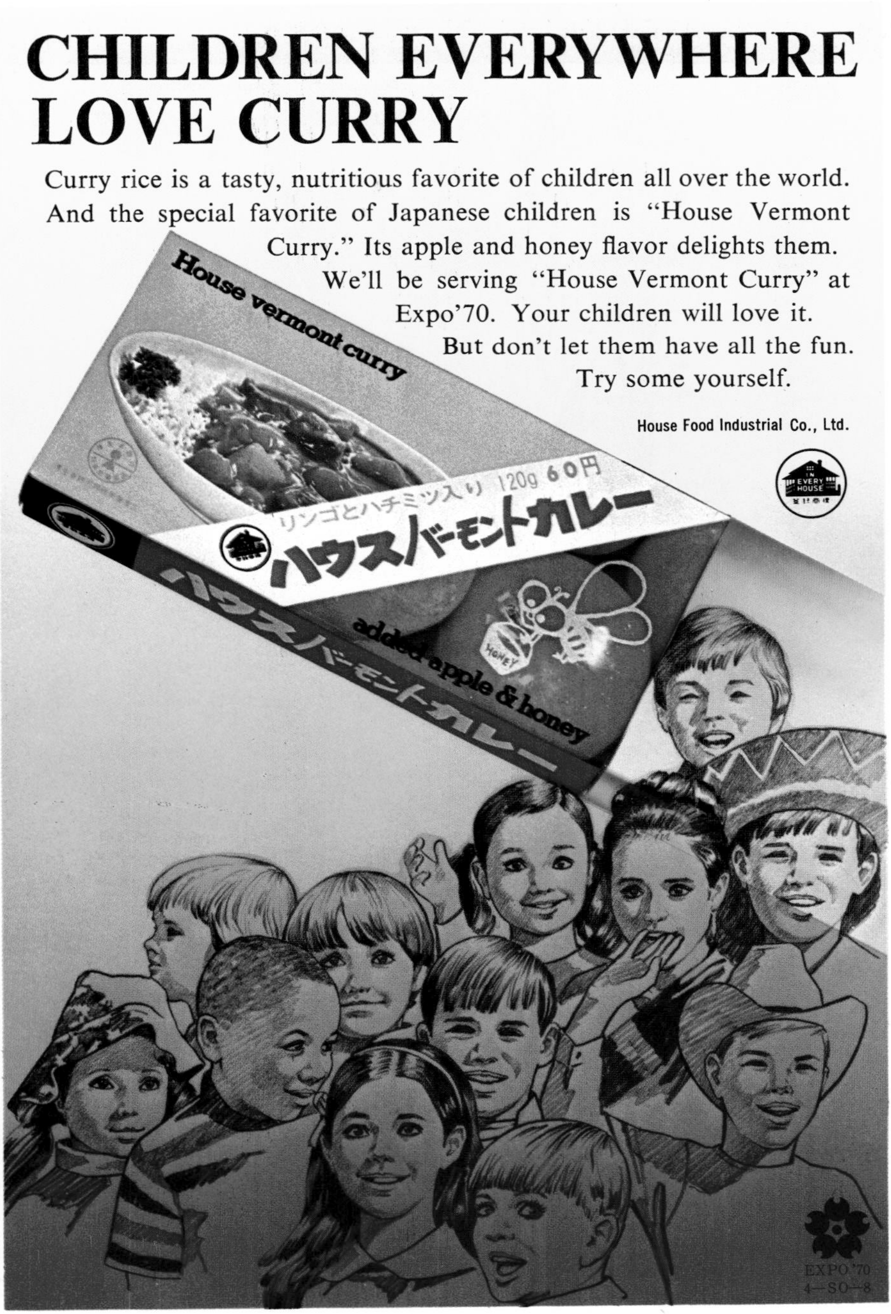

CHILDREN EVERYWHERE LOVE CURRY
Curry rice is a tasty, nutritious favorite of children all over the world. And the special favorite of Japanese children is "House Vermont Curry." Its apple and honey flavor delights them. We'll be serving "House Vermont Curry" at Expo'70. Your children will love it. But don't let them have all the fun. Try some yourself.
House Food Industrial Co., Ltd.
IN EVERY HOUSE
House vermont curry
リンゴとハチミツ入り 120g 60円
ハウスバーモントカレー
HONEY
added apple & honey
ハウスバーモントカレー
EXPO'70
4—SO—8

Restaurants in Pavilions

W: Western-style food
J: Japanese-style food
C: Chinese-style food

S: Self-service
T: Table-service

* ¥200–300 ** ¥300–400 *** ¥400–500

Pavilion	Type	No. of Seats	Price	Specialties	Service
Foreign Pavilions (in alphabetical order)					
Algeria		150		Cous-Cous, Wine	
American Park		500		Cafeteria, Steak House	
Argentina				Beef and Wine	
Belgium		260			S-T
British Columbia		Standing Seats		Fresh Fruit Juice & Hot Dog	
Bulgaria		180			
Burma		100		Authentic Burmese Food	
Ceylon		75		Ceylon Tea	
China		200		Authentic Chinese Cuisine	
Czechoslovakia		244		Pilsen Beer	
France		240		Cuisine française authentique	
Germany		390			
Hong Kong		210		Canton Dish	
India				Indian Curry	
Indonesia		200			
Iran		40		Coffee Shop	
Italy		213		Spaghetti, Noodle, Pizza	
Munich				Beer & Sausage	
Netherlands		200		Calf cutlet Dutch style; Herring, cheese and ham sandwiches	
New Zealand		120		Lamb Mutton Dish, Beer, Wine, Fish, Fruits.	
Pakistan		80		Choice delicacies Pakistani style	
Philippines					
Portugal		50		Wine	
Quebec		138			
Scandinavia		580		Bar-Salon-type	

Pavilion	Type	No. of Seats	Price	Specialties	Service
Switzerland		210		Dishes with Cheese from the Alps	
Turkey				Coffee Shop	
Uganda		30		Coffee and Tea	
U.S.S.R.		650		Russian, Gruziyan, Ukranian and other local dishes	

Japanese Pavilions (in alphabetical order)

Pavilion	Type	No. of Seats	Price	Specialties	Service
Chemical Industry	W	104	¥250—500		T
Fuji Group	W	652	**	Fried Chicken ¥300	S
Fujipan Robot	W	65	**		S
Furukawa	W	70		Sandwiches ¥200	S-T
Gas	W	88	***	Gratin Dish	T
Japanese Garden		50		Japanese Tea & Cakes	
Japanese Government		150			T
Kubota	J	36	*	Special Rice-Balls of Various Kinds	S
Livelihood Industry	WJC	259	¥80—1,000	Foreign-style Lunch ¥300	T
Local Autonomy	J	150	¥400—1,500	Tempura, Sukiyaki, Sushi, Unagi	T
Matsushita		50		Japanese Tea & Cakes	
Midori-Kan	J&W	200	¥50—300	Astrorama Lunch ¥300	S
Mitsubishi	W	120	**	Mitsubishi Lunch ¥300	S
Mitsui Group	W	105	¥100—2,000	Mixed Barbecue ¥400	T
Sanyo	W	70		Soft Ice Cream and Beverages to Eat	T
Suntory	W	50			

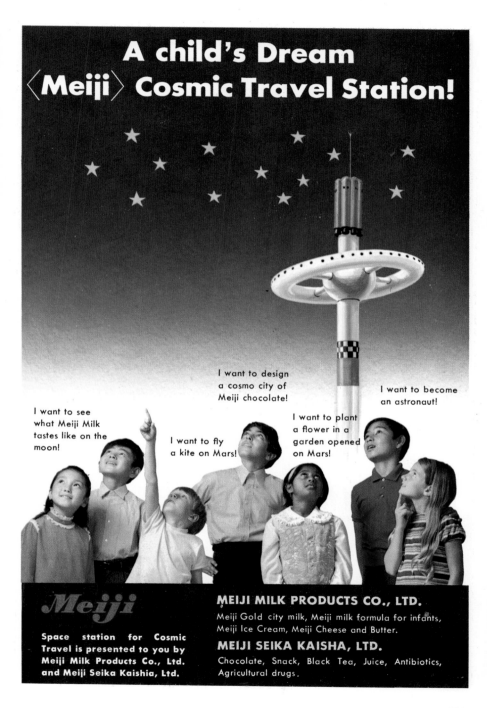

BE SMART-VISIT HANKYU

It takes you thirty years to visit every one of 300,000 stores in Osaka. It only takes thirty minutes to visit Hankyu wherever you are in this city. Same result you'll get: you'll find what you've wanted.

Hankyu, the largest department store in Osaka, is easily accessible from all major air and ground transportation and the site of Expo'70.

HANKYU DEPT. STORE

MAIN STORE:
UMEDA. OSAKA 06 (361) 1381
BRANCHES:
TOKYO-KOBE- SENRI

EXPOLAND
(Amusement Park)

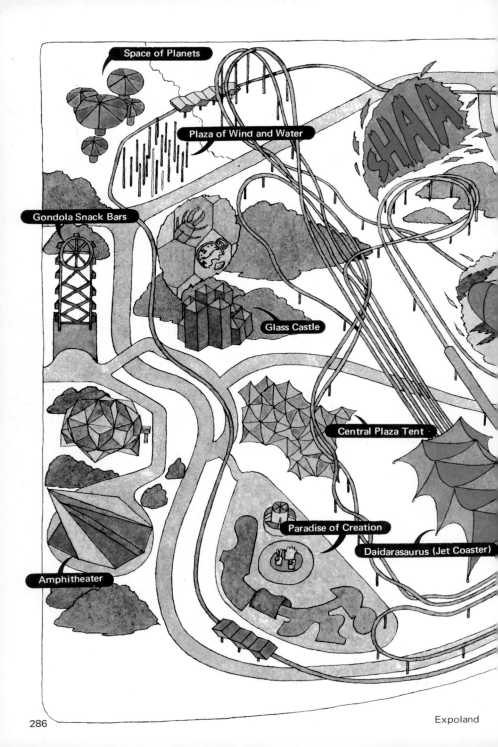

Space of Planets

Plaza of Wind and Water

Gondola Snack Bars

Glass Castle

Central Plaza Tent

Paradise of Creation

Daidarasaurus (Jet Coaster)

Amphitheater

Expoland

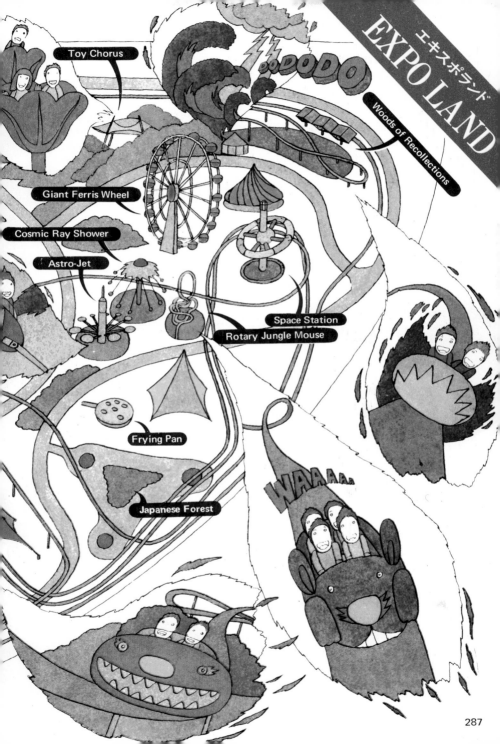

Expoland (Amusement Park)

Expoland is an amusement park — and more!

Its creators have divided it into six sections and have given each section a name. Fun and play is the idea throughout — but the emphasis is on creative enjoyment.

Plaza of Wind and Water

A forest of 66 thin, glass fiber poles. Five to 15 meters high (16 to 49 ft.) and all in bright colors they constantly move in the wind and are particularly striking when they are floodlit at night.

A "canal" with five fountain groupings runs through the area. A calm place to rest and relax.

From here a 30-meter-wide staircase takes you up to the Central Plaza.

Space of Planets

Surprise! At the entrance to Expoland, you will discover five huge red mushroom-shaped balloons as if for a jolly giant's birthday. They range up-to 30 meters — nearly 100 feet! — in diameter. And they are from 16 to 26 meters tall, looking as merry as you please. They represent the world of the unknown and appear as large shining planets when illuminated at night.

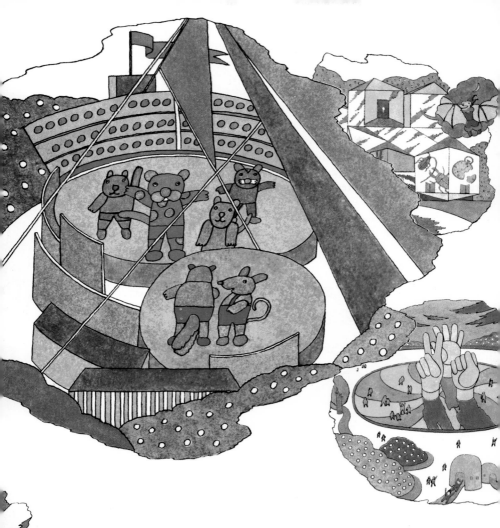

Land of One's Self

Here is a modern "Alice Through the Looking Glass" ... in the Glass Castle. Mirrors, glass, light and sound combine to offer an unusual experience. There are surprises everywhere. There's a room that changes itself ... another where everything appears topsy-turvy.

The "Paradise of Creation" is the name given to a special children's playground here. Everything is modeled after things of Old Japan. There are things to walk on, jump on, float on ... even a special garden for playing hide-and-seek. A visit here should be truly involving for a child.

The Expo Amphitheater is also located here. It is the site of many programs of special interest to children. For details, see page 238.

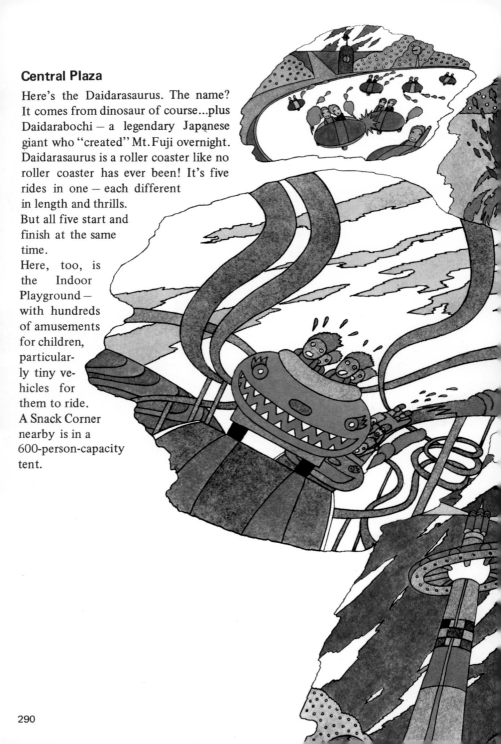

Central Plaza

Here's the Daidarasaurus. The name?
It comes from dinosaur of course...plus
Daidarabochi — a legendary Japanese
giant who "created" Mt. Fuji overnight.
Daidarasaurus is a roller coaster like no
roller coaster has ever been! It's five
rides in one — each different
in length and thrills.
But all five start and
finish at the same
time.

Here, too, is
the Indoor
Playground —
with hundreds
of amusements
for children,
particular-
ly tiny ve-
hicles for
them to ride.
A Snack Corner
nearby is in a
600-person-capacity
tent.

Ride Center

There's something here for everyone. The Space Station goes up 35 meters (115 ft.) inside a space-rocket-type tower. The Rotary Jungle Mouse revolves around a turntable and then dashes pell mell down its winding track. The Hurricane is like being on a ship during a storm. The Astrojet is like taking a space trip. Shooting the Rapids is just that — down a swift artificial stream. The Giant Ferris Wheel — 40 meters high (131 ft.) — goes around in 8 minutes and promises a grand view of all Expo from the top.

Woods of Recollections ,

A bit of fantasy. Where merry-go-round horses leave their circular confines and "romp" through flowers, forest, fountains and ponds. A Doll's Corner – with very special wagons to ride on. A Fun House where fairy tales come to life.

A forest made up of Japanese trees. Minirail. Locomotives. Live animals. Restaurants. Souvenir shops. And, just in case, a lost children's center!

Expoland

Laterna Magika (Magic Lamp)

Laterna Magika was performed, for the first time and with enormous success, at the 1958 World Exhibition in Brussels. Thereafter, it was received enthusiastically during a tour of many great world cities. It was also one of the highlights of Expo 67 in Montreal. Laterna Magika as an art form is a synthesis of theater, ballet and music combined with very advanced stage and lighting techniques; it is based on film projection simultaneous with live acting. The 60 performers and the 40-ton stage setting were brought from Czechoslovakia, where this revolutionary entertainment was discovered and developed.

294

WORLD EXPOSITIONS AND JAPAN

History of World Expositions

1853 "Crystal Palace" of New York World's Fair

1851 "Crystal Palace" of the first Great Exhibition

1851 — LONDON

This first Great Exhibition became famous for the "Crystal Palace," a revolutionary, 21-acre building of iron, glass and wood initially erected in Hyde Park. Included among a geat variety of new articles displayed were false teeth, artificial legs and a Colt revolver.

1853 — NEW YORK

This was the first world's fair held in America. Here, too, was erected a "Crystal Palace." The industrial age of Europe spread rapidly through the United States following this exposition.

1851 Visitors from the country at the first Great Exhibition

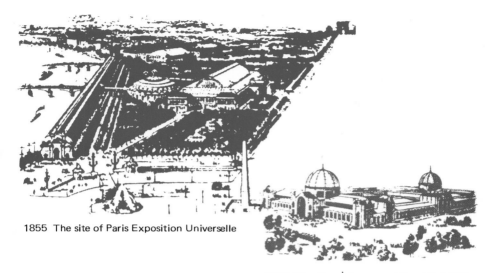

1855 The site of Paris Exposition Universelle

1862 The site of the second Great Exhibition

1855 – PARIS

Napoleon III was the force behind this Exposition Universelle. It centered on the "Industrial Palace" but a museum of fine arts was added. About 1,600 head of livestock were assembled and a special section was set up to display daily necessities, textiles and manufactured goods.

1851 Singer Sewing Machine

1851 Colt Revolver

1862 – LONDON

Though this exhibition was smaller in scale than the first one, articles designed to improve people's lives were prominent in the exhibits. In accordance with this new emphasis, a great variety of educational aids were featured.

1853 Otis Elevator at New York World's Fair

1862 Whitworth Drilling Machine

1862 New Printing Machine

1867 A view of Paris Exposition Site

1876 Buildings
at the Philadelphia Centennial

1873 The site of the Vienna Exposition

1867 — PARIS

Foreign buildings reflecting the color of their nationality gave an early example of a truly cosmopolitan world's fair atmosphere. Making their debut: electrical equipment, gas lamps, ball bearings. Krupp's huge gun, weighing 50,000 kilograms, drew particular attention. Japanese goods made their appearance, as well.

1873 — VIENNA

The exposition site was a beautiful forest park on the banks of the Danube. A lookout platform, gained by elevator, was constructed on the dome of the main building. Stage and music presentations were given and the Japanese Government participated officially for the first time.

1876–PHILADELPHIA

In addition to the usual main building at the Centennial Exposition, pavilions were built to house featured articles. Telephones, air-brake systems, dual-channel telegraphy, sewing machines and typewriters made their debut. Pullman coaches and sleeping cars also gained attention.

1867 Krupp's Huge Cannon

1876 Starting of Euris Engine

1867 Automatic Electromagnetic Power Generator

298

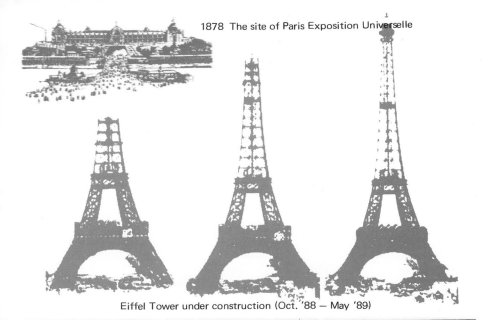

1878 The site of Paris Exposition Universelle

Eiffel Tower under construction (Oct. '88 — May '89)

1878 — PARIS

Telephones and type-writers, displayed for the first time in Europe, attracted much interest. But one of the biggest features, with an aquarium, was a huge captive balloon which carried 50 persons 500 meters into the sky several times a day. It was decided to hold inter-national conventions at each world exposition henceforth.

1889 — PARIS

The 300-meter-high Eiffel Tower became a symbol of technology and a pre-cedent for the construction of a theme building at world's fairs. The exposi-tion was the first to use electric lamps to light the site; electrically-illuminat-ed fountains were a special feature.

1893 — CHICAGO

The globe's first elevat-ed electric railway was con-structed between Chicago itself and the World's Co-lumbian Exhibition. Enter-tainment was a big feature, with a grand Midway fea-turing a newfangled Ferris wheel and also Buffalo Bill's Wild West Show.

1878 Edison's Gramophone Record at Paris Exposition

1893 The Inside of the Chicago Columbian Exhibition

1889 Exposition Train

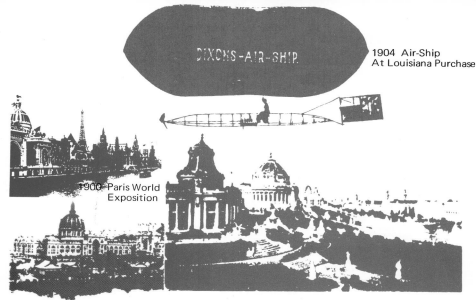

1904 Air-Ship
At Louisiana Purchase

1900 Paris World
Exposition

1893 Chicago Columbian Exhibition   1904 St. Louis World's Fair

1900 — PARIS

Enthusiasm for world expositions was unprecedented as 50 million people visited. Features included many bicycles, autos, X-ray equipment, wireless telegraphy, moving pictures backed by phonographic sound, Ferris' wheel for the first time in Europe and an illuminated "Water Castle" as well as a "Palace of Fantasy."

1904 — ST. LOUIS

"I'll meet you in St. Louis, Louis," and the big attractions at the fair were a display of 160 automobiles and an experiment in wireless telegraphy. As a forerunner of the fast-approaching aviation age, a special airfield was constructed.

1915—SAN FRANCISC

With culture as its nucleus, the Panama-Pacific Exposition, marking the opening of the Panama Canal, attempted to create an artistic harmony between architecture and sculpture, wall painting and color. It was the first world's fair in which some visitors flew by airplane and for which movie advertisements were used.

1900 Façade of Ceramics Palace

1904 Model-T Ford
at Louisiana Purchase

300

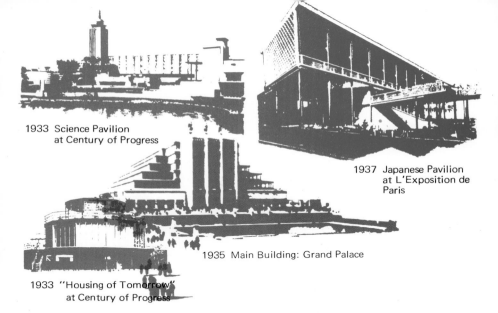

1933 Science Pavilion
at Century of Progress

1937 Japanese Pavilion
at L'Exposition de
Paris

1935 Main Building: Grand Palace

1933 "Housing of Tomorrow"
at Century of Progress

1933 – 34 CHICAGO

A theme was proclaimed, "Century of Progress," and a precedent was thus established. Pre-fabricated, windowless buildings with air-conditioning and artificial illumination radicalized interior display methods. The "Transparent Man" and a Gondola attached to a huge balloon were special attractions.

1935 – BRUSSELS

With the theme "Peace through Races," 350 buildings, large and small, and halls were built around a large 'palace.' There was also a huge stadium accommodating 75,000 people.

1937 – PARIS

The theme was "Exposition of Arts and Techniques" with the subtheme "Arts and Techniques in Modern Life." France introduced early developments in television. Picasso painted "Guernica" on the wall of the Spanish Pavilion.

1937 "Guernica" by Picasso at L'Exposition of 1937

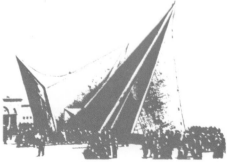

1958 The Man-made Satellite
at Brussels World Exhibition

1939 Aviation Pavilion at New York World's Fair, 1939—40

1958 Philips Pavilion designed by Le Corbusier
at Brussels Universal and
International Exhibition

1939—40—NEW YORK

1958 — BRUSSELS

"World of Tomorrow" was the theme and, in addition to the Nylon Pavilion, the tape recorder and television gained attention. A Time Capsul was sealed, to be only opened again in 5,000 years.

Based on the theme "Scientific Civilization and Humanism," the fair had as its symbol structure the Atomium. The Soviet Union exhibited the first man-made satellites and the United States built the world's largest free-span circular structure.

1939 The Television Set
at New York World's Fair

1958 "Atomium" at Brussels
Universal and International Exhibition

1967 Habitat 67 at Expo 67

1962 A view of the Century 21 Exposition with
Space Needle and Science Pavilion

1962 — SEATTLE

Century 21 Exposition.
"Mankind of the Space
Age" was the theme and
a 180-meter-high tower,
Space Needle, with a rotary observation deck atop,
was a special feature. A
1.9-kilometer monorail carried visitors from the city
center to the site and an
electronic computer system counted them.

1967 — MONTREAL

Canada's world exposition, nicknamed Expo67,
had as its theme "Man and
His World." New tent-type
buildings appeared and the
United States had a huge
geodesic dome. Display
methods became very
dynamic, with radical developments in motion picture
technique. Habitat 67 was
a grand and seemingly random collection of unitized,
prefabricated apartments.

1970 — OSAKA

1962 Space Costume
at Century 21 Exposition

1967 Multiple Screen at Expo 67

TODAY OUR WORLD EXPANDS

Welcome to Japan! It is a real pleasure for us, Dainippon Pharmaceutical Co., to make your acquaintance and thus to expand our world.

We serve all mankind through our fine medicines and pharmaceuticals. Closely working with leading American and European pharmaceutical companies, we have a large circle of friends around the world. Yet, it is a distinct pleasure to widen this circle by making your acquaintance.

At the same time, we look forward to enriching this relationship. As the oldest pharmaceutical company in Japan, we are in a unique position to minister to people's needs. Our experience and traditions coupled with our technology enable us to promise greater service in the future —to you—your neighbor—the world.

ESTD. 1897 **Ⓟ Dainippon Pharmaceutical Co., Ltd.**

25 Doshomachi 3-chome, Higashi-ku, Osaka
Tokyo Branch: 7, Nihonbashi Honcho 2-chome, Chuo-ku, Tokyo

Japan and World Expositions
──── Parallels in History ────

World expositions have been with us now, in varying intervals, for nearly 120 years. They have gone by many names: Great Exhibitions, World's Fairs, Expositions Universelles and, in Japanese, Hakurankai. Now "universal and international exhibitions" seem to have settled on a universal and international name, Expo, thanks to Montreal's Expo 67.

But this history of world expositions has been paralleled by that of Japan, both histories leading inevitably to Osaka's EXPO'70. Only 16 years after the first world exposition was held, the Emperor was restored as the actual head of Japanese government; a constitution followed and Japan hurdled her long feudalism to plunge whole-heartedly into the modern technological age.

World expositions were there to introduce Japan to her fellow nations from which she had been isolated so long. Also to introduce them to Japan. And as Japan enthusiastically participated in these world expositions, the call went up for Japan to host a gala fair of her own. What follows is history.

In 1851, on the eve of Japan's break with a 200-year-old policy of isolation, the first Great Exhibition was held in London, England. Two years after the Exposition ended, Commodore Perry from the United States sailed into the port of Uraga and dramatically altered the course of Japan's history.

First Japanese at Exposition

During the reign of the Tokugawa shoguns, a first mission was sent to the United States in 1860. One year later another mission was sent to Europe and the Japanese were thus first able to witness an Exposition, in London.

Japanese products, on a small and informal scale, were exhibited — mostly paper and wooden articles ordered from Japanese merchants by the British Consul or by foreign merchants in Yokohama. The relationship between Japan and World Expositions had begun.

Participation in the Exposition at Paris

For the World Exposition at Paris in 1867 the Japanese government formally sent for the first time representative products to be displayed. A Japanese Pavilion was erected; Japanese lacquerware, ceramics and paper products won scores of prizes. Kurimoto Akinokami, a member of the Tokugawa Shogunate, first translated "exposition" into Japanese and "hakurankai" became the term used ever since.

Participation at Vienna

The first participation for the Meiji government of Japan in an international exposition was at Vienna in 1873. With great success, Japan sent its usual products and also displayed on a large scale the customs and practices of the Orient, then almost totally unknown to Europeans.

In industry, Japan was almost completely dependent upon Western technology and machinery. Wishing to become independent, it decided to include among the 77 delegates to the Vienna Exposition 66 technical engineers. These experts not only viewed the technical advances on display at the Exposition but also visited work shops and factories, staying on after the Exposition. Back in Japan, these men wrote a monumental, 96-volume Report on the Exposition that was not only filled with precious technical information but also opened the door to the manufacturing of a whole host of new products.

Domestic Exposition

After the Exposition in London, domestic expositions became popular in Japan. To stimulate business within the country, the first Domestic Industrial Exposition was held in Tokyo in 1877 with many favorable results. By 1903, the fifth exposition was being held; the electric train made its debut at the fourth one, Canada opened a pavilion at the fifth. The size of the expositions grew. In 1907 there was still another Tokyo Industrial Exposition. The Taisho Exposition in 1914, the Peace Commemoration Exposition in 1922, the Osaka Exposition and many others followed.

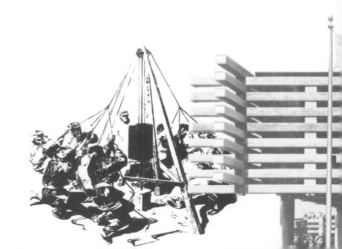

Steps toward an International Exposition

Although through the years Japan took part in the International Expositions held in other countries, and in 1910 participated in the Japan-Britain Exposition in London, as early as 1877 the desire to stage an international exposition in Japan was being felt — first voiced by Tsugumichi Saigo, Minister of Agriculture and Commerce. According to certain documents, specialists were invited from the United States in 1907 to give an opinion on the feasibility of an International Exposition in Japan. The advice was to wait another 10 years.

In 1928, 35 nations met in Paris to sign a Convention concerning International Exhibitions. Japan was among the signers. By 1930, Japan was ready to meet the demands for staging an international exposition. The Japanese government formally requested to have a 1940 Exposition in Tokyo to commemorate the 2,600th year of the country's foundation. Preparations were under way — and brought suddenly to a standstill when war broke out.

Dream Comes True

Because of the war and its aftermath, relations between Japan and the International Exhibitions Bureau were severed. But in 1963 the organization again requested Japan's participation. A certain self-confidence engendered by the success of the Tokyo Olympics promoted Japan once again to consider hosting an international exposition. In January of 1965, Japan ratified the Convention concerning International Exhibitions thus becoming the 32nd member nation. In that year it made formal application to hold a 1970 World Exposition in the Senri Hills near Osaka city. The following September the proposal was accepted and Japan became the third nation since the war to host a "general exhibition of the first category."

ENJOY A HEARTY WELCOME AT EXPO'70 AND HANSHIN

Hanshin Department Store, conveniently located in front of Osaka Station of the National Railways, is closer to the EXPO'70 site than all other department stores.

1 Umeda, Kita-ku, Osaka

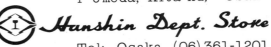
Hanshin Dept. Store

Tel: Osaka (06) 361-1201

Osaka and Its Environs

SUITA City — the Seat of EXPO'70

(Population 250,000; area 36.6 square kilometers).

Suita was formerly a collection of rice paddies and a marshalling yard of the National Railways. However, with the construction of the apartment complexes of Senri New Town, it is rapidly becoming a modern city. Since many workers and students living in Suita commute to Osaka, the city is a satellite of Osaka. With the opening of Expo, various city plans have been accelerated, and Suita is looking forward to being a city of beauty as well as of comfort.

OSAKA (Population 3,110,000; area 202 square kilometers).

Osaka, at the mouth of the Yodo River, is Japan's greatest commercial and industrial city. At the beginning of its history, it had been the Emperor's residence. During the Feudal Ages, Toyotomi-Hideyoshi built Osaka Castle where all activities were centered. With the fall of the castle, the shogunate power over the country passed to the Tokugawas and the center of power was moved to Edo (Tokyo). For the next 400 years, Osaka flourished chiefly as a merchant town, developing a peculiar tradesmen's culture.

While continuing its long history as a great center of merchandising, the city developed new industries quickly after World War I, concentrating mainly on the manufacture of textiles and machinery.

Canals and moats cut through the city, and with close to 1,500 bridges, one was reminded of the streets of Amsterdam. However, in recent years, this aspect has undergone a complete change. The construction of elevated highways and the increase of tall building have changed the skyline of the city so much that even long-time residents sometimes get lost.

Due to the tremendous motorization of Japan, Osaka is linked by super highways to Kobe in the west and the great cities of Kyoto, Nagoya, Yokohama, and Tokyo to the east. Even the old railway facilities have changed and now the New Tokaido Line trains can travel the distance of 553 kilometers to Tokyo in three hours. Jet planes reach Tokyo in only 45 minutes. In 1969, Osaka International Airport was remodeled. Expansion and consolidation was completed and many international flights come in and out of Osaka.

For a quick view of the city, a bus tour with an English-speaking guide is recommended. Rates for an afternoon tour are about $5.00, a night tour costs about $12.00. In this, the capital of hard workers on one hand, and pleasure-loving, food-loving people on the other, entertainment centers and drinking and dining areas become very active and brilliant neon lights brighten the night. You can experience the energy of Osaka yourself, particularly on the night tour.

KOBE (Population 1,240,000: area 534 square kilometers).

Backed by a line of mountains and facing the calm Inland Sea, Kobe is a beautiful harbor city with a moderate climate. It has been a commercial port for 800 years. After 1867, it experienced great growth as a trading port. Many foreign ships anchor in the harbor and foreign trading firms line the seashore. To a Japanese, this city is filled with the exotic. Kobe Beef means delicious beef; Western-style food, bread, and candies became popular more quickly here than in other cities.

This city and its surroundings, sandwiched between the sea and mountains, may be the ideal place to rest after a busy tour of EXPO'70.

KYOTO (Population 1,400,000: area 610 square kilometers).

There is probably no foreigner who has visited Japan and missed seeing Kyoto. This is because other cities have been Europeanized and Americanized, but Kyoto remains a genuine Japanese city. In 784 the Emperor established the capital in Kyoto which remained the capital for a thousand years.

Even after the Tokugawa Shogunate moved its government offices to Edo (Tokyo), it remained the home of the Emperor.

Fortunately, Kyoto being situated inland in a basin, it has experienced few natural disasters. It was spared from air raids during the war and escaped other man-made disasters. Thus many old artifacts still exist. Plan a leisurely visit to Kyoto Gosho, Nijyo Castle and other old shrines and temples and the Japanese gardens. Bus tours with English-speaking guides give you a glimpse of everything, and help you select the places to see again when you have more time. To really enjoy and appreciate the old temples and gardens, you should spend at least a half-day at each spot. Unlike the ancient ruins of Pompeii, the Acropolis or the Kiza, Kyoto's historic relics still live today.

Kinkakuji (The Golden Pavilion), Ginkakuji (The Silver Pavilion), Daitokuji, Koetsuji, Chionin, Nanzenji, Heian Shrine, Shugakuinrikyu, Daigoji, Ryoanji, Saihoji, Ujibyodoin, and others too numerous to mention are "musts" in Kyoto.

The cherry blossoms are especially beautiful at the Heian Shrine and Daigoji in the spring. The heart of the Japanese people is concealed in the rock garden of Ryoanji. For a taste of Japanese cultural activities, Kyoto is ideal for the Tea Ceremony, the Noh Drama, and classical Japanese dances.

Unlike Osaka whose people were merchants, Kyoto was filled with Imperial nobles. Their traditional arts and food have been passed on, which makes Kyoto an ideal place to taste elegant Japanese food, in authentic settings. You can buy fine art work for gifts. For those on a limited budget who desire inexpensive souvenirs, there is a wide range of Japanese clothing and miscellaneous articles to choose from, not only in Kyoto, but in Osaka, Kobe and other places. Also, there are tax-free shops for tourists in every big central shopping area.

The hearts of the common people can be understood in the festivals which have been held for hundreds of years. To a foreigner, a festival is interesting not only because it is something novel, but also because it lets him peek into a corner of the heart of the people. Kyoto is the capital of festivals. Special dates are

mountains. Traces of its grandeur can still be seen.

Along with the indigenous belief in the Gods of Nature which dates from earliest Japan, a new religion, Buddhism, came from the Chinese continent and began to flourish under the patronage of the Imperial Household. An awesome bronze Buddha 16.22 meters high is a symbol of this period.

reserved for each event; therefore, check the schedule to be sure you can see the festival of your choice.

The Great Buddha and Shrines
(Nara, the old capital — 30 minutes from Osaka by express train).

Nara, like Kyoto, is an old capital city. About 1,250 years ago, a magnificent capital for the Emperor was started in the basin surrounded by green

The ancient wooden structure housing the Great Buddha is the world's largest. Within the Todaiji in which the Great Buddha is seated, there are also the Minami Daimon, Shoro and Hokkedo. The Nigatsudo is famous for the water fetching procession at midnight in the Second Month of the old calendar, March 13th of the present calendar. Shosoin, and numerous other Buddhist figures along with fine arts

and industrial art works designated as National Treasures are housed in buildings which themselves are National Treasures.

Not only are there National Treasures in the Todaiji, but also the Five Story Pagoda within the Kofukuji, which is reflected in the Sarusawa Pond. Shinyakushiji, Hokkeji, Toshodaiji in the suburbs of Nishinokyo, Yakushiji and others, make Nara the storehouse of National Treasures.

When you tire a bit of the Buddhas and fine art works, look towards the Torii of the Kasugataisha and you will find a peaceful sight in the lanterns (lighted at the Spring Equinox and on August 15th) between the rows of Japanese cedar trees and the many tame deer nudging at passersby.

This area is called Yamatoji, and the origins of the Japanese are traced to this site. The highlight of a tour of Yamatoji is probably the Horyuji because its wooden frame has amazingly survived the damage by fire. It has been repaired over and over for the past 1,300 years. You should not miss seeing this temple, not only because it is old, but also, because of the beauty of the altar and the splendor of the cultural treasures, sculptures, paintings, and industrial art works contained in it.

Left:
A Statue of Buddha in Nara
by Kenkichi Sugimoto

A Glimpse of Modern Japan

The land of geishas and cherry blossoms is changing. High-speed expressways, pizza parlors, skyscraper office buildings and American movies may be the first thing that catches a visitor's attention. But soon he will notice that Western things have not yet supplanted Oriental customs and traditions. Instead, East and West live side by side in Japan, which is the unique appeal in 1970 of this country's big cities.

The daytime crowds are office workers dressed in Western suits and miniskirts. But in the evening, the men often change to kimono for watching TV at home. And on special occasions, the young girls, giggling in coffee shops over a soft drink, proudly wear a kimono for which they paid two months' salary.

Families who still prefer rice, soup and pickled vegetables for breakfast now use an electric rice cooker that saves the housewife an hour's sleep in the morning. The Japanese may be dextrous with a fork when eating western food, but for a Japanese meal, only chopsticks will do.

Japan is an archipelago of four main islands – Hokkaido, Honshu (where Osaka and Tokyo are situated), Shikoku and Kyushu – plus thousands of smaller islands, in a total area about equal to California. It lies on a volcanic belt, which accounts for the many earthquakes that occasionally, as in 1923, cause immense destruction.

Since 80% of the land is mountainous, Japan's 100 million people crowd into the arable portions, giving this country on the average the highest population density in the world. The crowding, on streets, highways, houses, theaters and stores, impresses Western visitors as almost phenomenal.

The average Japanese family, of 3.8 persons, is housed in a space of 730 square feet. Ferro-concrete, multi-family apartment buildings, whose exteriors resemble Western housing projects, are now being constructed in increasing numbers. A sitting room in Western style, furnished with chairs and tables, is becoming popular. But the interior of most Japanese homes, even newly-built ones, still presents a unique picture. The floors are most often "*tatami*" straw mats. Shoes are taken off at the entrance, so as not to dirty or damage the tatami. The living-dining room becomes the bedroom at night, when mattresses (futon) are taken out of their storage closet and spread on the tatami floor. Central heating is a rarity; instead, the rooms are heated as needed by kerosene or gas space heaters. Although 90.5% of all homes now have washing machines and 89.4% have electric refrigerators, the size of these appliances is about a half that of U.S. appliances, to suit the smaller dimensions of the Japanese home. 94% of all homes have TV sets.

Japan's standard of living is definitely on the rise, visible in these appliances, in the increasing consumption of meat, in the greater amount of money the people are spending on clothing and leisure. Predictions have been made that Japan will have the world's highest standard of living by

the year A.D. 2000. Right now, although Japan's gross national product ranks third, the standard of living is 20th among the nations.

Japan's spectacular recovery after World War II is called a miracle of the 20th century, although her industrial development brings its own price of industrial problems such as air pollution and over-urbanization.

Family life is changing, too. The multi-generation household is now giving way to the narrower circle of

Although Japanese must surely be one of the world's most difficult languages to read (two phonetic syllabaries of 46 characters each, plus a

parents and children. Wives, according to the Constitution at least, are equal to their husbands. Women have the right to vote, and 9 million women now hold jobs outside their homes.

minimum of 1,800 Kanji characters taken from the Chinese), Japan's literacy rate is still among the highest in the world. Daily newspapers have a total circulation of 45 million. Nine

A Glimpse of Modern Japan

years of school are compulsory, and attendance is 99.9%.

The post-war Constitution of Japan provides for democratic government divided into legislative (bicameral), executive and judicial branches. Japan's parliament is called the Diet. For the past two decades, the party system has been dominated by the Liberal-Democrats, the opposition resting in the Socialists, Democratic Socialists, Communists and Komeito.

His Majesty the Emperor of Japan, once regarded as the descendant of the Sun Goddess, is now, according to the Constitution, a symbol of the unity of the Japanese people. He is the 124th emperor of the Imperial line that has reigned since the beginning of Japan's history. He is also an expert marine biologist.

Next in line to succeed the Emperor is H.I.H., Crown Prince Akihito, who now has three children.

The Emperor has four other living children. The Imperial Family lives in the heart of Tokyo, in a palace surrounded by 250 acres of land.

Tokyo is the world's biggest city, but its population of 11 million people live in self-sufficient residential neighborhoods that are like villages, away from the downtown shopping-office areas. The best way to see the "real" Japan is to walk through one of these typical neighborhoods.

You can meet Japanese people on a personal level through the home-visit programs that have been set up in Tokyo, Kyoto, Kobe, Nagoya and Yokohama. The families who have volunteered to open their homes to foreign visitors speak English, French or German. You will be invited for an hour or two after dinner (around 7:30 p.m.), a visit which may lead to a friendly relationship and a glimpse into the "real Japan" of today. Information about this program can be obtained through the Japan Tourist Information Center, Kotani Bldg., 4 Yurakucho 1-chome, Chiyoda-ku,

Tokyo.

A shopping trip is another way to see modern life in Japan. The big department stores are organized on more or less the same plan, floor by floor; on the first floor, you will find an information counter with maps of the store in English, and English-speaking service clerks.

Hotel or shopping center arcades are another good source for shopping sprees. A fascinating collection of

A Glimpse of Modern Japan

shops and boutiques can be found on the smaller streets such as those behind the Ginza in Tokyo, or in the Shinsaibashi area in Osaka.

Japan is a shopper's paradise for such items as cultured pearls, textiles, pottery, porcelain, lacquerware, dolls, fans, bamboo utensils and furniture, cameras and optical goods, watches, transistor radios, umbrellas, cloisonne,

ivory, paper products, folkcraft and swords. Tourists are entitled to buy certain items tax-free, which means a discount up to 20 per cent. Inquire at your hotel. Antiques, curios and fine arts are also excellent buys, especially in Kyoto (Shinmonzen Street).

The sports and drama forms originated centuries ago are still going strong in modern Japan, along with baseball and imported musicals. There are six sumo tournaments a year, and

tourists would particularly enjoy watching an afternoon's match from a box seat. Judo, once a secret art of the samurai, karate and other martial arts are still taught and practiced.

Kabuki is a fascinating theatre form. An actress invented this style of drama in the 16th century, but somehow women were subsequently barred from its stage. So all the actors are men, though the female impersonators, with their movements, high voices, elaborate costumes and wigs, make their roles entirely believable. The story is usually high tragedy in slow motion, the actors dance their roles or speak in an unnatural but effective wail, while drums and shamisens provide a fitting background atmosphere.

Bunraku uses elaborate puppets manipulated by three men on stage. Even the puppet's eyes, mouth and facial expressions change with the script. A fourth man speaks the words, with a shamisen accompanist. Bunraku was developed in Osaka in the 17th century.

Noh players wear masks and their intense acting is heightened by the music of drums and flutes, a chanting chorus and the starkly simple backdrops.

The Imperial Household and Meiji Shrine schedule Bugaku performances twice a year. This theatre form, the oldest in Japan (dating back to the 9th century), is a super-stately ballet of magnificently costumed men; at the side of the platform sit musicians almost as elaborately dressed, singing and playing slow music.

The traditional visual arts of Japan still have a strong influence. The ancient scroll paintings, screens, woodblock prints, calligraphy and those artifacts that are considered national treasures (antique porcelain, pottery and household decorations) can be seen in museums. But artists nowadays still paint screens, scrolls and prints, while many Japanese families sit down on January 1 with brush and ink to produce their best possible specimen of calligraphy, as a lucky way to start the New Year.

The west shows its influence in the modern paintings and prints displayed in the dozens of small galleries, in the crowded schedule of concerts of Western music, with native or imported performers, of ballet and of drama.

The Japanese also like the brash revues inspired by Western productions. The Kokusai Theatre in Asakusa, Tokyo, features the world's longest Rockette-type line of girls, kicking in time to ear-splitting music; the program also offers spectacular staging feats such as waterfalls and blazing castles. A recent performance of the Takarazuka All-Girl Revue (Tokyo and Takarazuka City near Osaka) presented a musical play based on Wuthering Heights. The Nichigeki Theatre (Tokyo) changes its gaudy fare of skits, song and dance to suit the season.

Night life in Japan can mean many things, at many price levels. Western-style hotels have lounges where bands and combos provide good music for dancing. The neighborhoods of Akasaka, Roppongi, Shibuya, Shinjuku and Asakusa in Tokyo, and the Dotonbori in Osaka, are full of bars and restaurants that stay open late. Many night clubs have shows, some featuring foreign stars; here too, there is a cover charge. Many tour companies will guide the tourist through a smorgasbord of the high spots of big city night life.

Daytime tours are purposely varied to suit the range of tourist interests, from industrial trips through Osaka's main commercial enterprises, to arts and crafts trips through the small villages outside Tokyo. Your travel agents or the information desk of your hotel in Japan can advise you of the scope of tours offered.

Painting on pages 314—315:
Red Leaves at Toganoo, Kyoto
by Kaii Higashiyama

Painting on pages 316—317:
Cool of the Evening
(Kyoto's Shugaku-in Detached Palace)
by Kaii Higashiyama

A Glimpse of Modern Japan

資生堂化粧品

SHISEIDO
COSMETICS
TOKYO · NEW YORK · PARIS

At the Table — Japanese Taste

Japanese food is truly exotic. Sampling it should be one of the highlights of your visit. Don't miss this opportunity to give yourself a real taste treat.

In working up an appetite for Japanese food, remember that your taste buds and stomach must be the judge. Don't let your eyes scare you away from a delicious tidbit just because it doesn't look good. Don't be put off by an explanation that describes Japanese food in unappetizing ways.

A case in point is sashimi, which most people call raw fish. This creates a picture of biting through scales, fins and bones while the fish squirms in your grasp. Such is not the case. The secret of sashimi lies in the way the cook slices the fish and in the soy sauce which you spice to your own taste with a local relish called wasabi. If you really like fish, give sashimi a try. Chances are that you will like it. Beer or heated sake goes well with sashimi. If you prefer, restaurants will serve cold sake.

Sukiyaki

Sukiyaki is the Japanese dish with the widest international appeal. Thin slices of beef are mixed with Japanese vegetables. These include onions, vermicelli (shirataki) and bean curd (tofu). Everything is cooked in a shallow pan with a sauce made of sweet sake, soy sauce and sugar. Each diner helps himself from the cooking pan, placing his portion in his own dish to let it cool. The sukiyaki can be dipped into a beaten egg to enhance the flavor. Rice is usually served towards the end of the meal, but may be ordered with the sukiyaki.

Tempura

Tempura, different kinds of fish and vegetables fried in deep oil, is delicious and gives some familiar foods a delightful new taste. Shrimp, cuttle fish and shell fish are among the varieties used. When eating tempura, you dip it into a sauce made of grated Japanese radish (daikon), dried bonito stock, sweet sake and soy sauce. The grated radish adds to the taste and helps digestion.

If you enter a first-class tempura restaurant, put yourself in the hands of the cook. This is usually less expensive and assures a steady flow of delightful morsels.

Sushi

Sushi is a Japanese favorite which was developed a few hundred years ago. It varies in ingredients, shape and taste according to the locality in which it was developed. Boiled rice is flavored with a little vinegar and salt. Sugar is sometimes added. After it is cooled, it is served in a variety of ways with sashimi, shell fish, shrimp and cuttle fish. A very popular styles, nigiri-zushi, which originated in Tokyo while the city was still called Edo, has the slice of fish placed on top of the ball of rice. Eggs, cucumbers and "nori" are other ingredients. Nori is actually sea weed, but don't let your ears fool you. It is a delightful food seasoner. Norimaki, rice and vegetables rolled in nori, is called by some the Japanese sandwich.

Kabayaki

Kabayaki is the Japanese name for roasted eels. These are a delicacy and many restaurants specialize in serving them. The head and bones are removed and the body sliced and broiled over a charcoal fire. Afterwards it is garnished with a thick sauce, roasted, and eaten while hot. A good way to introduce yourself to kabayaki is to order a dish called "unagi donburi." This is a bowl of rice topped with slices of roasted eel in portions that let you savor the flavor.

For your Speaking Pleasure

You wish to add to the pleasure of your trip by mastering a few everyday Japanese expressions. Fine. The expressions are quite easy to memorize. However, success in using them depends almost completely on your pronunciation. Japanese pronunciation is fairly easy. Yet, if homegrown accents creep in, they can make expressions completely unintelligible.

Japanese does not have letters. It has signs which correspond to the sound of syllables. These sounds never change. If you pronounce them as the Japanese do, your ability to communicate will expand considerably. Skipping the full semester course, we offer some general rules which should contribute to your speaking pleasure.

The basic Japanese sounds are pronounced approximately as follows:
"a" (ah) "i" (tick) "u" (rook) "e" (wreck) "o" (more) "g" (sometimes as in 'get' usually at the beginning of words, and sometimes as the "ng" in

'sing' in the middle.)
No matter what consonant precedes these sounds, they don't change.
In Japanese each syllable receives the same stress.
Long vowels are doubled.
Double consonants are doubled, as in the English word "unnatural."

A suggestion. When Japanese sounds are written in letters, one set is written "ra, ri, ru, re, ro." However, Japanese does not have the pure "r" sound. The English "l" is closer to the correct Japanese pronunciation. If you use the "l" sound instead of the "r", your Japanese will be easier to understand.

One last suggestion. Don't jitterbug with Japanese, waltz with it. Smoothly. Gracefully. The phrase for "Thank you" is written "Arigato gozaimasu." Say, Ahligahto gozahimahsu. That lettering may look funny, but if you say it smoothly, your pronunciation won't be.

324

Greetings

*Good morning.	Ohayō.
*Hello.	Konnichi wa.
	(used during the day)
*Good evening.	Komban wa.
*Welcome.	Yōkoso.
*Hi.	Yā.
	(used by young men only)
*Good-bye	Sayōnara, or Sainara (Osaka)
*Good night.	Oyasumi nasai.
*Good-bye, sir.	Shitsurei shimasu.
*So long.	Jā, mata.
(Bye, now.)	
*Fare ye well.	Saraba.
	(now used in jest only)
*See you again.	Mata aimashō.
*Please come again.	Mata dōzo.
*Hey! Say!	Chotto. Moshi-moshi.
*Congratulations!	Omedetō.

Do you speak English?

*Do you speak English?	Eigo hanashi masuka?
*Do you understand me?	Wakari masuka?
*Does anybody here speak English?	Dareka eigo hanaseru hito imasenka?
*Where can I find somebody who speaks English?	Dokokani eigo hanaseru hito imasenka?
*I don't understand you.	Wakarimasen.

How do you do.
How are you?

*How do you do.	Hajime mashite.
*How are you?	Gokigen ikaga (desuka)?
*Say, what's new?	Yā dōdai? or Dōdane?
*How're you feeling?	Genki?
*I'm fine. Thank you.	Genki desu.
*My name is John Smith.	John Smith desu, or John Smith to mōshimasu.

For your Speaking Pleasure

Help!

*Help!
*Someone come quick!
*First-aid station.
*My kid got hurt!
*My wife isn't feeling well.

Tasukete!
Dareka hayaku kite!
Kyū-kyū jo.
Kodomo ga kegashita!
Kanai ga byōki desu.

Thank you. Excuse me.
Please. Yes. No.

*Thank you.

*Thanks a lot.
*Thanks.
*Thank you very much indeed.
*You're welcome.
  Not at all.
*No thank you.
*Excuse me, or I'm sorry.

*Please.
*Please go right ahead.
*Yes.
*Yes, of course.
*No.
*Certainly not.

Arigatō.
Ōkini. (Osaka, Kyoto, Kobe)
Dōmo arigatō.
Dōmo.
Dōmo arigatō gozai mashita.
Iie.
Dō itashimashite.
Iya, kekkō.
Gomen nasai.
Shitsurei.
Dōzo.
Dōzo, dōzo.
Hai (or Ē).
Ē, mochiron.
Iie. Chigaimasu.
Iya, dame dame.
Akan, akan. (Blunt refusal used by Osakans
            meaning "Nothing doing.")

Who? What? Where? Which?
When? What time? How much?

*Who?	Dare? or Donata?
*Who're you?	Anata donata? or Anata wa donata desuka?
*What?	Nani?
*What's this?	Kore nani? or Korewa nandesuka?
*Where are we now?	Koko doko? or Kokowa doko desuka?
*Where?	Doko?
*Which?	Dore?
*Where do I get a train ticket for Expo?	Bampaku yuki densha no kippu wa dokode kaimasuka?
*Does this train go to Expo?	Kono densha wa Bampaku yuki desuka?
*Which train is for Expo?	Bampaku yuki densha wa dore desuka?
*When?	Itsu?
*What time?	Nanji?
*What time do we get there?	Itsu sokoni tsukimasuka?
*How much?	Ikura? or Oikura?
*I'll take this.	Kore kudasai.
*Let me take a look at this (that).	Kore (Are) misete kudasai.

For Your Speaking Pleasure

COMPENDIUM
OF
DATA

Japan World Exposition

Honorary President: H.I.H. Crown Prince Akihito

President: Eisaku Sato

Commissioner General of the Japanese Government: Toru Haguiwara

Officials and directors of
The Japan Association
For The 1970 World Exposition

President (Permanent Director):
Taizo Ishizaka

Vice Presidents (Permanent Directors):
Shozo Hotta
Yoshishige Ashihara
Goro Inoue
Shigeo Nagano
Yoshimaru Kanno

Permanent Directors:
Tadashi Adachi
Shinobu Ichikawa
Gisen Sato
Kaoru Chuma

Secretary General (Permanent Director):
Shunichi Suzuki

Executive Director (Permanent Director):
Tatsusaburo Satoi

Directors:
Shiro Akabori
Koichiro Asakai
Masashi Isano
Satoshi Isozaki
Heitaro Inagaki
Seisuke Inada
Junzo Imamichi
Kanji Ueda
Kogoro Uemura
Takio Ouda
Toru Osawa
Masao Ohashi
Ryozo Okuda
Daizo Odawara
Saburo Kajiwara
Motohiko Kanai
Fujitaro Kanasashi
Seiji Kaya
Torao Kawazu
Kazutaka Kikawada
Takeo Kitajima
Hidezaburo Kurushima
Mikine Kuwahara
Ataru Kobayashi
Shoji Koyama
Shiho Sakanishi
Takeshi Sakurada
Tatsuo Suyama
Seiichiro Takahashi

Minoru Takita
Taro Takemi
Satoru Tanaka
Motoo Tsuchikawa
Kiyoshi Tomii
Soichi Tominaga
Heidayu Nakagawa
Yasujiro Nakamura

Torazo Ninagawa
Kinichiro Nozaki
Kichihei Hara
Takashi Hirayama
Shintaro Fukushima
Toshikatsu Horii
Kenzo Horiki
Teizo Horikoshi
Yoshinori Maeda
Hiroshi Mizoguchi
Tatsuo Miyazaki
Kunitake Muroga
Seihachiro Yagi
Daigoro Yasukawa
Genzaemon Yamamoto
Haruo Yamamoto
Yuichi Yuasa
Seizo Yoshimura
Shigeru Yonezawa
Naoji Yorozu

Auditors:
Takashi Yokota
Rokuro Tsuda

Chief Secretary:
Teizo Horikoshi

Secretaries:
Toshio Morioka
Tetsuro Nakagawa
Hisatsugu Tokunaga
Kyonosuke Ibe
Eiji Kageyama
Naraichi Tanaka
Susumu Shimomura

Members of Expert Committees

Theme Committee: Shiro Akabori
Masaru Ibuka
Jiro Osaragi
Saburo Ohkita
Seiji Kaya
Shigeki Kaizuka

Takeo Kuwabara
Ayako Sono
Kenzo Tange
Seiichi Tohata
Masataka Toyoda
Saburo Matsukata
Shigeharu Matsumoto
Ryu Murayama
Hideki Yukawa

Information and Publicity Committee:
Kozo Kawakami
Kimiji Ishikawa
Kosuke Katsuno
Kozaburo Odanaka
Hidetoshi Kato
Manabu Kanematsu
Nagamasa Kawakita
Shigeo Kimura
Taiji Nakamura
Saburo Sakai
Ayako Totsuka
Fumio Nishisaka
Yasuhiro Naito
Eijiro Fujise
Hideo Matsuyama
Nobuo Motoyoshi
Susumu Eijiri

Art Exhibition Committee:
Takaaki Matsushita
Michiaki Kawakita
Atsuo Imaizumi
Ryoichi Imamura
Teruo Ueno
Jo Okada
Osamu Kurata
Ryuken Sawa
Masaru Sekino
Kenzo Tange
Zenryu Tsukamoto
Yoshinobu Masuda
Chisaburo Yamada
Jiro Yoshihara

Expo Site Transportation Committee
Chairman: Kikumatsu Hirai
Tsurukichi Imaoka
Eiji Kometani
Isamu Saeki
Hideo Shima
Tsuyoshi Shirabe
Kenzo Tange
Kaichiro Nezu
Matsutaro Fujii
Yasushi Matsudaira
Yoshinosuke Yasoshima
Kaoru Mori

Finance Committee
Chairman: Kogoro Uemura

Permanent Committee:
Chohei Asada
Yoshishige Ashihara

Tadashi Adachi
Masashi Isano
Shinobu Ichikawa
Goro Inoue
Yoshizane Iwasa
Kazuo Ueda
Kyubee Kanai
Katsuji Kawamata
Kiyoshi Kawarabayashi
Kazutaka Kikawada
Yoshio Sakurauchi
Kiichiro Sato
Wataru Tajitsu
Motoo Tsuchikawa
Takeo Terao
Mochinaga Nakagawa
Shigeo Nagano
Sohei Nakayama
Kanichiro Hirai
Keiichi Hirose
Shozo Hotta
Teizo Horikoshi
Konosuke Matsushita
Daigoro Yasukawa
Takashi Yokota

Executive Committee:
Kyonosuke Ibe
Eiji Kageyama
Ryojiro Kurita
Hiroshi Satani
Tatsusaburo Satoi
Tsutomu Shiwa
Kosaku Tachibana
Hisatsugu Tokunaga
Tetsuro Nakagawa
Nihachiro Hanamura
Masao Hama
Masaru Hayakawa
Yukio Hara
Shigeo Matsumoto
Mitsuyoshi Muneoka
Toshio Morioka
Seiichi Yamashita

Official Movie Production Committee:
Shinichi Abe
Shinbi Iida
Kunisuke Ito
Susumu Ejiri
Hidekuni Ohuchi
Taro Okamoto
Masaru Katsumi
Nagamasa Kawakita
Kunihiko Fukuhara
Takeo Kuwabara
Kenzo Tange
Suketaro Taguchi
Yutaka Tamura
Yoshitake Tsushima
Naoki Togawa
Soichi Tominaga
Michio Tokunaga
Tamotsu Inoue

Yoshiharu Matsumoto
Hideo Matsuyama

Construction Advisors:
Shigeru Ito
Masahiko Yokoyama
Kenzo Tohata
Ryo Tanahashi
Eika Takayama
Eiji Kometani
Akira Sato

Design Advisors: Masaru Katsumi
Iwataro Koike
Chiyo Tanaka
Zenichi Mano
Ryuichi Hamaguchi

Entertainment Advisors:
Hidemi Kon
Yoshinori Maeda
Junzo Imamichi
Rikie Suzuki
Ikuma Dan
Nagamasa Kawakita

Expo Hostess Guidance Advisors:
Fujiko Hoshino
Tomiko Sen
Charlotte Sata

Art Advisors: Seisuke Inada
Sueji Umehara
Namio Egami
Yukio Kobayashi
Hidemi Kon
Teiichi Hijikata
Shinjo Mochizuki
Yukio Yashiro
Shojiro Ishibashi
Noboru Goto
Kaichiro Nezu
Morisada Hosokawa
Jiro Enjoji

Display Design Advisors:
Katsuhei Toyoguchi
Isamu Kenmochi

Nucleus Facility Producer:
Kenzo Tange

Architects Cooperating with Producer:
Asao Fukuda
(Festival Plaza)
Kuniichi Hikotani
(Guest House)
Masato Ohtaka
(Main Gate)
Kiyonori Kikutake
(Tower, International
Bazar)
Hiroji Kamiya
(Grand Roof)
Arata Isozaki
(Equipments)
Machio Ibusuki
(Expo Hall)

Atsushi Ueda
(Viewing Stand)
Kiyoshi Kawasaki
(Expo Museum of Fine
Arts)
Kunio Kato
(Gate: East, West,
South, North)
Koichi Sone
(Moving Walk, Facilities
in Plazas)
Koichiro Nezu
(Association Hqr. Bldg.)
Shigehiko Sugi
(Press Center)

Exhibition Producer of Theme:
Taro Okamoto

Exhibition Sub-Producers of Theme:
Shigeomi Hirano
(Management)
Tomoshige Ono
(Administration)
Noboru Kawazoe
(Mid-air level)
Sakyo Komatsu
(Underground level)
Susumu Okada
(Projection of pictures)
Toshiro Mayuzumi
(Sound)
Kazuhiko Chiba
(Ground level, Tower)

Entertainment Producers:
Kunisuke Ito
Takeo Watanabe
Misa Watanabe
Nobuo Fukuhara

Official Record Movie Production Headquarters
General Producer: Suketaro Taguchi

General Director: Senkichi Taniguchi

Secretary-General: Tadashi Moriwaki

Personnel list of the Japan Association for the 1970 World Exposition

Secretary General and General Director, Operation Headquarters:
Shunichi Suzuki

Deputy Secretary General and Deputy General Director, Operation Headquarters:
Yuji Hirai
Toshio Miyano
′ Eiji Hamanaka

Deputy Secretary General and General Director, Public Relations Headquarters:
Nobuo Imaeda

Chief of Protocol of Expo Association:
Tatsuo Suyama

Deputy Chief of Protocol of Expo Association:
Naokazu Okuda

Director, Protocol Office:
Keiichiro Kawahira

Director, Secretariat Office:
Fumihiko Hiroyama

Director, Coordination Office and attached to Operation Headquarters:
Tamotsu Akimoto

Chief Inspector, Inspectors' Office and Director, Administration Bureau and attached to Operation Headquarters:
Tatsuji Hamada

Director, Finance Bureau and attached to Operation Headquarters:
Yasumitsu Aoyama

Director, Funds Procurement Bureau:
Shintaro Hyodo

Director, External Relations Bureau:
Shotaro Takahashi

Director, Exhibition Bureau:
Masao Tobita

Director, First Operations Bureau:
Masayasu Asa

Director, Second Operations Bureau:
Mitsuo Hayashi

Director, Entertainment and Recreation Bureau:
Hitoshi Nakanishi

Director, Public Safety and Service Bureau:
Tadayuki Takagi

Director, Transport and Visitors Bureau:
Toshio Ueshima

Chief of Engineering and Deputy General Director, Operation Headquarters and Acting Director, Construction Bureau:
Yasuo Yamamoto

Chief, Supply and Installation Division of Construction Bureau:
Setsuro Tamai

Director, Information and Publicity Bureau:
Yoshichika Fujita

Director, Overseas Information and Publicity Bureau: Takeo Komatsu

Director, Tokyo Office:
Haruo Okumura

Director, New York Office:
Kiyoshi Kimura

Director, Expo Museum of Fine Arts:
Soichi Tominaga

Deputy Director, Expo Museum of Fine Arts: Masanori Sakamoto

Commander in chief, Expo Guard Corps:
Katsumi Tabuchi

Steering Committee of the Commissioners General of Section

Chairman:	Canada
Vice-Chairman:	Burma
Reporter:	Belgium
Members:	U.S.A.
	U.S.S.R.
	Australia
	France
	United Kingdom
	Thailand
	Mexico
	Saudi Arabia
	Czechoslovakia
	Ivory Coast
	Tanzania
	India
	Chile

Commissioners General for EXPO'70 (as of February 20, 1970)

Country	Commissioner General	Deputy Commissioner General
Canada	Patrick Reid	Jean Octeau Jacques C. Vaast
Korea	Jun Sok Han	Jin Hong Kim Hun Shik Min
U.S.A.	Howard L. Chernoff	Paul A. Modic Harold O. Wright
China	Chin-Chow Chu	Nan Wan Yang Wu Yu Liang
Netherlands	Jozef M.L. Th. Cals	J.H. van Gemert
Zambia	Bonaventure D. Chileshe	Gwendoline C. Konie
U.S.S.R.	Boris A. Borisov	A.I. Golovkin L.V. Pasholikov
Belgium	Guy Daufresne de la Chevalerie	Daniel Ellegiers Audré de Ville de Goyet
Germany	Alfred E. Schulz	Kurt Daniel
Switzerland	Max Troendle	John Brunner Werner Sutter
New Zealand	John Lloyd Fenaughty	Colin B. Murray Douglas L. Hard
Australia	Thomas K. Morrison	William Worth Charles A. Allen
France	René Sanson	Jacques Lieury Pierre Viriot
Bulgaria	Avakum Branitchev	Angel G. Angelov
Kuwait	Fahad Al-Sarawi	Khalid Al Far Mohamed Adnan Da'adouch
United Kingdom	John Figgess	William Bentley E.W. Swaine
Cuba	Carlos Lechuga	José M. Diaz Mirabal Santiago Díaz Paz
Turkey	Danis Tunaligil	
Portugal	Manuel Duarte Gaspar	Ruy G. de Brito e Cunha
Thailand	Ananda Bhoocha-oom	Chamnong Phahulrat
Philippines	Victor A. Lim	Adelfa Caugma Jesus Tanchanco
Algeria	Mohamed Hachemi Hannouz	
Mexico	Fernando Gamboa	Joaquin Gomboa
Scandinavia	Sven A. Hansson	Arild Isegg
★ Denmark	* N. Arnth Jensen	
★ Finland	* Olle Herold	
★ Iceland	* Gunnar Fridriksson	
★ Norway	* Nils Fredrik Aall	
★ Sweden	* Kjell Öberg	
Ethiopia	Hapte Sellassie Taffesse	Tula Gula
Laos	Chau Nith Nokham	Phanh Ngaosivathn Thotsakan Insisiengmay
Burma	Ye Goung	U Chit Khine U Ba Aye
Greece	Frank H. Scolinos	George A. Sioris Constatine Haratsaris

Country	Commissioner General	Deputy Commissioner General
Dominican Republic	Hans Heinsen	
Saudi Arabia	Bakri S. Shata	Abdullah T. Dabbagh
Czechoslovakia	Miroslav Galuška	Ladislav Košťa
		Zdeněk Koudelka
Ceylon	Herbert Ernest Tennekoon	A.M. Jayashinha
		E.V. Melder
Ivory Coast	Pierre Billon	
Tanzania	Sebastian Chale	F.R.K. Etuttu
Indonesia	D. Ashari	IR. Adnan Kusuma
Ghana	Samuel Patrick Ofei Kumi	
Cyprus	Alecos Koupparis	
Madagascar	Andrianampy Ramaholimihaso	
Uganda	Azarias Baryaruha	Bogere Kivumbi Ssembatya
Singapore	Lam Peng Loon	Lim Chew Kuan
		Chan Chor Cheung
Pakistan	Jamshed R. Rahim	Mohammad Aslam
		A.A. Qazi
Gabon	Daniel Assoumou	Innocent Nzyengui
India	H.D. Shourie	Raghbir Dyal
Chile	Sergio Silva	Ricardo Hüe
Vatican	Yoshigoroo Taguchi	Yoshiyuki Furuya
		Atsushi Hayashi
Viet-Nam	Buu Tho	Nguyen Phuoc Doe
		Ngo Khac Thiew
Colombia	German Rodriguez F.	Nestr Zarate
Nepal	Prakash Chand Thakur	Amar Raj Bhandary
Ecuador	Galo Valencia Vásquez	
Peru		Eduardo Ponce Vivanco
Italy	Alberico Casardi	Boris Biancheri Chiappori
		Pasquale de Toma
Central African Republic	Bernard Beloum	Michel Ouada
Argentina	Rodolfo Urbano Freyre	Jose Leon
		Rodrigues Zia
Brazil	Fabio Rhiody Yassuda	Miguel Alvaro
		Azario de Almeida
		Manuel Maria
		Fernández Alcázar
Nigeria	George Dove-Edwin	F.A. Ede
Abu Dhabi	Rashed Abdulla	
Iran	Anushirvan Rais	Sassan Jávan
Malaysia	Abdul Razak Majid	Rashid Eusoff Mamajiwalla
		Yew Hong Nieng
Afghanistan	Abdul Hakim Tabibi	Abdul Qadir Bakhtary
		Mohammed Isa Sayami
El Salvador	Carlos de Sola Wright	
Cambodia	Khek Vandy	
Malta	Paul J. Naudi	Michael G. Pizzuto
Venezuela	J.M. Pérez Morales	
United Arab Republic	Mohamed A El Hamzawi	A Kamal Abdul Salam
		Naser Madkour
Monaco	Hyacinthe Chiavassa	Takuya Wakabayashi
		Ruth Castellini

Country	Commissioner General	Deputy Commissioner General
Nicaragua	Carlos Manuel Perez Alonso	Willian Manuel Tapia Alemán
Panama	Napolen Franco	Benjamin Orejuela
Costa Rica	Federico Volio	Takeshi Wada
Uruguay		
Mauritius	A. Marcel Lagesse	
Sierra Leone		
Ireland	**Hugh Kilfeather	Frank Okuno
Japan	Toru Haguiwara	Tamotsu Inoue
		Yutaka Tamura

International Organization	Commissioner	Deputy Commissioner
United Nations	Shin-ichi Shibusawa	Kazuo Ichihashi
		*** Jacob Zuckerman
Asian Development Bank	D.C. Gunesekera	P.S. Hariharan
		W.A. Vawdrey
O.E.C.D.	James R. West	Howard Steensen
E.C.	Arthur Theunissen	Guy Simon

Territory	Commissioner General	Deputy Commissioner General
Hong Kong	Hugh Norman-Walker	N.J.V. Watt
		Grahame S. Blundell

Province	Commissioner	Deputy Commissioner
Quebec	Mitchel P. Boudriau	Normand Bernier
		Claude Servant
British Columbia	John J. Southworth	
Ontario	George Kitching	Frank Moritsugu
		Bruce R. Newton

State	Commissioner	Deputy Commissioner
Washington	Hugh A. Smith	Judson S. Wonderly
Hawaii	**John A. Burns	
Alaska	Robert B. Chernich	Yoshio Katsuyama

City	Commissioner	Deputy Commissioner
San Francisco	Charles von Loewenfeldt	George F. Curran
		Robert Strickland
Los Angeles	Bernard J. Caughlin	Kermit R. Sadler
		Kazuhisa Ohmori
Munich	Alfred E. Schulz	

Enterprise	Commissioner	Deputy Commissioner
Ampark Corporation	Allen Beach	K. Fujitsuka
		J. Kearns
Kodak- Nagase	Kenneth Raynor	George Leynolds
		Waichiro Ogawa

N.B.   *   **Honorary Commissioner General**
      **   **Acting Commissioner General or Acting Commissioner**
    ***   **UN Coordinator**

Representatives for Japanese Exhibitors

Exhibitor	Representative	Deputy Representatives
Japanese Government:	Eikichi Ito	Tsutomu Sumitomo Yoshihisa Harada Masao Miyake
The Preparatory Committee of the Local Governments' Pavilion:	Mikine Kuwahara	Motohiko Kanai Tatsuo Miyazaki
The Japan Monopoly Corporation:	Seiichi Makino	Tetsuo Tomofuji Tadayuki Ishii
Nippon Telegraph and Telephone Public Corporation: Kokusai Denshin Denwa Co., Ltd.:	Hiroji Kurokawa	Shosuke Endo Yoshio Sano
Japan Gas Association:	Hiroshi Anzai	Iwao Nishiyama Hiroshi Yasuda
Wacoal Inc. and Riccar Sewing Machine Co., Ltd.:	Koichi Tsukamoto	Shozo Hiraki Koichiro Kihara
The Federation of Electric Power Companies:	Hisao Mizuno	Masahiro Wada Seiichi Tanaka
The Sumitomo Pavilion Committee:	Toshio Sato	Etsuo Noguchi Masahiko Kodama
Takara Group:	Hidenobu Yoshikawa	Hidekazu Yoshikawa Hideharu Horie
The Japan Iron and Steel Federation:	Yoshihiro Inayama	Kenkichi Toshima Sojiro Kuroda
Fuji Group EXPO'70 Association:	Kunihiko Sasaki	Hiroshi Morihiro Hideo Sugasawa
Expo Textiles Association:	Toyosaburo Taniguchi	Kagayaki Miyazaki Shokichi Abe
Suntory, Ltd.:	Keizo Saji	Michio Torii Tatsuji Fujiwara
Kubota, Ltd.:	Kenzo Yoneda	Keitaro Hiro Nobuo Mizoguchi
The EXPO'70 Mitsui Group:	Kiichiro Sato	Kiyoshi Fujise Yutaka Kanda
Toshiba IHI Group:	Junji Hiraga	Masazo Natori Masao Mizushina
Pepsi-Cola Group for the 1970 World Exposition:	Katsuhiko Fujiyama	Katsuhiko Kawashima Russel F. Mooney
Exhibition Council of Japan Folk Crafts Museum, EXPO'70:	Gen Hirose	Keizo Asai Yoshiro Ohbayashi
Furukawa Pavilion Committee, EXPO'70:	Kanjiro Okada	Nobuo Nohara Masakazu Mizutani
Hitachi Group:	Shinkichi Hashimoto	Hiroshi Honma Toshihiko Kubo
Midori-Kai:	Yosomatsu Matsubara	Kanichi Nakayasu Yoshio Takayama
IBM Japan, Ltd.:	Sanae Inagaki	Yoshinori Horiguchi Hidehiko Ohta
Mitsubishi General Committee, EXPO'70:	Ichiro Terao	Shotaro Suzuki Takeshi Terajima
Ricoh San-Ai Group:	Mikio Tatebayashi	Iwao Yamamoto Tsuguo Hojin
Japan Automobile Manufacturers Association, Inc.:	Katsuji Kawamata	Tsutomu Nomiyama Yoshio Sakurai

Exhibitor	Representative	Deputy Representatives
Sanyo Electric Group:	Yuro Iue	Kaoru Iue Taichi Kameyama
Fuji Baking Co., Ltd.:	Jinjyu Funahashi	Masateru Funahashi Takeshi Funahashi
The Church of Jesus Christ of Latter-day Saints:	Bernard P. Brockbank	Edward Y. Okazaki Walter R. Bills
Joint Exhibition Association for EXPO'70:	Hiroyasu Yamaguchi	Masafumi Yasugi
Matsushita Electric:	Masaharu Matsushita	Tetsujiro Nakao Tsuyoji Fujio
Japan Chemical Industry Association:	Masao Fukushima	Kiyoshi Nakatsukasa Takeji Ohshima
Committee of the Christian Pavilion for EXPO'70:	Hinsuke Yashiro	Isamu Ohmura Takeo Igarashi

Donators of Various Facilities

Donators	Facilities Donated
The Federation of Bankers Associations of Japan The Dai-Ichi Bank, Ltd., The Mitsubishi Bank, Ltd., The Mitsui Bank, Ltd., The Fuji Bank, Ltd., The Sanwa Bank, Ltd., The Sumitomo Bank, Ltd., The Bank of Tokyo, Ltd., The Nippon Kogyo Bank, Ltd. (Industrial Bank of Japan), The Nippon Kangyo Bank, Ltd., The Kyowa Bank, Ltd., The Tokai Bank, Ltd., The Daiwa Bank, Ltd., The Long-Term Credit Bank of Japan, Ltd., The Hokkaido Takushoku Bank, Ltd., The Bank of Kobe, Ltd., The Hypothec Bank of Japan, Ltd.	Expo Museum of Fine Arts
The Trust Bank Association, Inc.	Expo Museum of Fine Arts
The Japan Federation of Securities Dealers' Associations	Expo Museum of Fine Arts
The Life Insurance Association of Japan	Expo Museum of Fine Arts
The Marine and Fire Insurance Association of Japan, Inc.	Expo Museum of Fine Arts
The Local Banks Association of Japan, Inc.	Expo Museum of Fine Arts
National Associations of Mutual Loans and Saving Banks	Expo Museum of Fine Arts
National Federation of Credit Association	Expo Museum of Fine Arts
The Federation of Electric Power Companies	Expo Hall
The Japan Iron and Steel Federation	Daidarasaurus
Japan Federation of Construction Contractors, Inc.	Daidarasaurus
Japan Automobile Manufacturers Association	Grand Fountain and Passenger Cars & Buses
The Japan Electric Machine Industry Association	Robot (Deme and Deku)
The Shipbuilders' Association of Japan	West Gate Overpass and North Overpass
The Cement Association of Japan	Guest House
Petroleum Association of Japan	East Gate and West Gate
Japan Light Metal Association	Mobile Toilet and Trailer
The Japan Society of Industrial Machinery Manufacturers	Escalators in the "Tower of the Sun"

Donators	Facilities Donated
Japan Chemical Fibers Association	Mushroom-Shaped Tents
Osaka Pharmaceutical Manufacturers' Association	East Clinic, West Clinic and First Aid
The Pharmaceutical Manufacturers' Association of Tokyo	Centers (Medical instruments and supplies)
The Osaka Household Medicines Manufacturers' Association	
Tokyo Home Remedy Industry Cooperation.	
Japan Foreign Trade Council, Inc.	Expo Club
Japan Ammonium Sulphate Industry Association	Fountains (In Front of Museum of Fine Arts)
The Japan Gas Association	Fountains (Wednesday Plaza)
The Association of Petrochemical Industries of Japan	Fountains
Japan Soda Industry Association	Fountains
Communication Industries Association of Japan	Lighting Facilities in Festival Plaza
Japan Mining Industry Association	General Lighting Facilities
The Japanese Electric Wire and Cable Makers' Association	General Lighting Facilities (Excursion Bus Parking Area)
The Japanese Shipowners' Association	Pond of Good Earth
Japan Paper and Pulp Association	Telephone Booths
Japan Electrical Construction Association, Inc.	General Lighting Facilities
The Japan Bearing Manufacturers Association	Night Lanes in Festival Plaza
Japan Camera Industry Association	Mushroom-Shaped Tents and National Days Bulletinboards
Japan Spinners' Association	Rest Corners (Expoland)
The Japan Warehousing Association, Inc.	Lending Services
Japan Association of Rolling Stock Manufacturers	Thursday Plaza Rest Area 1, 2, 3
Japan Porcelain Enamel Industry Association	Public Drinking Fountains, Washstand Basin
Motion Picture Producers Association of Japan, Inc.	Small Shelters
Mainichi Broadcasting System, Inc.	Strollers
Lotte Co., Ltd.	Strollers
Matsushita Electric Industrial Co., Ltd.	Strollers
Takeda Chemical Industries, Ltd.	Strollers
Sunstar Dentifrice Co., Ltd.	Strollers
The Nikka Whisky Distilling Co., Ltd.	Strollers
All Japan Lions Clubs	Aid Station for the Handicapped
Olivetti Corporation of Japan	Typewriters for Press Center
Takii Seeds Co., Ltd.	Entertainment Information Boards
Yomeishu Seizo Co., Ltd.	Mail Boxes
Nippon Paint Co., Ltd.	Scribbling Corner
Hatsuta Seisakusho Co., Ltd.	Portable and Movable Fire Extinguishers and Sign Boards
Nissho-Iwai Co., Ltd.	
Yamato Shokaki Co., Ltd.	
The Tokyo Marine and Fire Insurance Co., Ltd.	Site Information Boards
Shimazu Seisakusho Ltd.	Site Information Boards
Ito Ham Provisions Co., Ltd.	Gondola Snack Bars (Wednesday Plaza)
Minolta Camera Co., Ltd.	Lost Children Center
Morinaga Confectionery Co., Ltd.	Gondola Snack Bars (Thursday Plaza)
Morinaga Milk Industry Co., Ltd.	

Donators	Facilities Donated
Moon Bat Co., Ltd.	Umbrellas and Umbrella Stands
Bridgestone Tire Co., Ltd.	Shuttle Bus Stops and Excursion Bus Terminals
A. Türler and Co. (Switzerland)	Sundial
Kobeya Baking Co., Ltd.	Gondola Snack Bars (Saturday Plaza)
Chambers of Commerce and Industry of Japan	Flag Staffs (Festival Plaza)
Nagoya Railroad Co., Ltd.	Gondola Snack Bars (East Gate Plaza)
Toto Ltd. (Former Toyo Toki Co., Ltd.)	Sanitary Wares and Fittings there for in Symbol Zone
The Nisshin Oil Mills, Ltd.	Benches, Trash Bins and Ashtrays (Tuesday Plaza)
	Underwater Restaurant
Kikkoman Shoyu Co., Ltd.	
Manns Wine Co., Ltd.	
Kikko Foods Corporation	
Miyoshi Oil and Fat Co., Ltd.	Small Shelter, Benches, Trash Bins and Ashtrays
	Wheel Chairs
The Japan Railway Welfare Association	Wheel Chairs
Nichii	Benches (Expoland)
Kanematsu-Gosho Ltd.	
Hokushin Plywood Co., Ltd.	Amphitheater
Japan Junior Chamber of Commerce	Small Shelter, Drinking Cups, Benches, Trash Bins and Ashtrays (Monday Plaza)
Yamamoto Nori Co., Ltd.	
	Microphones for Festival Plaza
Primo Company Limited	Electric Cars (Expo Taxi)
Snow Brand Products Co., Ltd.	Benches, Trash Bins and Ashtrays (Wednesday Plaza)
Juchheim's Co., Ltd.	Fountains (in front of Expo Hall)
Sony Corporation	Small Shelter, Benches, Trash Bins and Ashtrays
Lions Club 302-W1	Symbol Garden in Creation Ground
Arabian Oil Company Ltd.	Large Shelters and Small Shelters (Around Pond and in Wednesday and Saturday Plazas)
The Daimaru Inc.	Electric Cars (Expo Rent-Car)
Shiseido Co., Ltd.	Small Shelters, Benches, Trash Bins and Ashtrays (Tuesday and Thursday Plazas)
Fukui and Co., Ltd.	
Japan Credit Federation of Retailers of Sake and Food	Small Shelters, Benches, Trash Bins and Ashtrays (Around Pond)
Pioneer Electronic Corporation	Speaker System for Festival Plaza
Kinki Coca-Cola Bottling Co., Ltd.	Mobile Viewing Stands, Mobile Stages, Wagon Stages and Trailer
Tokoname-city (Aichi Prefecture)	Porcelainware in the Garden, Porcelain Benches
Tasaki Pearl Co., Ltd.	Small Shelters, Benches, Trash Bins and Ashtrays (Sunday North Plaza)
Asahi Glass Co., Ltd.	Shelters (Expoland)
Fuso Pharmaceutical Industries Ltd.	Small Shelter, Benches, Trash Bins and Ashtrays (Around Pond)
Yakult Honsha Co., Ltd.	Gondola Snack Bars (Expoland)
Meiji Milk Products Co., Ltd.	Space Station

340

Donators	Facilities Donated
Meiji Seika Kaisha, Ltd.	Space Station
Tanaka Kikinzoku Kogyo K.K. Tanaka Electronics Industry Co., Ltd. Tanaka Matthey K.K. Electro Plating Engineers of Japan Ltd. Yamazaki Co., Ltd. K. Hattori & Co., Ltd.	Telegram and Telephone Centers, International Telegram and Telephone Centers EXPO'70 Official Time System, Clock & Information Booth and Rest Area (Around West Garden)
Japan Buddhist Federation	"Horinkaku" (Around West Gate)
The Kyoto Chamber of Commerce & Industry	Tea House in Japanese Garden
Nippon Express Co., Ltd.	General Lighting Facilities (Around Pond and Plazas)
NGK Insulators, Ltd. Noritake Co., Ltd.	Forest of Poles
Arbos Yakusho Co., Ltd.	Soap Containers and Liquid Soap for Washing Hands
Nishijin Textiles Industry Association Nishijin Kimono Textile Industry Association Nishijin Textile Museum	Tapestry for Reception Hall in Guest House
Nippon Sheet Glass Co., Ltd.	Glass Castle and Management Office
House Food Industrial Co., Ltd.	Glass Castle
Nippon Gakki Co., Ltd.	Glass Castle and Grand Pianos (Guest House, Expo Hall, Festival Plaza, Press Center, and Festival Hall) Electone (Expo Hall and Festival Plaza) and Other Percussions, etc. (Expo Hall).
Toa Electric Co., Ltd.	Radio Cars
Benedictine (France)	Small Shelters, Benches, Ashtrays and Drinking Cups (Tuesday Plaza)
Rotary-Japan World Exposition Committee	Expo Club
Shigaraki-cho (Shiga Prefecture)	Floor Tiles and Porcelain Wall Plates for Guest House
Tamura Electric Works Ltd.	Public Telephone Booths
Ishikawa Seito Co., Ltd.	Clinker Tiles (Near Main Gate)
Honny Chemicals Co., Ltd.	General Lighting Facilities (Around Pond and Rose Garden)
Nitto Electric Industry Co., Ltd.	Site Information Boards
Cow Brand Soap Kyoshinsha Co., Ltd.	Small Shelters, Benches and Ashtrays (Friday Plaza)
Rotary Club of Montreal Lakeshore Canada and 12 Rotary Clubs in Osaka and Suita Rotary Club	Peace Rose Garden
Chuetsu Shuzo Co., Ltd.	Benches, Trash Bins and Ashtrays (Around Pond)
Japan Air Lines Co., Ltd.	Royal Boxes in Festival Plaza
Kawai Musical Inst. Mfg. Co., Ltd.	Shallow Pond, Log Labyrinths, Spring See-Saw and Swamp-Jump, in Creation Ground and Grand Pianos (Amphitheater, Underwater Restaurant and Expo Club), Electone (Amphitheater) and Rhythmers (Creation Ground)
Misawa Homes Company Ltd.	Expoland West Rest Area

Donators

Kyoei Kaihatsu Co., Ltd.

Sanwa Shutter Mfg. Co., Ltd.
Yamagiwa Electric Co., Ltd.
Arita-machi (Saga Prefecture)
C. Kondo & Co., Ltd.
Osaka Crippled Children Society (Shimizu Fund)
Yokogawa-Hewlett-Packard, Ltd.
Daifuku Machinery Works, Ltd.
Sony Shoji Co., Ltd.
Sogo Dept. Store Co., Ltd.
The Disabled Veterans Association of Osaka
   Prefecture Higashi Sumiyoshi District
The Disabled Veterans' Wives Association of
   Osaka Prefecture Higashi Sumiyoshi District
Japan Copper Development Association

Victor Company of Japan, Ltd.
The Japan Iron and Steel Federation

The Mainichi Newspapers
Tokyo Shibaura Electric Co., Ltd.

Yuasa Battery Co., Ltd.
Suzuki Motor Co., Ltd.

Kokando Co., Ltd.

Klauss 17 Preservation Society

The Hokkaido Prefectural Government
The City of Sapporo
The Organizing Committee for the XIth Olympic
   Winter Games, Sapporo 1972
Toho Co., Ltd.
Osaka Dental Clinic Association
Senyo Kogyo Co., Ltd.
Fuji Photo Film Co., Ltd.
Nippon Steel Corporation
Matsushita Electric Industrial Co., Ltd.
Sanyo Electric Co., Ltd.

Facilities Donated

Crane Car with Dump for Trash
   Collection
Containers with Shutter
Chandeliers in Guest House
Wall Tiles in Expo Hall
Curtains in Expo Hall
Wheel Chairs
I.C.U. System and Restoring Devices
Trailer for Container
Tapestry for Expo Hall

Benches for the Handicapped

Bronze Memorial Tablets (VIP Rooms
   in Expo Plaza)
Projectors (Expo Hall)
Sculptures of Iron and Steel
   (Around Pond)

Electronic Information Boards
   (Expoland)
Electric Cars (Maintenance)

Benches, Trash Bins and Ashtrays
   (Thursday Plaza)
Locomotives to Expoland, Passenger Car,
   Station Master's Office
Shelters (Expoland)

Rest Area (Expoland)
Dental Clinic
Minirails

Curtains (Expo Hall)
Water Cooler
Electric Cycle Cars

List of Service Contributors

Contributors

Japan "IKEBANA" Art Association

Head Masters of Ground Tea Ceremony of Various
   Sects
Japan Green Tea Federation
Japan Doctresses Society

Osaka Prefecture Dentists' Society

Service

Flower arrangement in Guest House,
   Expo Club, etc.
Tea service for honorable guests at tea
   house in Japanese Garden
Same as preceding
Medical examination and treatment
   services by 6 doctresses
Dental examination and treatment
   services by 2 each of dentists and
   helpers; 1 office personnel

Contributors	Service
Osaka Prefecture Pharmacists Society	Dispensary services by one pharmacist
Japan Nursery Association	Nursery services by 6 nurses
Lions Club	Service by total of 12 persons per day; 2 office personnel
Osaka Prefecture Handicapped Children Association	Services for handicapped children by 15 persons and 2 office personnel
Girl Scout, Osaka Prefecture Branch	Stroller lending service, etc., 2,600 persons
International Wool Office	Sheep feeding service
Kuyo-Kai Representatives' Association of Various Schools of "Bon-Seki"	Flower Arrangement
Minolta Camera Co., Ltd.	52 "Lost Children's Friends"

Donators of Theme Exhibits and Facilities of Theme Exhibition

Donators	Theme Exhibition
Commissioners General of Each Participanting Country	Cooperators in collecting information for Photo Exhibition "Unknown People Supporting the World" (On the Ground)
Japan Camera Manufacturers Association Foundations	
International Education and Information Center Foundations	
Nippon Hoso Kyokai (NHK)	
Mochida Pharmaceutical Co., Ltd.	"Models of DNA Nucleic Acid and ATP Protein" (Underground)
Japan Television Network Co., Ltd.	"Song of Life," Cooperator in collecting films and producing this movie film (Underground)
Kodansha, Ltd.	"World Largest Picture-Book" (Aerial)
Nippon Hoso Kyokai (NHK)	"Commercial Communication Satellite, INTELSAT IV" (Aerial)
	"MANDARAMA" Cooperator in collecting films and producing this movie
Sharp Corporation	"Way of Discrepancy" and "Steps of Crisis" Cooperator in producing the movie (Aerial)

Customs

Do you have business with Japanese Customs? Look no further than the Expo Association Headquarters Annex. Anything to be used at Expo, any baggage arriving from abroad, any press or other materials for overseas — they'll look after it here. And at four branches throughout the Expo site.

Expo Site Facilities

"Sky Ride" (Aerial Cableway)
Constructed and Operated by
"Kinki Nippon Railway Co., Ltd."
Adults ¥200   Children ¥100

Concessions

The concessionaires listed here by area sell souvenirs bearing the EXPO'70 symbol, new products, and the specialties of countries from all over the world. In addition, 69 shops (in Group A) selling snacks and beverages and 13 confectionary shops (in Group C) are located near the Gates and in Expoland, Festival Plaza, monorail stations and various other spots within Expo.

Their concession locations are: East Gate (A-3, C-2), South Gate (A-2), West Gate (A-2, C-2), North Gate (A-2, C-1), Sunday Plaza North (A-2), and South (A-2), Monday Plaza (A-2), Thursday Plaza (A-3), Second Friday Plaza (A-1), Pond-A Area (A-2), Pond-C Area (A-3), Pond-E Area (A-2), Festival Plaza (A-2), Symbol Area North Plaza (A-2, C-1), Main Gate North (A-3, C-2), Main Gate South (A-1), Tower Plaza (A-2), Wednesday Plaza Station (A-2), West Gate Station (A-4), Japanese Garden Station (A-2), Expoland Station (A-2), Expoland (A-8), Central Bus Parking Area (A-2, C-2), West Bus Parking Area (A-2, C-1), Rest Area at West Bus Parking Area (A-3), and North Bus Parking Area (A-2, C-1).

Area	Name of Shop (Company)	Commodity
East Gate	Souvenir Shop	Souvenirs
	Tazaki Pearl Co., Ltd.	Pearl products
	Souvenir Shop	Souvenirs
South Gate	Souvenir Shop	Souvenirs
	Souvenir Shop	Souvenirs
West Gate	Souvenir Shop	Souvenirs
	Daimaru, Inc.	Daily necessities and general sundry goods
	Souvenir Shop	Souvenirs
	Marusho	
	Tsukiboshi Rubber Ind. Co., Ltd.	Gent's suits, hats, canvas shoes, raincoats, etc.
North Gate	Segami Seiyakusho	Medicines, medical supplies, and cosmetics
	Tazaki Pearl Co., Ltd.	Pearl products
	Souvenir Shop	Souvenirs
Sunday Plaza (North)	Souvenir Shop	Souvenirs
	Japan M G C Society	Models and toys
(South)	Souvenir Shop	Souvenirs
	Osaka Tobacco Dealers Cooperative Association	Tobacco
Monday Plaza	Souvenir Shop	Souvenirs
	Morimoto Bussan K.K.	Japan's folk art objects
	Ricoh	Watches
Tuesday Plaza	Republic of Korea	Korean laver
		Folk art and industrial art objects
	India	
	Viet Nam	
	Republic of China	
	Canada	Beverages, maple sirup, maple sugar
	Canada	Apples
	Souvenir Shop	Souvenirs
Wednesday Plaza	Souvenir Shop	Souvenirs

Area	Name of Shop (Company)	Commodity
Wednesday Plaza	The United Nations	Souvenirs Beverages and provisions and bread
	Burma	Textile goods
	Burma	
	Switzerland	Soft ice cream and chocolate
	Portugal	Juice
	Souvenir Shop	Souvenirs
Thursday Plaza	Furukawa Sangyo K.K.	Models of Furukawa Pavilion and Souvenirs
	Tobacco Cooperative Society	Tobacco
	Mitsui Metal Industry Co., Ltd.	Gold cups, other souvenirs and products of Mitsui Group companies
	Dainippon Printing Co., Ltd.	
Friday Plaza	Czechoslovakia	
	Hong Kong	Books
	United Kingdom	
	Colombia	
	Bulgaria	Juice, nectar and provisions
	Souvenir Shop	Souvenirs
	Republic of China	Pineapples, canned goods and juice
	Brazil	
Saturday Plaza	India	
	Italy	Bizantin arts and leather goods
	U.S.S.R.	Folk art objects, vodka and amber products
	U.S.S.R.	"
	Belgium	Belgian waffles and doughnuts
	Souvenir Shop	Souvenirs
	Iran	
	Turkey	
Pond-A	Pakistan	
	Nepal	
Pond-B	France	French bread, canned goods and provisions
	France	"
	Philippines	Hats and wooden goods (spoons, forks)
Pond-C	Hawaii	
	New Zealand	Milk products and soft ice cream
	New Zealand	"
Pond-D	Netherlands	
	Thailand	
Pond-E	Kokumin	Medicines and medical supplies
	Daimaru, Inc.	Daily necessities and general sundry goods
Monorail Japanese Garden	Belgium	Belgian waffles and doughnuts
	Saudi Arabia	
Monorail Expoland	Nippon Seal Co., Ltd.	Etiquette brushes and Souvenirs

Area	Name of Shop (Company)	Commodity
Central Gate Theme Hall	Souvenir Shop	Souvenirs
	Souvenir Shop	Souvenirs
	Souvenir Shop	Souvenirs
	The Nippon Kangyo Bank (3 concessions)	Exhibit and sales of raffles
	Japan Hat Association	Hats, etc.
	Kyodo Printing Co., Ltd.	
	Osaka Tobacco Dealers Cooperative Association	Tobacco
	Foreign Specialty Shop	
	Osaka Tobacco Dealers Cooperative Association	Tobacco
Symbol Area North Plaza	Souvenir Shop	Souvenirs
	Textile Shop	Textile goods and accessaries
Central Gate (South)	Souvenir Shop	Souvenirs
Tower Plaza	Belgium	Belgian waffles and doughnuts
	Australia	Ice cream and provisions
	Pakistan	
	Belgium	Belgian waffles and doughnuts
	Australia	Ice cream and provisions
	Souvenir Shop	Souvenirs
Central Bus Parking Area	Souvenir Shop	Souvenirs
	Shiseido	Cosmetics
Expoland	Souvenir Shop	Souvenirs
	Hattori Tokeiten	Watches and clocks
	Konishiroku Photo Shop Unitica Rayon	Color-photo cards of EXPO'70
	Republic of China	
	Iran	
	Turkey	
	Mainichi Broadcasting Co., Ltd. (MBS)	Commodities developed for young people
	Daigaku-Do	Cigarette lighters, festival glasses,
	Japan Gas Ligher Development Association	telescopes and binoculars
	Pakistan	
	France	
	U.S.S.R.	Folk art objects, industrial art objects, vodka and amber products
	U.S.S.R.	"
	U.S.S.R.	"
	Philippines	Hats and wooden goods (forks, spoons)
	Philippines	"
	Foreign Specialty Shop	
International Bazaar	Belgium	Flour and juice
	Republic of Korea	Korean laver, Folk-art objects and ash trays, etc.
	Bulgaria	
	Thailand	Leather goods
	Thailand	
	Algeria	
	Colombia	
	Hawaii	Jewelry, fruit juices and instant coffee

Area	Name of Shop (Company)	Commodity
International Bazaar	Hawaii	Confectionery and cosmetics
	Indonesia	Leather goods and foot-wear
	Indonesia	"
	Turkey	Embroidery goods, leather goods, beverages, and tobacco
	Turkey	Woolen textiles
	Algeria	
	Pakistan	Embroidery goods and leather goods
	Pakistan	"
	Tanzania	Natural honey
	France	Perfume, parasols, handkerchiefs and accessories
	France	Delicacies, cheese made from sheep milk, and eau de cologne
	Hong Kong	Ball-point pens and wigs
	U.S.S.R.	Perfume, folk art object, industrial art objects, vodka, amber and fish products
	U.S.S.R.	Watches, Cognac, tobacco, wines, chocolate and confectionery
	United Nations	Stamps, souvenirs, etc.
	Republic of China	Canned goods
	United Kingdom	Scotch whiskey and British foodstuffs
	Netherlands	Cheese, butter, milk products and sausages
	Netherlands	Chocolate, confectionery, ham, bacon and tobacco
	Germany	Blades, stamps, confectionary etc.
	Brazil	
	Argentina	
	Argentina	
	Philippines	
	Philippines	
	Germany	Perfume
	Germany	"
	Switzerland	Chocolate, soft ice cream, etc.
	Switzerland	Embroidered handkerchiefs
	Colombia	Coffee, leather goods, woolen goods, confectionery and fruit juices
	United Kingdom	Scotch whiskey and British foodstuffs
	New Zealand	Milk products and ice cream
	Iran	Tobacco, embroidery goods and hand-made shoes
	Iran	Sheepskin products and soap
	Greece	Liquors, fruit juice and provisions
	Greece	
	Canada	
	Canada	
	Ghana	
	Laos	Tobacco and ivory goods
	Republic of China	
	Czechoslovakia	Salami, cheese, bacon and ham
	Czechoslovakia	
	India	
	India	Black tea, fruit juice, leather goods, straw goods and woolen goods
	India	Embroidery goods, shoes and synthetic precious stones
	Italy	Leather accessories and Bizantin arts
	Italy	"
	Hong Kong	Ball-point pens and wigs

Index

Index

Acknowledgements

**Valuable assistance
in the preparation
of this book was given by:**
Canadian Government Travel Bureau
CBS-Sony Records Inc.
Chunichi Shimbun/Tokyo Shimbun
Expo Museum of Fine Arts
Gendai Geijutsu Kenkyusho
K. Hattori & Co., Ltd.
Kadokawa Shoten
Morinaga Milk Industry Co., Ltd.
Nippon Electric Co., Ltd.
Nippon Grammophon Co., Ltd.
Shinchosha
Shufu-no Tomo Sha
St. Joseph's College
Theatre EXPO'70

Index of Advertisers

EXPO'70 Official Guide

¥300

Printed February 1, 1970
Published March 10, 1970

Publisher: Shunichi Suzuki
Compiled with the cooperation
of Dentsu Advertising Ltd.
EXPO'70 Official Guide Committee
(Chairman: Haruo Chijiiwa)
Printed by
Toppan Printing Co., Ltd.
Published by
the Japan Association
for the 1970 World Exposition
Suita City, Osaka, Japan
(Address all inquiries to:
Information and Publicity
Bureau of the Association)
Circulation Agent:
Tokyo Shuppan Hanbai Co., Ltd.

Printed in Japan

Getting to the Site

by train

National Railways	━━━━━
Private Railways	━━━━━
Osaka Municipal Subways	═══════

1. To Main Gate: by Subway Midosuji Line (No.1).
2. To West Gate: by Hankyu Railway's Senri Line.
3. To West Gate: by Subway Sakaisuji Line (No.6).
4. To East Gate: by bus from Ibaraki station which connects with National Railways' Tokaido Line.
5. To East Gate: by bus from Ibarakishi station which connects with Hankyu's Kyoto Line.
6. To Main Gate: by bus from Minami Ibaraki station which connects with Hankyu's Kyoto Line.
7. To Main Gate: by National Railway's New Tokaido Line, transferring at Shin-

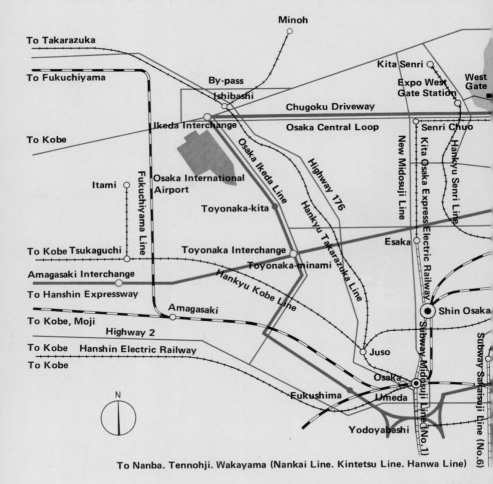

To Nanba. Tennohji. Wakayama (Nankai Line. Kintetsu Line. Hanwa Line)

by car

Expressway	━━━━
Highway	────

1. From Tokyo and Nagoya: by Tomei and Meishin Expressways, Ibaraki Interchange, Highway 171, and Sainomoto Settsu North Line (Road). Or along Tomei and Meishin Expressways to Suita Interchange.
2. From Kyoto: through Highway 171 and Sainomoto Settsu North Line, or through Meishin Expressway.